SHARED GOVERNANCE FOR NURSING

A Creative Approach to Professional Accountability

Timothy Porter-O'Grady, EdD, RN
Sharon Finnigan, RN

Affiliated Dynamics, Inc.
and
St. Joseph's Hospital
Atlanta, Georgia

AN ASPEN PUBLICATION®
Aspen Publishers, Inc.
Rockville, Maryland
1984

Library of Congress Cataloging in Publication Data

Porter-O'Grady, Timothy.
Shared governance for nursing.
"An Aspen publication."
Includes bibliographies and index.
1. Nursing service administration. 2. Hospitals – Administration.
1. Finnigan, Sharon. II. Title.
RT89.P6 1984   362.1'73'068 84-16814
ISBN: 0-89443-874-3

Editorial Services: Martha Sasser

Library of Congress Catalog Card Number: 84-16814
ISBN: 0-89443-874-3

Printed in the United States of America

3 4 5

To the nursing leadership, both clinical and managerial, at Saint Joseph's Hospital, Atlanta, Georgia. Its belief, commitment, and perseverance served to inspire and encourage the authors to pursue nursing organizational excellence in spite of a common lack of belief in its possibility.

Table of Contents

Foreword

Today's professional nurse values competency. Included within this value is the desire to assume accountability to clearly articulate what nursing practice entails, define excellence in that practice, and determine, through evaluation, the quality of care provided, as well as the competence of the practitioner.

Since the majority of nurses continue to practice in the institutional setting, the challenge has been to facilitate a process of professional governance within an established hierarchical organization. This requires clear definition of what professional governance is, with thoughtful deliberation as to how to achieve the principles of accountability. It requires valuing a decentralized approach to governance and management thus demonstrating that people should retain as much influence as possible about the decisions that affect their work and working environment, their professional development, and their personal fulfillment.

The authors have placed in your hands the tools to move a professional nursing staff toward full professional accountability. They have demonstrated creativity and risk taking—but more important, great trust and respect of today's professionals. Their willingness to share this evolving model should be applauded, and their challenge to replicate and move the model to the next level of refinement accepted. Only by accepting their challenge will nursing achieve professional maturity. Thank you Tim Porter-O'Grady and Sharon Finnigan for sharing your model and giving the nursing community the benefit of your hard work!

Barbara A. Donaho, R.N., M.A.
Associate Vice President for
Professional Services
Sisters of Mercy Health Corporation
Farmington Hills, Michigan

Preface

This book is directed to all nurses and others interested in creating a professional work environment that reflects the desire for a higher level of accountable patient care. All nurses have a stake in their workplace and its nursing practice activities. Indeed, the workplace problems verbalized most frequently by nurses in hospitals have a great impact on performance, levels of satisfaction, and productivity.

The primary focus of this book is the creation of a work environment that reflects the values and professional practice behaviors articulated by nurses. Its central theme is the systematic development of a professional workplace for nurses. Its practice-based text carries the reader through each phase of shared governance, from concept to systems integration. Special emphasis is given to the logical progression away from the traditional bureaucratic organization to a new structure that supports shared governance.

The authors maintain that it is possible to build into the hospital system a nursing organization that reflects in practice the best that nurses have to offer. A shared governance system removes the artificial constraints that prohibit the nurse from fulfilling her professional objectives. The design of the new organizational structure establishes a basis for nursing accountability and the internal mechanisms that support it—without management coercion. Shared governance in nursing offers a way in which the profession of nursing in hospitals can become truly professional, with all the status, opportunities, and values that implies.

Tim Porter-O'Grady, Ed.D., R.N.
Sharon Finnigan, R.N.

Authors' Note

Throughout this book, physicians are usually referred to as being male, primarily because the hospital environment has traditionally been staffed by male physicians. For similar reasons, nurses are referred to as female. The authors realize that today many physicians are women and many nurses are men. The reference to these professions as being primarily male or female is in no way intended to be sexist, but is rather intended to convey the historical perspective necessary for an understanding of the concept of shared governance.

Acknowledgments

The authors would like to thank and extend their heartfelt appreciation to the following individuals who participated in the development and refinement of this text.

First to our nursing colleagues in practice, who provided the anxiety, need, and impetus for consideration of alternative strategies for organizing and governing professional nurses.

To Mr. Kenneth Wheeler, Chief Executive Officer, Saint Joseph's Hospital, Atlanta, Georgia, and to our administrative peers whose insight, comments, anxiety, and commitment to shared governance in nursing helped to develop and refine the system into a workable structure.

To Patticolleen Runfola, whose patience and editorial and clerical assistance were invaluable.

To all the people at Saint Joseph's Hospital whose tolerance, patience, and support of nursing administration and the nursing organization made this book possible.

Finally, to our colleagues in nursing at Saint Joseph's Hospital in Atlanta, Georgia, and in other institutions across the country who have struggled to make the profession of nursing whole and who continue to devise ways in which it can grow and be viable for the benefit of nurses everywhere.

Introduction

Nursing is at the crossroads. Changes in the health care delivery system, in economics, and in social conditions in the United States are having an impact on all of its citizens. Because of its central role in the delivery of health care services, nursing is greatly affected by the changes in social and public policy and in economic circumstances. Concomitant with these changes, there have been changes in the roles and expectations of women. Because of the new opportunities that have accrued to women through the assertion of their rightful place in social institutions, the profession of nursing has been changed dramatically, both internally and externally. Internally, women are raising their expectations, demands, and desires for responsibility, equality, and full participation in decisions affecting not only patient care but the health care delivery system as a whole. Externally, they are demanding equal opportunities and roles in our society. In the process, they have increasingly moved into careers other than nursing, thereby diminishing the attraction of nursing as a career and reducing the enrollments in nursing schools.

These dramatic changes in nursing and health care delivery systems have been the subject of many national studies. These studies have focused on issues related to satisfaction, staffing levels, career choices, motivation, participation, and organizational relationships. All have indicated the need for fundamental changes in nursing organization and practice. Their recommendations seem to point toward certain key changes:

- increasing the economic value of nurses
- creating a workplace that is satisfying and rewarding
- increasing the participation of nursing staff in decisions that affect their practice and profession

Thus, certain fundamental changes need to be encouraged in the health care delivery system to facilitate the utilization of nurses, both as a resource and as key members of the health care delivery team. Indeed, broad-based studies of the nursing profession emphasize the need for greater involvement by nurses in decisions at the policy, operational, and practice levels. Hospitals are being encouraged to broaden their utilization of nurses, to initiate mechanisms and create environments that will raise the functioning level and sense of satisfaction of the nursing staff.

This book outlines a process and related mechanisms that address, in an integrated way, the complex transition to an organizational structure that provides for the full utilization of the nursing resource. It also proposes a system for maintaining an operational framework for the new organizational structure. This system—called shared governance in nursing—is designed to reflect the professional character of the participants in the nursing organization and to promote certain positive behaviors and practices. Within this organizational framework, the text describes a mechanism for making the necessary internal alterations to provide ongoing support of the professional role of nursing in the delivery of health care services. Other components of the shared governance system provide multiple approaches to the creation of a professional structure for nursing. Depending upon the needs, position, and goals of the institution, and regardless of the ultimate design of the structure it may use to achieve shared governance, the mechanics are essentially the same—the establishment of a system in which staff participate fully in all activities that have an impact on their work and ultimate goal: meaningful patient care.

The text is primarily descriptive. While theoretical applications provide a basis for strategies for organizational change and movement to a shared governance system, the central focus is on application. All too often in the literature of nursing, the value and theoretical articulation of a procedural system is presented, but without the provision of adequate and meaningful tools. In this case, it is hoped that the presentation will itself serve as a toolbox of thoughts and ideas to foster the full development of the nursing professional and the nursing profession within an organizational context. The ideas, concepts, and processes suggested here will, we hope, provide impetus for the generation of further ideas, processes, and concepts in those institutions that seek to apply a professional framework to their nursing organizations. In this way, our book should serve as a valuable stimulant for those institutions and agencies that are striving for higher levels of growth in their nursing organizations.

However, the present volume in no way purports to be the last word on the implementation of shared governance systems. Much like the concept it discusses, it is rather like an overview of the underlying framework of a building to which additional walls, ceilings, windows, and other refinements must be added. A more comprehensive text on nursing governance structures and strategies will undoubtedly become available as more institutions and agencies tackle the various issues involved in the development of shared governance systems and share their particular experiences— their successes and their failures—with their colleagues in the nursing profession.

In any event, having been personally involved in the establishment of a shared governance organizational system for nursing in a 300-bed community hospital, the authors can testify that the results achieved were far beyond our expectations as change agents and the expectations of the professional staff with whom we worked. Since the circumstances and conditions existing in that hospital were very similar to those in hospitals in other parts of the country, we firmly believe the same results can be achieved in other institutions that desire growth and enhanced quality in their nursing organizations.

Thus, this book is offered to our colleagues as a beginning point in their efforts to design and implement a truly professional organization for the practice of nursing. In all such efforts, we support them—and so will their nursing staff.

CQI - owners of rb process
(impact on work)

Chapter 1

Traditional, Contemporary, and Future Perspectives on Nursing

TRADITIONAL PERSPECTIVES—WHERE HAVE WE BEEN!

Nursing has had an exciting and dramatic history, one fraught with alternating advances and pitfalls. Perhaps the one thing that makes nursing's history unique is that it parallels the long and arduous struggle of women to establish their identities and to create "spaces" for themselves in a tradition of male-dominated societies. The struggle has had many setbacks. Because of the traditional belief that women are strongly influenced by their emotional drives, they have borne the burden of responsibility for various ills in our social systems.[1] Though history recognizes many outstanding women, the fact that there have been comparatively fewer such women than men indicates that, for the most part, women's roles have traditionally been subservient to men's.[2]

More recently, the struggle to validate and provide a meaningful place for nursing in the nation's health care delivery system has been linked to the struggle for women's rights. Like many institutions in the United States, our health care system is replete with traditional biases—including sexism, racism, privilege (social class and professional), and isolationism—all of which have affected the status and growth of our hospitals.[3]

Hospitals: The Birthplace of Nursing in America

Hospitals came into their own in America between 1900 and 1910. In this period, over a thousand new hospitals were built. Most of these were small and operated in the interests of individual doctors or small physician groups. In these establishments the rudiments of nursing care came into existence. Because they were primarily in the business of "selling" nursing services provided exclusively by women, many of these hospitals became lucrative institutions for their owners. Thus the formalized approach

1

to nursing education was established.[4] Still, much of the nursing education provided in such settings merely reinforced the traditional view of the role of women in our society. Housekeeping, feeding, comforting, and the implementation of simple treatment orders by the physician constituted the core of nursing activity. Additionally, nurses were required to take care of the individual needs of the physician and to act in his best interests. Today, some might still argue that not much has changed in 80 years![5]

In that early period, schools of nursing became closely associated with the hospital structure and reflected the hospital's values in their organization and curricula. Because they were not independently financed, the nursing schools had to depend upon the hospitals for financial support. Of course, this support did not come without some obligation to the hospitals. For example, hospitals began to demand specific work commitments from nursing students in exchange for "free" room and board and a nursing education. Nursing schools soon developed systems that utilized nursing students to staff a hospital around the clock. In other words, for little investment, the hospital received "free" nursing care. To support this system, a rigorous disciplinary process, along with an esprit-de-corps approach, created a militaristic facade to assure student support for the rigid hierarchy and authoritarian structure. This served to strengthen and perpetuate the hospital's control over its environment and its "indentured servants," the nursing students.[6]

Thus, the primary role of the nursing profession was to train nurses to assume the basic responsibility of hospital and medical care for patients. Since nurses were closely aligned with the hospital's work environment rather than with the academic environment associated with universities and colleges, the emphasis was on practice-related activities, often supported by a theoretical framework provided by the physicians. As the hospital developed within our society, nursing evolved in the same organizational and operational mode. Consequently, changes associated with nursing had to be viewed in the context of those same changes as they affect the hospital.

Moreover, since most schools of nursing were subject to the authority of their sponsoring hospital, decisions made by the nursing school superintendents were subject to review by the administrative officers of the hospital. The nursing school did not enjoy the autonomy available to the medical profession. And, since the hospital was an economic entity—that is, it had to make money in competition with other hospitals and health services—most of the decisions that affected its operation fell within the economic framework of the hospital as a business. Nursing was an integral part of the structure and therefore was especially influenced by these decisions. As a result, abuses of the nursing resource arose. Frequently, inappropriate scheduling of nursing students was made for 12- to 16-hour shifts.[7] The selling of student nursing services outside the hospital became a common source of revenue for the hospital.[8] Often the students were barely knowledgeable regarding the cases for which they were expected to assume accountability. Within the hospital, nursing students were frequently assigned to cases beyond their level of competence. When in need of expert support for difficult cases, the apprentice student often found that her only resource was another nursing student, who may have been the "nurse in charge" on the evening or night shift. These practices continued for most of the century.[9] Indeed, many of the current conflicts and concerns in nursing are clearly the result of these earlier circumstances and influences. Only in the past 20 or so years have most of these practices fallen into disfavor. Today, legislation that protects the rights of all workers has largely eliminated these abuses in the health care field. At the same time, nursing leaders in the hospital environment have moved the profession from its period of subservience to its present status as a complex, knowledgeable, and highly technological profession.

Education and Social Transformation

The movement of nursing education away from the control of the hospital into the academic mainstream is perhaps the greatest achievement of organized nursing to date. Despite the attending debate and dissension, this move has strengthened the profession, enabling it to assert its independence and grow as a unique discipline. Yet, because of many nurses' strong ties to the hospital schools where they received their training, there has been much lag in the profession's efforts to confront the many complex issues related to health care and nursing today.

As Joann Ashley points out in her controversial book, *Hospitals, Paternalism, and the Role of the Nurse,*[10] those outside the profession have not always had the best interests of the profession at heart. Also, the continuing rigid hierarchy of the hospital bureaucracy, supported by some nursing organizations, has, for the most part, tended to reinforce the status quo and keep the practicing nurse at the lowest levels of the hospital organizational and decision-making system. Physicians specifically and administrators indirectly have been concerned and affronted by the continuing evolution in the quality and level of nursing education. Many in the medical profession feared that the growing quality and quantity of nursing education would pose a threat by creating competition by nurses for the roles of physicians. Particularly during the 1920s and 1930s, the medical professional organizations raised objections to the direction nursing education was taking in defining, independently and internally, the role of nursing in the health care system.[11]

Nevertheless, the work of the early leaders in nursing—Levinia Dock, Adelaid Nutting, Isabelle Hampton Rob, Lillian Wald, and others—continue to build a strong basis for the subsequent development of nursing. The gains made in establishing nursing as an independent profession were to a great extent due to the diligent and detailed work of these leaders. Similarly, since the 1940s, much of nursing education has been redefined as a relatively independent discipline. These changes have paralleled developments in the medical sciences. As a result of new developments and technologies within the unique nursing framework, schools of nursing have been gaining more and more independence in defining curriculum content and scope of practice and in addressing specific practice issues related to the development of the individual nurse.

Within the last 20 or 30 years, most of the work in the profession has focused on establishing an academic basis upon which nursing practice can build. On this foundation, the increased utilization of nurses and the expansion of nursing practice into all areas of health care delivery have been cornerstones in the development of the nursing profession. As the education of women became more generally accepted, women seeking opportunities in nursing have been availing themselves of graduate and continuing education in a variety of health-related fields. Today, opportunities for graduate education in nursing extend from specified clinical practice areas to public health, administration, and even public policy.

Perhaps the most pervasive problem within the nursing profession, and for women generally in our society, continues to be the socialization process that continues to make women victims of their own upbringing.[12] As a result of this process, the independence, assertiveness, and ability of women to operate within our male-oriented and male-dominated society have been significantly limited. Concomitantly, the nursing profession's development has been slow and tedious; the successes have not been measured in giant leaps. Thus, a thorough understanding of the socialization of the nurse as a woman and of the implications of this within the professional environment of nursing is an important corollary to changing self-perceptions. A short review of this socialization process will help to establish a conceptual base upon which the individual nurse can make some judgments regarding influences within the system that have an impact on her practice and her control of that practice.

Women's Sex-Role Stereotyping

The reader might ask, "Why are we discussing sex roles in a book concerned with a new organizational approach to nursing practice in the hospital?'' The answer stems from the fact that sex-role issues influence all behaviors in the social setting. The child's sex is a major factor in influencing that child's behavior and social responses, beginning with the mother and father. Discussions centering on who the child will be lead the two parents to respond differently in terms of the baby's perceived needs in preparing for its role in life. For example, when a parent thinks of a boy, characteristics traditionally considered masculine, *rough, strong, firm, tough, sports, competition, responsibility, president,* and a host of similar terms come to mind. The same process occurs when thinking about a girl, only the characteristics for her are significantly different. The parents may think in terms traditionally considered to be feminine qualities— for example, *vulnerable, gentle, pretty, sweet, caring, sensitive, comforting,* and *nurturing.* These characteristic images remain with the family while the child is growing up and are constantly reinforced by the society at large. Children are taught to fulfill their prescribed roles in play, in learning, and in relating to their parents, other elders, and to the community.[13]

These experiences strongly affect our responses to life's circumstances—to peers in the workplace, to a spouse in the home, or to friends in a social framework. Specifically, anything we might do to alter our situation or circumstances is going to have a dramatic impact upon our response to organizational change. We are not always aware why the situations we confront during a normal work day cause the kinds of responses in us that result in satisfaction, joy, frustration, or rage. Sometimes there are other more insidious manifestations of the effects of our living situation upon our lives. Physiological symptoms such as backache, headaches, or stress reactions, are frequently evidence of our response to the situations and circumstances we often find ourselves living in and with. These responses lead us to ask why we feel what we do about these things and we find that there is often not a clear, readily available answer which can help us relieve our concern. What we may not readily realize is that some of these problems can easily be associated with our internal adaptation to circumstances over which we have exerted limited control in the course of our lives.

Much of how we respond to most normal work-related or organizational situations is determined by the socialization process we have experienced to that moment. The way our parents and others have responded to our needs, the values they have instilled in us, and the way they have behaved toward us and toward each other have all been major influences on how we behave in the work environment. This has a very special relevance to nursing. Because it is primarily a female profession, nursing has many of the characteristics that reflect the socialization of women. The way the individual nurse responds to stress, interacts with others, thinks, carries out work obligations, and feels about herself and her place in the work arena will have a distinct impact on how she exists and how others perceive her in the social milieu.[14]

With this background of familial and social adaptation, the young woman, facing choices related to education or employment, has been traditionally limited to fields deemed appropriate to her sex. With few exceptions, she has made choices reflecting the gentle and nurturant qualities regarded by society as appropriate for women. Until this past decade, marriage, teaching, nursing, or other "supportive" work were the major choices available to women without penalty. Even now, women respond slowly to broader opportunities for career and employment because of the dissonance between their socialization and the role demands of the various opportunities now available to them.[15]

Traditionally, when a woman chose to go into nursing, she almost always found that sex-role stereotyping was strongly reinforced in the training school and in the hospital work environment. The men were the administrators and/or the physicians—both positions of control and authority. The school was tightly controlled and had a rigid list of rules that proper "ladies" would uphold and maintain. These rules were promulgated to enforce behavioral discipline and to protect the women from the "ravages of sin" and other social ills. In fact, they served primarily to maintain the social order of the hospital and to indicate clearly to all initiates the nature of the male-dominated hierarchy in the hospital and the roles they were to fulfill in it. The whole training process of the nursing student in the hospital reinforced these rules and images. When the nurse graduated, her only guideline for successful operation in the hospital environment was to behave in a manner consistent with her training.

CONTEMPORARY PERSPECTIVES—NURSING AND TECHNOLOGY

Despite these strong traditional influences, the U.S. health care delivery system has undergone radical growth and change in the past two decades. The advent of high technology and its resulting demands have created a dramatic change in the learning and working environment of nurses. Professional nursing organizations have made major strides in redefining nursing practice and education to confront the growth in the health care field and to anticipate meaningful responses. Yet the new external demands on nursing and the internal needs for growth have imposed major emotional and sociological stresses on both the nurse and the profession. Conflicts between traditional role behaviors and modern expectations have created difficulties in adjustment for the individual nurse. New terms like *burnout* and *reality shock* have become common.

Women's Interaction with Other Women

From the earliest stages of their developmental processes, women have been taught strategies and behaviors that frequently have put them at odds with one another. The values most often ascribed to the sex role of girls also frequently created circumstances that led to a fundamental mistrust of one another as women.

Young girls are socialized in the belief that popularity, good looks, desirability, and personality are all-important characteristics and should be a part of the girl's image as she develops. Because of the high degree of exclusiveness these characteristics demand, many girls' groups tend to exhibit jealousies, favor seeking, and cliquish language, dress, and interests and thereby exclude some individuals. The girl's interpersonal strategies emphasize the use of "feminine skills" rather than dominance and aggression, both of which have traditionally been considered unfeminine. Traditionally, "feminine" skills are frequently manifested in manipulative behavior, behind-the-scenes maneuvering, gossip, and discrete jockeying for favorable position in the prevailing peer group. As the girl begins to move into womanhood, a new element, sexual relationships with men, enters the picture and creates an additional dramatic impact on relationships with other women. Though much of the previous socialization has prepared the girl for a role as homemaker and support person, the sexual relationship with a man begins to take precedence, often producing conflict with or distrust of other women. This frequently results in intense competition with each other for the favors of men.[16]

Such underlying distrusts and conflicts often lead to a fear of forming any alliances or relationships with other women that may threaten a growing relationship with a man. Because men are not only the locus of power in the society but are traditionally the object and outcome of a woman's developmental process, a woman frequently feels safe only when she performs those behaviors that do not interfere with her relationships with the key male individuals in her life. For such women, the perceived need for popularity and acceptance leads them to value their ability to please, to look good, to be liked, and to act "nice." The capabilities that are regarded as essential to leadership—the ability to negotiate, persuade, persist, exert power, and debate on an equal footing with peers—generally are not incorporated in their repertoire of adult skills. Indeed, it frequently appears that such women are drilled in exhibiting behaviors that prepare them to fail at professional, peer, and work relationships, before even beginning on a course leading them into the work milieu.

Yet it is frequently this framework of thinking and behaving that a young woman brings to the beginning phases of her orientation to nursing. In fact, it may be the very motive prompting her to select nursing as a career. She may have seen it as the appropriate pathway by which she can actualize nurturant and supportive behaviors in a socially acceptable manner, without the risk of creating internal cognitive conflicts with her fundamental value base. And in many ways, those in the nursing profession may validate these beliefs through their reinforcing behaviors.[17]

Within the nursing profession, this behavioral process can produce apparently unconnected conflicts between hospital-based and academic-based nurses, related specifically to expectations in the workplace. The nurse trained in the hospital framework has been socialized to expect something different from the workplace than has the nurse who has received her education in an academic setting. The academic nurse has been periodically inserted into the hospital framework through a curriculum that calls for clinical experience to complement a conceptual base. In contrast, the hospital-based nurse has experienced her entire learning process in the context of the hospital. For her, it has been not only a learning experience but also a living experience. There has been no broader frame of reference for her. Needless to say, these diverging learning processes can produce serious relational conflicts among nurses in the hospital organization.

Thus, in the practice environment, basic concepts and values engendered in learning programs can generate conflict regarding the adequacy of the clinical base of the practicing nurse. The other side of the argument involves the nurse's ability to see beyond the immediate clinical application of nursing practice, to look more clearly at the impact of nursing intervention beyond the hospital walls. Regardless of the solution to specific issues, however, the work environment in most hospitals remains constant and the organizational structure frequently reflects the same hierarchical framework it always has. The same basic statement is thus relayed to all nurses regardless of their preparation: "You occupy the same position in the organization you always have; you will therefore have the same degree of significance that position implies."

In the last decade, technological demands alone have required dramatic changes in both the knowledge base and the skills of the practicing nurse, both in and out of the hospital. Frequently there has been little time to adapt to one technique or care strategy before another better and more effective approach is suggested. It has often seemed that the only constant in the life of the nurse was the certainty of imminent change. Because inconsistency is a permanent companion to today's nurse, the need for responsiveness and flexibility in the organization is not just advisable but actually required. Although many of those in the nursing hierarchy have been caring and responsive to staff needs, elements of discord, mistrust, and competition remain between the practicing nurse and those responsible for management of the organization. This is, of course, combined with preexisting mistrust that many nurses have toward one another, both in their relationships and in their ability to practice effectively.

Modern Perceptions of Women's Roles

In the last decade many changes have occurred in society that affect both the roles and the work dynamics of women. Many employment barriers have been broken down, and few areas of business and professional life are closed to women who are interested and capable of fulfilling the demands of work in those areas. Many former sex-role stereotypes are vanishing and being replaced by attitudes and expectations that equate women and men in fulfilling responsibilities in the work arena.

Response to these changes seems slowest in the health care delivery system. The medical hierarchical system is still the model of choice in the delivery of health services. This remains true despite the fact that a varied mix of well-prepared health care providers exist in a number of different specialties. The medical model permits nonphysician practitioners, such as nurse-midwives and nurse anesthetists, to provide services only after a thorough review of their credentials and complete subordination of their activities to medical review and approval. This approach has limited the application of multidisciplinary approaches to health care services, notably in most community hospitals across the country. This problem has been less evident in university-affiliated hospitals in large urban centers. Even there, however, most professional activities are within the purview of various medical review bodies that are required to approve all forms of interactions with patients.

Much of this activity is supported by law. One of the most sacred relationships in our society exists between physician and patient. The law permits interference in that relationship in very few instances, and then only in the most exceptional circumstances. As a result, the physician operates at the center of the health care delivery system, and all its activities revolve around his or her locus of control. Of course, this places other health care professionals in roles subservient to that of the physician.

In the hospital environment, as in any situation in which an individual has considerable power over work circumstances and interpersonal relationships, a wide variety of practice behavior is evident. Thus, there has always been a broad base of response to the needs of this group. Also, since physicians generally are independent entrepreneurs or business persons, control over their activities becomes nearly impossible. Thus, the situation is one in which accountability for delivery of a service may be spread over a broad base, yet that delivery requires the mandate of an individual for its undertaking. Obviously, relationships within this situation are complex. Complicating this further is the fact that this controlling force—the physician——is recognized as an independent component of the hospital system. Few other systems exist in which the operating agency (the hospital) has limited control over access, utilization, or disposition of its product (in this case, the patient). In addition, the independent entrepreneurs (the physicians) may utilize whatever services they deem necessary, with few limitations on their behavior. It is no wonder that hospitals are complex and often volatile organizations.

THE NURSING PROFESSION'S PERCEPTIONS OF ITS WORK ENVIRONMENT

Perhaps one of the more serious discrepancies in the development of nursing relates to the profession's understanding of the political framework within which it operates. Because women were not part of the decision-making structure of most hospitals, except for carrying out policy, strategies for establishing power relationships in nursing were not easily developed. It is unlikely that such strategies would have been valuable early on, because the social framework did not permit women to form the kind of coalitions necessary for such relationships. Most women would have found such relationships in profound contrast to their own perceptions of their positions, both in relationship to one another and to society in general. When women did attempt to establish power relationships, they usually did so over issues related to social or moral causes and not necessarily over women's rights.

Most of the societal changes that influence day-to-day activity are made quietly, in the legislative arenas of municipalities, counties, states, and the nation. The same process is carried out in the board rooms and administrative offices of businesses and hospitals every day. Yet it is from these very operational arenas that women, especially nurses, have been absent during the development of the nursing profession and the growth of the health care delivery system. As a result, nurses have been handicapped in developing skills needed to function in such arenas. Strategies for making meaningful change and knowledge of the political mechanics involved are just now being integrated into the development of nurses as they prepare to confront the "real world" issues affecting their practice.

Nurses' fear and misunderstanding of the value of developing power, both individual and collective, is a related matter. Again, the socialization process of women has tended to create the view that the pursuit of power and its attendant behaviors and risks are neither feminine nor necessary. So power relationships in the hospital remained essentially unchanged for a century of nursing. Even today very little evidence exists that the power ratio between nursing and other administrative services in hospitals has changed much. The administrative team is still heavily dominated by other service administrators, the majority of whom are men. Although this is beginning to change somewhat, it is doing so only as more women enter other administrative specialties and move away from the close association with nursing that may have hindered them from expanding their skills and their power base in the organization.

The lack of appropriately prepared nursing administrators has been one of the major factors in the absence of a clear power base for nursing. Even today, most nursing administrators are inadequately prepared for their administrative roles in the organization. Frequently, from the very start of the formalization of the nursing profession, the nurse perceived as being the strongest, either personally or clinically, has been given management authority for the nursing service. Obviously, what with the socialization of women and the preparation of nurses, this person was perhaps the least prepared individual to assume such responsibility. Yet the practice was undertaken repeatedly in many hospitals across the country.[18]

Thus, a wide variety of well-prepared nursing administrators has not been available. In all honesty, hospitals probably selected the people who, in their judgment, best reflected the characteristics deemed most appropriate to the role of nurse manager. The absence of the kind of resources in nursing that would eventually be available in other hospital administrative services has continued to limit the number of people prepared to assume administrative roles in the hospital's executive arena.[19]

Nursing is not yet "out of the woods" in this area. Most nursing administrators in this country still are not as well prepared in administration as the administrators in other major hospital service areas. Most of those other individuals have master's level preparation in hospital administration and have had an approved residency in a practice environment before assuming their role as a hospital administrative officer. Not so in nursing. Most nursing administrators with master's degrees are prepared for clinical positions and are not exposed in their graduate programs to significant courses in business, health, or nursing management.[20]

Nurses with graduate degrees account for only the minority of nursing administrators practicing at the executive level. Thus, the majority are prepared at no more than the diploma or baccalaureate level. Less than 5 percent of all nursing managers have graduate administrative education appropriate to the role of chief nursing officer.

It becomes clear at this point why it has been difficult for the nurse manager to compete, on a par with other administrators, for resources and power in the hospital institution. Knowledge of finance, accounting, social influences, strategy planning and marketing, human relations management, productivity, and operational management processes is missing from the nursing administrator's skill base. A host of other needed talents and insights are also provided by exposure to the academic disciplines necessary for development of an adequate knowledge base.[21]

The Status of Nursing

Nursing's status in the organization is also involved here. Status is an outcome of what is expressed from within an individual or organization and how that expression is perceived externally. Those with a strong self-image and the commitment and resources necessary to reinforce it usually present that strong image to others. It is that image and not any so-called real image that is important and is commonly thought of when people refer to the individual or group involved. Generally, then, it is the public's image or perception of a group that becomes the group's political or social image. Professionalism, ethics, service, principles and the like—although essential—do not always make up the image held by others. Consider society's perception of physicians and lawyers, engineers and teachers. Each group has a strong sense of its own standards and practices, but the public served by each often has an entirely different perception of its members and activities.

Nursing is in a similar position. One need only recall how nurses are presented in soap operas, dramas, serials, and other media to get an idea of how they are perceived socially. Such perception parallels that of women in general, but neither does any favor to the prevailing image of nursing held by the public and members of other health professions. Viewing a nurse as a competent, knowledgeable, capable professional is difficult for those whose only exposure to nurses prior to hospitalization has left the image of a man-chasing, subservient, obedient, compliant individual with no mind of her own, someone whose most significant decision is which doctor to date. Some may argue that in many of our institutions, that image may indeed be correct, but it does no good to work for change when a nurse cannot break out of a preordained cultural mold that pre-describes her role and its limitations.

Many of those perceptions are reinforced by nurses themselves. Conversations among nursing professionals frequently create a depressing view of what is going on in the profession—in practice, education, and politics. While nurses may gripe about how they are presented in the media, they are sometimes rougher than the media in their descriptions of themselves to others. Nurses often expect to demonstrate commitment to fairly rigid criteria, thus priming themselves for failure. Instead of debating and negotiating solutions to internal issues, nurses frequently broadcast their disagreements to all. This lack of resolution provokes interest in other bodies of health professionals to help nurses solve some of their critical issues and get them back on their feet again. Here, again, nurses reinforce the dependency image.

FUTURE PERSPECTIVES—THE CHALLENGE AHEAD

One could easily decide that nursing's current condition is such as to render its future pretty hopeless. However, the truth is not so bleak. The nursing profession is not breathing its last breath, nor has it fully arrived at a position of leadership in health care. Radical changes in the system and the accelerated growth in technology for the delivery of patient care have changed the practice and the roles of nurses, as well as influencing some of the fundamental relationships between the disciplines essential to appropriate patient care.

Despite limitations on the growth of nursing, significant change has occurred that would have been inconceivable a decade or two ago. The women's movement and the strengthening of women's political influence have had a tremendous impact on the power women have in today's society. Many new laws have been passed assuring women's rights and augmenting their access to positions of power and authority. Various regulations also assure that women, when appropriately prepared, have the same rights to promotion and privilege as their male counterparts. Although there has been major change in the legislative area, however, response to those changes has frequently been slow, especially in nursing.

Most of the work of nursing is considered a service role, not a primary decision-making role, especially in hospitals. Greater evidence of nurses having major decision-making roles exists for those in private practice or public service. Behavior in hospitals is beginning to change, however, because of some unplanned but significant events. In the last decade a higher level of preparation and performance has been required to meet the needs of technology. Fewer auxiliary nursing personnel have been required, while the need for registered nurses has grown, and grown at a rate that has outstripped the resources available. As a result, a significant shortage of nurses has occurred. At the same time, many nurses were discovering that the practice environment failed to meet their personal needs or made them feel alienated through its nonresponsiveness. This shortfall created a great interest in the plight and the role of nurses in the hospital.

To remedy the nursing shortage, hospitals made a great effort to attract nurses by addressing compensation and benefits programs. Innovations and supportive programs designed to help improve the work life of the nurse were developed and continue to be created. Bicultural training, internships, career development programs, tuition assistance, variable staffing, primary nursing, joint practice, and many other innovative programs became part of the daily professional life of nurses in many institutions across the country. Also, physicians have been sensitized to the needs of nurses, especially in terms of how they treat and behave toward nurses. While there has been less success with these efforts, some changes have occurred even here. Because of various protections against arbitrary action in employment, it is not as easy as it once was for a physician to have a nurse dismissed. In most institutions the nursing management team is accountable for the employment of nursing staff. The days when nurses must live under the threat of what a physician might do to them on a whim are, it is hoped, gone.

Although testimony at the public hearings of the National Commission on Nursing in 1981 revealed dramatic problems relating to nursing in some institutions, many unique and creative responses to the needs of nurses were also revealed.[22] These included flexible scheduling, more decentralization of decision making, nurse–physician liaison groups, education–service liaison committees, and other institution-specific responses. The formation of the National Commission on Nursing in 1980 had a very positive impact on the profession. That impact was produced not so much by what was said as by the fact that a heightened awareness reinforced, in the minds of nurses and others, some issues already of concern to them. The involvement of a broad variety of health leadership made the work of this three-year commission especially meaningful. The fact that it was sponsored by the American Hospital Association (AHA), a conservative influence on hospitals' relationships with nursing since the beginning of this century, was an additional benefit.

The final report of the National Commission on Nursing documented and committed the AHA, through its 1983 convention delegates' approval of its content, to support many beliefs that nurses had long held vital in meeting basic administrative and practice needs of hospital nurses.[23] At the heart of the commission's report are recommendations that address such issues as expanding and improving nurse–physician relationships, trustee interaction with nursing, nurses' participation in developing health policy at every level, baccalaureate education, professional satisfaction and autonomy, and nursing research. The effort has done much to focus a new kind of attention on the profession and the nurse's role in the delivery of health services.

Various other activities are currently being undertaken to better address nursing needs. The American Academy of Nursing report on magnet hospitals identifies 30 hospitals that have designed unique, creative approaches to the management of nursing resources.[24] These hospitals are representative of many that have been seeking and developing strategies to raise the status and value of nurses and nursing, both in their institutions and in communities in various settings around the country.

Today's overall attitude toward nursing leadership has changed from what it was in the past. A higher level of sophistication and astuteness is evident in the leadership, and people involved in nursing are more cognizant of the political and social obligations that accompany inroads in the power arena. There is a front-line expectation of participation at the highest levels of organizations and governments, rather than the old second-class-citizen attitude and its consequent attempts to attain first-class citizenship. Concomitant with the same expectations in the women's movement, nursing is beginning to anticipate major changes in the marketplace and to respond to that anticipation, rather than waiting for the changes to happen and then reacting, frequently too late. The onset of the prospective payment system legislation and nursing's response to its limitations, as well as the many implications for patient care, is a good example.

This country's health care delivery system is undergoing radical change, and nursing is at the forefront of a number of new challenges. Many new alternate mechanisms for delivering nursing services, including the prospective payment system, requires imagination and foresight.

It is an exciting time for nursing. Much work will be necessary within institutions to make them truly representative of the professional model of nursing behavior. We cannot expect professional behavior and judgment from nurses if we do not believe they are capable of such behavior. We must provide mechanisms that will help identify and articulate those behaviors in practice. The framework for practice—the work environment—is one of the fundamental bases from which the growth of nursing activities within the hospital will spring. The nursing administrator's primary responsibility is to assure that the appropriate environment for that growth exists.

The question often asked by nursing administrators is, "What is that environment and how do I provide it?" Current information suggests that nurses must be autonomous yet interdependent, peer related yet accountable, professional yet caring, independent yet involved; and they must participate in key decision making at all levels of the organization. We know that these specifics are necessary for nursing in institutions to assume full responsibility in health care delivery, but how can we encourage staff members already overburdened with the responsibility for providing patient care to get involved in the necessary processes? Can we get them interested enough? Can we afford it economically? Finally, what opposition from administrators, medical staff, and others will nursing staff meet when assuming a strong leadership role?

Change is possible. Nursing can achieve what it wants in the hospital by undertaking the necessary risks and by following the appropriate strategies for obtaining success. The profession can become the cornerstone of success for any hospital and a prime mover in the future of health care if nurses know what to do, what they want, and how to proceed to achieve that outcome. The place to begin is within the profession. Creating a professional organizational framework provides an environment that evokes professional behavior. Eliminating from that environment any opportunity to behave in any other way assures the appropriate reinforcement of desired actions.

It appears that we are living in a time that is ripe for major social and professional growth for women in general and for nurses specifically. The organizational model discussed in this text is designed to encourage and provide a framework for actualizing these changes within an institutional focus. The concept can be applied to any setting where nurses practice, however. By moving toward a shared governance system, the nurse has a chance, for the first time, to become a fully participating and practicing professional—equal to any challange or opportunity.

NOTES

1. M. S. Teitelbaum, ed., *Sex Differences, Social and Biological Perspectives* (New York: Anchor Books, 1976).

2. B. Yarburg and I. Arafat, "Current Sex Role Conceptions and Conflicts," *Sex Roles?* (1975): 1, 2, 137.

3. John Stuart Mill and Harriet Taylor Mill, *Essays on Sex Equality*, ed. Alice S. Rossi (Chicago: University of Chicago Press, 1970).

4. J. Ashley, *Hospitals, Paternalism and the Role of the Nurse* (New York: Teachers College Press, 1977), pp. 1–15.

5. Richard Beard, "The Trained Nurse of the Future," *Journal of the American Medical Association*, December 1913, pp. 2150–2153.

6. _____, "Report on the Joint Session of the Council on Medical Education and the American Council on Hospital Service," *Journal of the American Medical Association*, April 1933, p. 1179.

7. _____, *Committee for the Study of Nursing Education, Nursing and Nursing Education in the United States* (New York: Macmillan Company, 1923).

8. G. W. Olson, "How the Small Hospital May Be Made Self Supporting," *Transactions of the American Hospital Association*, 1913.

9. Isakil Stewart, "Movement for Shorter Hours in Nurses Training Schools," *American Journal of Nursing*, March 1919, pp. 439–441.

10. Ashley, *Hospitals, Paternalism*, pp. ix, x.

11. J. Ashley, "Report of the Committee of Nurses and Nursing Education," *Journal of the American Medical Association*, April 1927, pp. 1175-1180.

12. R. Friedman, R. Richart, and R. Vande Wille, *Sex Differences in Behavior*, (New York: John Wiley and Sons, 1975).

13. L. Pogrebin, *Growing Up Free: Raising Your Child in the 80s* (New York: McGraw-Hill Company, 1980), pp. 49–54.

14. Ibid., pp. 119–122.

15. Ibid., pp. 492–513.

16. Ibid., pp. 50–51.

17. Ibid., pp. 30–54.

18. M. Poulin, "Education for Nursing Administrators: An Epilogue," *Nursing Administration Quarterly* 3, no. 4 (1979): 45–51.

19. R. Rotkovich, "A Clinical Component in Education for Nursing Administration," *Nursing Outlook*, October 1979, pp. 668–671.

20. _____, *National League for Nursing, Masters Degree Education in Nursing, 1982* (New York: The League, 1983).

21. B. Stevens, "Education in Nursing Administration," *Supervisor Nurse*, March 1977, pp. 19–23.

22. _____, *Summary of Public Hearings, National Commission on Nursing* (Chicago: American Hospital Association, 1981).

23. _____, *Summary Report and Recommendations, National Commission on Nursing* (Chicago: American Hospital Association, 1983).

24. _____ *Magnet Hospitals' Attraction and Retention of Professional Nurses, American Academy of Nursing* (Kansas City: American Nurses Association, 1983).

Chapter 2

In the Bureaucratic Tradition

THE HISTORICAL PERSPECTIVE

In thinking about the term *bureaucracy*, the first organizational structures that come to mind, especially in the Western world, are those commonly associated with government. Preceding these was the governance form maintained by religious institutions. It is in this context that much of our traditional thinking about organizations arises. In the Western world in particular, the formidable structures of the Church and the Holy Roman Empire were some of the sources of the origins of organization. Through the early centuries, the Roman Catholic Church had a major influence on the thinking and operational style of European society. After the Protestant revolution, the formation of nation states was the next significant social change. With the development of these states, more change in the style of organization occurred. The military–religious authoritarian structure has remained essentially unchanged and influences organization to this day.

The industrial revolution did not bring much change in organizational structures. If anything, it reinforced in industry the characteristics that were already entrenched in government and the military. Labor was considered the basic component of the production process. As such, it was subject to the governance and control of the organizational elite. Labor became inextricably aligned with the "production" psychology—so much so that it was viewed solely within this context. Rarely was labor considered holistically, in a way embuing people, the components of labor, with social, intellectual, or spiritual needs. Consequently there was no need to incorporate any allowance for those needs into either the workplace or its philosophy. In this environment the workers—the basic units of production—became divorced from their personal "wholeness." This attitude has prevailed well into the twentieth century and is the basic belief woven through the fabric of the work setting.

Within this context, Max Weber, the father of bureaucracy, solidified the thinking justifying bureaucracy as the form of governance most effective for Western industrial man.[1] Further, he believed that this was the preferable organizational structure for institutions and defined work relationships within this framework. The structure's purpose was to maximize efficiency and to centralize control; this would provide for unified action aimed at controlling the organization. As a result, the organization was layered with hierarchies of control, and each ascending level had an expanded scope of accountability. The systems developed to support this approach relied heavily on vertical communication and management strategies and on narrow spans of control to ensure that the institution was operating within a clearly predefined set of directives.

As already mentioned, this organizational strategy remains in place in most organizations in the United States. Almost all hospitals use this design as the basic organizational structure. The organizational charts of most hospitals usually delineate clearly the lines of direct control and management within the traditional confines described by the bureaucratic system (see Figure 2-1). Reporting relationships and position placement thus become central issues to the leadership, with positions close to the top levels becoming the most desirable ones. In the bureaucratic approach, policy making, direction setting, and other mandates of the organization are generated within a narrow hierarchic range at the very top levels. Most of the other levels are located to ensure that the organization's mandates and rules and regulations which are designed to achieve established goals, are reinforced and maintained.

As organizations have grown and become very complex, various approaches to maintaining this basic framework have been undertaken. Decentralization is a strategy often undertaken to make the work and control mechanisms mesh more effectively and efficiently without sacrificing productivity. The element of structural control also remains a large part of most decentralization strategies. Decentralization of most traditional organizations usually occurs as a result of complex growth or major diversification.[2] While the decision-making process and structure remain essentially unchanged, the strategy has separate, parallel hierarchic organizational charts reflecting the pyramidal relationships and a process for connecting the "pieces" of the organization to its top rungs to preserve the integrity of the system.

Inherent in the design of the bureaucratic organization are behaviors that represent this design in the human workplace. The purposes of the organization are identified by one group: those within the controlling and policy-making framework of the system, rather than those responsible for seeing that such direction is undertaken by the organization. The third

Figure 2-1 Bureaucratic Model

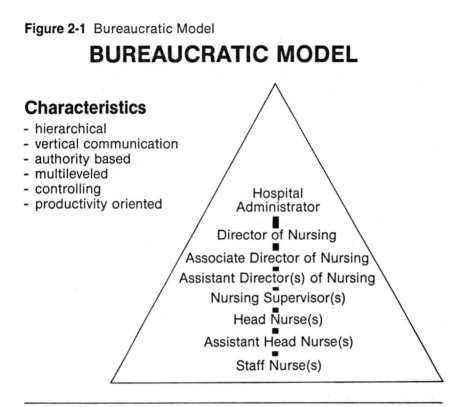

BUREAUCRATIC MODEL

Characteristics

- hierarchical
- vertical communication
- authority based
- multileveled
- controlling
- productivity oriented

Hospital
Administrator

Director of Nursing

Associate Director of Nursing

Assistant Director(s) of Nursing

Nursing Supervisor(s)

Head Nurse(s)

Assistant Head Nurse(s)

Staff Nurse(s)

---

group contains those individuals charged with carrying out day-to-day activities that are necessary to meet the organization's objectives. These workers make up the vast work force that is the majority of workers in the system. This system is frequently identified as the production model of organization.

Supporting theoretical processes were built into this bureaucratic system. One of the most widely read theorists of his time, Frederick Taylor was commonly identified as the father of scientific management.[3] Taylor's school of management focused on the tasks done by workers in pursuit of the objectives of the organization. Scientific management theorists believed that the best way to increase output was to improve the techniques applied to the work being done. Taylor viewed the people involved as the instruments through which the organization achieved its goals. He and his colleagues felt that these workers, like machinery, could be more efficiently utilized by the organization if certain changes and efficiencies could be incorporated into the workplace or into the workers themselves (see Figure 2-2).

Figure 2-2 Hospital Organizational Characteristics

ORGANIZATIONAL PERFORMANCE CHARACTERISTICS		
Characteristics	Nonprofessional	Professional
Structure	Tight Control High Degree Structure	Low Structure
Distribution of Influence	Low Total Influence Centered at Top	Even Distribution of Influence
Superior-Subordinate Relations	Directive Low Freedom	Participation High Degree of Freedom
Colleague Relations	High Coordination Few Differences	Diffuse Relations Low Correlation Many Differences
Time Orientation	Immediate, Short Term	Long Range
Goal Orientation	Technical High Task	Professional Scientific High Interactional
Management Style	Task Centered High Control	Task and Relationship Orientation

It was within this system that such exercises as time and motion studies, work task analysis, performance measurement, and a variety of other statistical processes were undertaken. Incentive for making these efficiencies work could be offered in the form of monetary rewards that would increase the worker's income to the extent that production expectations could be achieved. In this system the role of the organization's managers was to establish production outputs, and to assure that work strategies were developed to ensure that those outputs were maintained and increased when the demand for production was raised by key leadership.

The bureaucratic system did much to help industrialized society to grow and business and factory processes to become highly productive. It did much, certainly, to assure America's predominance in the free industrialized world. Combined with what appeared to be unlimited human and mineral resources, these systems created a model industrial society. Paradise was not free of problems, however. The bureaucratic system was designed to maintain the predominance of the main units of free enterprise—business and industry. But focus on output, tasks, and productivity did little to satisfy the individual needs and wants of the workers in these settings. The workers responsible for carrying out the work of the system usually received little human response to their needs. It was not long before the workers' need for protection became predominant and major changes occurred; workers of the United States were in the lead. Union organizing became a primary tool of the American worker, and before long the union became a legitimate part of industrialized society.

Unions brought a new focus to industry. Industrial leadership reluctantly participated in the collective bargaining process, either because it was mandated by law or was the only forum through which business could communicate with its employees. The fundamental behaviors associated with this practice have remained essentially unchanged; the worker–employer relationship exists today in much the same framework as it always has, retaining its adversarial nature. It is less violent, however, than was the case in the past.

THE BUREAUCRACY TODAY

The bureaucracy remains the most prominent form of organization. The system still represents the overriding organizational choice of this country's institutions, including hospitals. The bureaucracy allows power, authority, and accountability to remain relatively centralized within the control of top management. It fosters behaviors that parallel the kind of structure in which few hold the bulk of power and control.

The bureaucracy has been the structure of choice in the hospital industry since its inception. Most hospitals, regardless of size, reflect the basic characteristics of this organizational model. Much has been done to decentralize decision making in the hospital; however, the organizational design reflects all the characteristics of bureaucratic design regardless of how the organization may have "flattened" its decision-making system.

Although the bureaucratic system remains the chosen approach in most hospitals, major changes have occurred in the last two decades in managers' thinking about the organization's relationship to employees. Researchers and administrators have focused on attempts to change the behavioral components of the manager's relationship to the worker. Many theorists and managers believe that if the organization's feelings toward its employees become more positive, and if employee–management communications and relationships become more open, the work environment will be more conducive to increased productivity. In other words, the better management treats the worker, the better the worker will perform for management.

Basic structures of organizational design have been discussed and redrawn, redefined, and renovated; however, much of the early organizational structure defined by Taylor and his associates remains essentially in place in hospitals. Many people in the health care field recognize that hospitals have perhaps been the slowest to adapt human relations strategies to the workplace, yet there may be no environment that needs such strategies more. These newer management concepts focus on developing the managers and management skills necessary to provide leadership in relating the organization's needs to the work practices of the workers. A basic understanding of these processes is essential for a manager to fulfill minimal performance expectations.

Development of Human Management Theory

Perhaps no theory of psychological development has had as much impact as that developed by Abraham Maslow; it identifies a human "hierarchy of needs."[4] He postulates that at the lowest level are physiologic needs, those oriented to safety and security, and those for social affiliation. As we approach higher levels of the hierarchy, individuals begin to require recognition and esteem; eventually they aspire to self-determination or self-actualization. Maslow states that the needs hierarchy forms the basis of all human activities. Understanding Maslow's theory of hierarchical needs and how it applies to work and human dynamics has become an essential part of the manager's role, for the manager must deal with individuals at various levels of the bureaucratic hierarchy and must attempt to coordinate and integrate human resources and activities for a broad-based group of people in the workplace.

Building on the Hawthorne studies, Douglas McGregor recognized that traditional organizations—with their centralized decision-making structures, the superior–subordinates pyramid organization, and external control of the individual's work—corroborated certain assumptions about human nature and work.[5,6] He built the following hypothesis. According to Theory X, he pointed out, most people prefer to be directed; they are not interested in obtaining responsibility and want to be safe and secure above all else. Concomitant with this philosophy is the belief that people are motivated only by money, fringe benefits, and the threat of punishment. McGregor pointed out that Theory X managers attempt to structure, control, and closely supervise all employees. This type of manager demonstrates external control and believes that such control is clearly appropriate for dealing with unmotivated, inadequate, and immature people.

McGregor believed that Theory X did not adequately or appropriately describe the true motivating forces underlying human action. He therefore developed an alternative theory of human behavior that he called Theory Y; it assumed that people are not by nature lazy, unreliable, irresponsible, or immature. He believed that people can be basically self-directed and creative if properly motivated and permitted to express creativity. McGregor held that the essential task of management in the bureaucratic framework was to permit, to the extent possible, the individual employee's potential to be exposed and set free. He believed that properly motivated people will best achieve their goals by directing their efforts toward accomplishing the organization's goals. His approach was a radical departure from traditional management concepts.

Chris Argyris built further on the dynamics of the assumptions of Theory X and Theory Y.[7] He compared bureaucratic (pyramidal) practice and humanistic democratic practice and noted some rather distinct differences. Following bureaucratic or pyramidal values, he believed, led to poor, shallow, and mistrustful relationships in the workplace. On the other hand, when an organization adhered to the humanistic and democratic values associated with Theory Y, trusting and authentic relationships developed resulting in improved interpersonal competence, intergroup cooperation, and increased flexibility among people and, ultimately, in increased organizational effectiveness. From these studies, Argyris developed the immaturity–maturity theory, which reflects his belief that individuals move on a continuum of growth. When expectations of their behavior change, they move from behaviors reflecting immaturity to those reflecting maturity. Through assessment of the environment and a structured, well-designed program for human development in the organization, the manager can encourage employees from immature behavior to that consistent with mature or democratic, humanistic values.

Frederick Herzberg of the University of Utah believes that complex sets of behaviors are at work reflecting different values in the organization.[8] He believes that these are reflected in two kinds of factors: hygienic factors and motivating factors. According to Herzberg, hygienic factors are reflected through the organization's policies and administration, supervision, working conditions, interpersonal relations, money, status, and security. Although he believes that these hygienic factors are essential for maintaining a stable environment, they do not by themselves motivate the employee to further productive activity. Herzberg believes motivating factors are intrinsic to the individual or the job itself. Examples of such factors are achievement, recognition for accomplishment, challenging work, increased responsibility, growth, and development. These kinds of factors reflect the interests, needs, and values of the employee as well as his or her need for growth and development beyond hygienic factors. When people are properly motivated in terms of these intrinsic factors, their productivity and personal satisfaction can be enhanced.

Rensis Likert studied prevailing management styles of organizations and arranged them on a continuum of four basic systems.[9] System One reflects managers as having no confidence or trust in subordinates and rarely involving them in the decision-making or management process. The majority of decisions are made and goal setting done by top-level administrators; the results are issued throughout the organization. McGregor's traditional Theory X behaviors are highly evident at this level.

In System Two, Likert sees management as having paternalistic confidence and trust in employees, such as that in a master–servant relationship. Still, most goal setting and decision making occur at the top levels, though some decisions are reached at definite and prescribed places in the organizational structure. This system still reflects a superior–subordinate sense of fear and caution.

In System Three, management begins to give evidence of having a substantial, though not complete, confidence and trust in subordinates. Still at the top levels are such things as policy formation and general decisions affecting the direction of the organization. There are more specific objective decisions made at lower levels, however, and a moderate amount of superior–subordinate interaction and trust exists.

In System Four, Likert sees management as having complete confidence and trust in subordinates. Participation in all matters relating to the organization's work, activity, and decisions is dispersed throughout the organization as the manager feels appropriate. Decisions thus reflect both the needs of the organization and of the employees who serve it. This kind of organization is characterized by extensive and friendly superior–subordinate interaction, with a high degree of confidence, trust, and participation. Likert validated his concept in hundreds of studies conducted nationally in private and public enterprises. His studies indicated that, although this system of human resource management was considered the most appropriate, it was used most rarely in institutions in both the business and health communities. Changing organizations to function according to System Four involves the ability to coordinate the highly complex issue of alternating human and organizational behavior.

Building on the work of Eric Berne, many managers have attempted to incorporate concepts of transactional analysis (TA) into the traditional organizational environment.[10] Adapting Berne's concept to management, Dorothy Jongewood identified two types of transactions as useful for managers: complementary and crossed.[11] Complementary transactions reflect open communications between individuals and reduce the amount of dissonance between communicators; appropriate, expected responses are likely. Crossed transactions result from closing communication, at least temporarily. The response in crossed transactions is neither expected nor appropriate; it may be out of context in terms of the sender's intent, or it may be received in an inexact manner. Through careful understanding and use of the TA approach, the well-informed manager can help eliminate barriers to open communication in the organization and facilitate the development of more positive interaction.

No overview of traditional management would be complete without reference to Peter Drucker, father of modern management.[12] Drucker believes in participatory organizations that provide for structure sufficient to maintain the organization's integrity, while permitting appropriate involvement in goal identification and decision-making processes at the lowest possible levels of the organization. He believes in individual autonomy and that every member of the organization should participate in working toward the goals established for the organization. Using these open strategies, he believes, can positively affect the management functions of leading, organizing, planning, and controlling a complex organization. Management is a science that must be learned, according to Drucker, and this learning must be reflected in the manager's behavior. He has further indicated that, to the extent that these concepts are not learned and incorporated into the leaders' management function, successful outcomes for the organization may be limited.

Since the initiation of the scientific management school and the human relations school, many people have sought to combine the concepts of the two schools of thought into one total approach to leadership theory.

Cartwright and Sandler conclude that all group activities culminate in two basic ones: meeting group objectives and maintaining the group itself.[13] Meeting group objectives is characterized by behaviors that focus on goal achievement, planning, and establishing structure. Group maintenance is reflected both through harmonious relations between members and emphasis on individual contributions to group activities.

In its effort to identify characteristics of leadership, the Bureau of Business Research at Ohio State University focused on two patterns or dimensions of leadership: initiation of structure and consideration.[14] The first pattern—initiation of structure—is outlined as the establishment of organizational patterns, lines of communication, and procedure. Structure should center on behavior that facilitates trust, respect, friendship, and mutual relations between leader and subordinates. Based on studies of these behaviors, four quadrants with two separate axes were identified to indicate the mix of these behaviors. Each of the four quadrants indicated a leader's behavior pattern: high structure–low consideration (high initiating-structure axis), high consideration–high structure, and low consideration–low structure.

Building on the Ohio State University leadership concept, Blake and Mouton have developed a leadership model they call a managerial grid.[15] Five types of leadership are located on the four quadrants of the Ohio State University leadership model. The grid indicates the leader's concern for production (task) and for people (relationships). The production concern is aligned on a horizontal axis scaled to measure the leader's degree of production (task) orientation. Concern for people is aligned along a vertical axis scaled to measure the degree of people (relationship) orientation of the leader.

Leadership styles are identified by the researchers as part of their management grid. "Impoverished" leadership, the first of the five leadership types, indicates a low level of concern for either production or people; this type barely meets requirements for work tasks and organizational membership. Impoverished leadership receives one point for concern for both people and production.

"Country club" leadership indicates a well-developed concern for people; it creates a friendly, warm atmosphere that facilitates interpersonal relationships. This receives nine points on a concern-for-people axis and one point on the concern-for-production axis.

"Task" leadership behavior indicates strong support for efficiency of production and for arranging conditions that will facilitate work output. Task leadership receives a score of nine on the concern-for-production axis and a score of one on the concern-for-people axis.

"Team" leadership behavior is directed toward maintaining optimal work output while encouraging and developing a high level of morale and personal satisfaction. Team behavior is scored nine on concern for production and nine on concern for people.

The fifth type of leadership, "middle-of-the-road" behavior, indicates an adequate level of work performance and output balanced with maintaining a satisfactory level of morale in work group members. This behavior is given a score of five on both the concern-for-people axis and the concern-for-production axis.

Although the managerial grid studies and Ohio State University's research are similar, the "concern for" factor allows room for a purely attitudinal dimension, while Ohio State University's studies primarily indicate a behavioral dimension and examine others' perceptions of leaders' actions.[16]

Studies by Likert indicate some general patterns of leadership by managers with a record of high productivity.[17] Likert discovered that high performance is closely related to the manager's focus on human relations and to work group members' commitment to high performance goals.

Likert indicates that production-centered or job-centered managers have lower production records. His studies revealed that managers with high production levels clearly identified work objectives and allowed subordinates the freedom to meet them. This discovery establishes definitively the existence of a relationship between production performance and work group interrelationships.

In his studies on adaptive leader behavior, Fiedler suggests that a number of behaviors evident in various leadership styles will be effective or ineffective depending upon situational variables.[18] In his leadership contingency model, he identifies three major variables that may determine whether a leader will be effective or ineffective: task structure, position power, and personal relations with group members. This model identifies eight combinations of these three variables. Each of the eight combinations indicates a leadership situation. The most favorable situation for the leader, according to Fiedler, is one in which the leader is well liked by members, has a position of power, and has a clearly defined task structure. Through his studies attempting to determine the best leadership style (task centered or relationship centered), Fiedler has concluded (through use of his Least Preferred Co-worker's [LPC] scale and Assume Similarity Between Opposites [ASO] scale) that task-centered leaders may perform well in situations that are either strongly favorable or strongly unfavorable to them.[19] Relationship-centered leaders may perform best in situations that are intermediately favorable.

The empirical studies already described have shown that theories centered on production (task) and on people (relationship) have developed from both the scientific management and human relations schools of thought. These studies indicate that elements of both production and people have an impact on leadership process, group performance, and interaction. A third factor, the situation in which a leader operates, is also part of the leadership process and has a considerable influence on whether it is effective or ineffective. Various models have been developed to outline the relationship between task theory and relationship theory. Various leadership theories and models indicate that, regarding the leader and his or her interaction with the follower, this relationship plays a significant role in the relative effectiveness of the leader, the individual, and the work group as a whole.[20]

THE NURSE IN THE HOSPITAL BUREAUCRACY

The hospital's interest in the role of the nurse as administrator, supervisor, and manager is increasing.[21] Many studies indicate that in the traditional bureaucracy, the examples set by an individual manager have a profound influence on the attitude and performance of others.[22] Since a nurse administrator in this system has considerable influence over others, their perception of her or him affects the administrator's ability to exercise management responsibility fully. Historically, the administrator in the traditional institutional clinical setting has been perceived as holding major responsibility for the nursing care that occurred in the institution. The nurse administrator was responsible for nursing students, practical nurses, and other registered nurses. As health institutions have grown, offering a multitude of services, and clinical nursing units have become more complex, the nursing administrator's role has expanded to include the planning, implementation, and evaluation of all nursing services.[23]

During the 1970s, registered nurses made significant advances through a series of legal and organizational initiatives that have established a clear legal accountability and responsibility, both individually and collectively, for nursing care rendered in institutions.[24] Such changes dramatically affected the role of the nursing administrator, changing it from one of clinical supervision as a chief nurse to a more varied and complex managerial and administrative function, no longer including clinical involvement. The bureaucratic framework emphasized her role in managing financial, environmental, structural, and relational concerns, placing unprecedented demands on her and requiring leadership skills and knowledge not previously a part of her basic preparation.[25] With more than 7,000 hospitals in the United States employing approximately 800,000 registered nurses and 600,000 auxiliary nursing personnel, the need for leadership knowledge and skill in administering the human complexity inherent in the delivery of nursing care becomes evident.[26]

Professional nurses share a desire to provide the highest quality patient care possible. Maintaining direct and positive communication among professional nurses is essential to fulfilling the desire for quality patient care. To maintain communicative interaction, each participant must be clearly aware of the individual expectations and collective expectations of both the group and the organization. Open lines of communication among group members relate directly to their knowledge of the expectations of the individual and the organization. Working with others involves a constant change in interaction and demands a controlled, constructive role that fosters communication.[27]

MODIFYING THE BUREAUCRATIC STRUCTURE

One of the organizational designs that has been commonly incorporated into current organizational and human resource management models is the matrix model. The matrix model is designed to bring the decision-making components of the organization to its operational levels. In nursing the model provides an opportunity for nurses at the practice level of the organization to exercise some role in the decision-making process. The matrix model, through its three unique qualities, lends itself well to nursing:

1. It is decentralized and focuses on the tasks to be done.
2. The tasks are directed to the overall objectives of the organization.
3. The tasks are usually short term, lasting anywhere from a few days to several years.[28]

Since there are many functional units (specialty clinical and administrative areas) in the nursing organization, much of the work occurs at the operational level. Bringing the functional decision-making power and accountability to the unit level facilitates the work of the unit. In the matrix model, resources essential to accomplishing the work are removed from the hierarchic arrangement and made available to the practicing nurse. Therefore, she may have access to a clinical specialist, a staffing coordinator, or a unit manager without having to use the traditional management track to obtain that support. Clearly, communication systems and strategies are important in this approach because many lateral relationships are invested in a matrix structure. Communication strategies take on a special significance in a matrix structure set up in a large multispecialty hospital where units may be diverse and segregated from one another.

In the matrix organization integrity is maintained by a strong central planning and governing function that combines all the system's parts for reporting purposes and for developing the central plan and strategy for implementing overall goals and objectives of the nursing service. In this approach the final locus of control and decision center are usually part of the nursing administrator's role. Dissemination of accountability filters down and through the organization's management track; thus, the further in or down the hierarchy the individual manager resides, the less accountability he or she has. That accountability is complemented by the responsibility attached to specified roles that focus on unique task or work categories usually designed to support nursing activities or to assume some of the tasks once considered part of the practicing nurse's role. Often, new tasks or responsibilities not formerly part of the organization's work focus are incorporated into the nursing function; the new work then becomes the function of a specialized individual who either assumes accountability for the function or assists the nursing staff in fulfilling responsibilities associated with the new role (see Figure 2-3).

Figure 2-3 Matrix Model

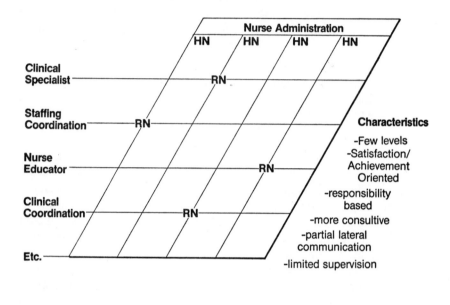

Regardless of the approach used by hospitals, it is within the context of the bureaucratic system that new designs or approaches are being explored, yet the bureaucratic system is proving to be the obstacle inhibiting organizational change. This is especially true in relation to professional nursing in the hospital context. The basic issue relates specifically to the conflict in fundamental definitions between bureaucratic organization and professional practice (see Figure 2-4).

In attempting to bring appropriate structure to the professional nursing environment, however, hospital organizations bring the conflict in definitions to the forefront. A bureaucratic organization by definition requires a highly ordered structure within which the purposes and functions of the organization can unfold. In order to maintain the relationship between order and function, a highly hierarchic system of internal controls are put in place to ensure the integrity of the system. Responsibility flows down and up a rigidly predefined ladder, with the key locus of decision and power resting at the apex of the organization. The primary and central communication linkages are vertical since authority is derived through that relationship.

Figure 2-4 How Dissonance Arises between the Bureaucratic
Organization and Professional Practice

dissonance

BUREAUCRATIC ORGANIZATION	PROFESSIONAL PRACTICE
ordered	consultive
hierarchical	collaborative
controlled	knowledge based
vertical	lateral communication
authoritative	judgment rendering
structured	developmental
administrative	standard centered
pyramidal	measurable
policy governed	interdependent

dissonance

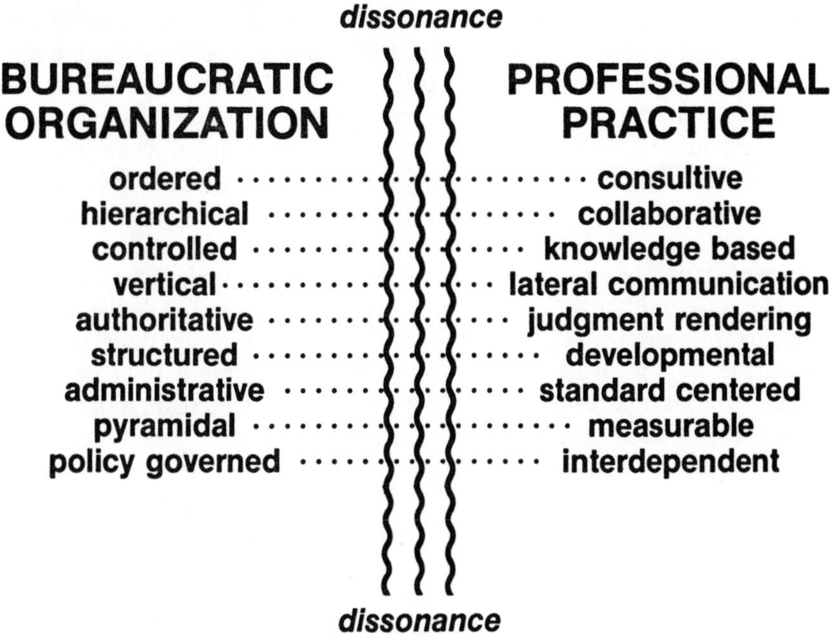

Supporting the organizational pyramid are operationally generated mandates that apply structure and value to the decision-making system and provide the behavioral overlay that ensures compliance within the system. This component is frequently identified as the policy or procedural element. These controls and derivations or similar elements provide the "glue" that holds most such organizations together. Around these elements is a host of traditions, values, and behaviors that serve as the cultural milieu of the organization. Often, these processes become the major work of the organization's management, who fight and struggle to keep the rules, policy, processes, and mandates in place. In assuming this role, management enables the organization to function smoothly and affirms the value and importance of the structure to work and outcomes. The key statement, however, is quite different from the one perhaps intended by the system's custodians: control of the system and all its parts lies elsewhere than in the arena where the work of the organization is done.

The obvious message in these organizations is that the power base and all it implies lie outside the workers' realm of influence or control; it operates independent of the individual function of work. It is this reality that has led, for the most part, to the need for labor unions and their assumption of responsibility for the quality of work life. The bureaucratic system fundamentally disregards valuing the individual in the work setting, requiring that special and separate benefits must be provided in the bureaucratic organization to value the worker. When the system failed to recognize that value, external systems were developed to address such issues.

The problem of the bureaucratic system is compounded when attempts are made to integrate it with the professional work group. In the hospital setting, members of the largest professional group—nurses—have been dealing for decades with the outcome of the fundamental conflict between the organization and professional role delineations. Against the backdrop of a hierarchic organizational system, nursing attempted to define itself in terms characteristically reserved for the behavior of professionals. In the past 20 years the profession at large has focused more fully on those definitions that reflect the character of professional nursing practice in any setting. It has become clear that these definitions are not well integrated in the traditional organizational structure. Indeed, they may be a threat to it.

Professional needs engender a 180-degree shift from the traditional organizational structure. Such terms as *collaborative, consultative,* and *joint relations* conjure up an image different from that synonymous with a bureaucratic structure. Professional practices emphasize—indeed, they demand—more lateral relationships and communication channels that cross hierarchic boundaries. Consistent with this, a valuation of the unique knowledge and skills of the professional must be assured. The fact that professionals render judgments based on their knowledge and interpretation of various signs and facts strongly indicates the need for a new supporting structure. Couching all these behavioral variables in professional terms indicates the underlying interdependence professionals must have if they are to practice their professions. When this interdependence is neither valued nor provided for, professional practice is impossible. When this occurs, the role and function of the professional are reduced to those of a technician carrying out by rote the demands of a system that expects more but makes no provision for it.

It should come as no surprise that nurses do not practice at levels consistent with professional expectations. In most organizations, such practice is virtually impossible. In fact, the values of bureaucracy actually prevent professional behavior. A review of some conflicts between structure and function for professional nurses in the bureaucratic structure may help illustrate this point.

In a bureaucratic organization the value of policy is considerable. Because the organization cannot function without the mandate of protocol and process, the necessity of policy takes on special significance. In fact, policy holds an inordinate amount of importance in the organization. Policy and procedure committees in nursing divisions are responsible for formulating the rules and mandates that articulate nursing behavior and practice. These roles are so clearly entrenched in the nursing service that operating without them is inconceivable. When a nurse quotes the policy and procedure manual to justify or support some behavior, it is gospel. Woe be the nurse whose judgment or practice was in some manner inconsistent with the organization's policy mandate.

Accepting such a mechanism in the bureaucratic organization is inconsistent with the basic tenets of the profession. What the policy and procedure manual replaces is the informed and appropriate judgment of the professional exercising her duties. Because the organization must protect its interests from possible misjudgment by its employees, it minimizes risks by establishing a common boundary within which all employee activities are measured. The professional has come to believe that participating in this manner is, in fact, assisting the hospital in its efforts to protect the patient. One must ask, however, "Protect the patient from whom and what?" The reader may conclude, as many in the profession have, that patients may not be protected from anything by such well defined and clearly articulated policies and procedures. If anything, patients may be endangered by a document that follows a standard, universal "cookbook" approach to their needs.

For years our colleagues in the medical profession have declined to participate in anything that would place definitive limits on their prerogative to make judgments on the specific medical needs unique to the individual patients they serve. They have clearly recognized that prescribed practice parameters do not adequately address the many variables met in the clinical environment. On the other hand, nurses have not only fully participated in this "fencing off acceptable behavior and practice"; they have often led the way in doing so. As those who spend most of their time in the clinical setting can attest, patients rarely fall into neatly packaged categories. Where they may share a common diagnosis, they may have distinctly different manifestations. In addition, patients bring different cultural, social, educational, environmental, and personal variables to their illness or health care situation. Using standardized responses on these variables, as outlined in policy and procedure, is a futile effort at best. Nurses' general lack of reference to most hospital policy and procedure manuals attests to the perceived real value attached to these manuals by nurses.

The move by the professional nurse to generate standards upon which sound practice judgment can be based is commendable. Establishing standards provides a baseline from which practice can spring, instead of constraints within which it is often frustrated. Other hospitals, however, are changing the name of the process but not its nature. A significant difference exists between a standard that provides a minimum baseline from which practice will grow and policy and procedure that defines the limits of behavior and nursing practice. The former facilitates the development and creativity essential to sound nursing practice, whereas the latter merely defines the limits of behavior. One is freeing; the other, constricting. Standards are intended to meet broad-based patient needs in rendering care, while the other is directed toward protecting the institution from the possibility of liability and, perhaps, from practitioner incompetence.

Trust—A Key Element in Fostering Change

With this argument, the matter of trust arises. Because professionals are interdependent, trust is an essential component of their relationship. It would not stretch a nurse's imagination to state that trust is an often sought but most elusive element in nurses' relationships with each other and with the institution in which they practice. Since trust, though often articulated, is not the cornerstone of the bureaucratic organization, there is no inherent motivator in the system to encourage its development. The "us–them" syndrome fostered by bureaucratic structures all but precludes the development of collaborative, meaningful interactions that are fundamental to the development of professional trust.

Trust also has special implications for practice and intraprofessional support. When other professionals have problems related to the service they render, they seek assistance from colleagues, advice from peers. If necessary, they search the literature to find an appropriate approach. This behavior pattern is notably absent from the practice of professional nurses in most institutions. Nurses have not learned or incorporated into their behavior those skills indicative of professionals in communion with each other. Although such skills have been supported in the modern nurse's education, they have not been given the same value by the employing institution. In other words, the employing institution neither expects nor supports these professional relationship skills. Again, the behavior is inconsistent with the bureaucratic organization's view of its employees. If encouraged to the logical extent of professional practice, such behavior could endanger the integrity of the hierarchy central to most current hospital systems.

The Nurse–Physician Relationship

Another key component in the bureaucratic tradition of hospitals is the conflict between nurses and physicians. This conflict is reflective of the system itself. While many creative approaches to medical and nursing interaction can be attempted in traditional organizational designs, there will always be a struggle to maintain the lines of communication and interaction. This is primarily because the system does not inherently encourage the peer colleagueship necessary to make those interactions self-generating.

The physician is an entrepreneur. He is, in fact, the primary customer of the hospital. The product of the physician, and the hospital, is the service that leads to the wellness or accommodation of the patient. The important point here, however, is that the physician is the central player in this team arrangement. Because of his importance to the hospital's success, the hospital is obviously going to do all in its power to meet his needs and to support his continuing to bring patients to the hospital. As previously pointed out, physicians already have many rather entrenched ideas about the role of the hospital, women, and nurses, as well as a number of preconceived notions about his place in the system. Although these ideas were not formally encouraged in his medical training, neither were they discouraged in the training process. Physicians have come to believe that the hospital is there to serve their needs and those they perceive for their patients. The hospital has supported and perpetuated this belief by developing systems and relationships that facilitate physicians' concepts about roles in the hospital and their primacy in the clinical process.

The physician's primacy and accelerated position in the traditional organization do not change merely because others are growing personally and professionally, becoming more assertive in delineating their own roles, responsibilities, and relationships to medical staff. The reality of this interaction is reflected in the nurse's need to seek approval or prior consent—in essence, to ask permission to become more directly involved in decisions affecting patient care and treatment. The right of ownership maintained and protected by the physician in this framework is an intervening, unchanging variable that always influences the nature of the interaction between nurse and physician. That interaction can never change as long as one party to it has an ascendant position and the other, a dependent role. Where there is stress and "noise" in the relationship, the tendency for unilateral solution exists and always favors the dominant party. This process underlies the historical relationship between nurse and physician and still continues in most hospitals, reflecting ongoing bureaucratic traditions and behaviors.

The Quest for Accountability

The internal bureaucratic structure of the nursing organization is a further constraint on the development of the individual nurse that is necessary if professional practice is to become commonplace. The rallying word in most nursing practice settings is *accountability*. Frequently, from the moment the new student hits the classroom and the clinical setting, the term becomes a part of her vocabulary and thought process. It is a term that will follow her for her entire nursing career. The problem with accountability, however, is that it is more expectation than reality. Nursing management frequently complains that nurses in most settings do not demonstrate appropriate accountability. This should come as no surprise. Nurses have an inordinate amount of insulation from the realities of exercising accountability. That they do not demonstrate accountability in practice is not surprising; it should be expected.

Nursing management has assumed all the system's activities that are commonly associated with the exercise of internally generated accountability. If problems arise in practice (with other care givers, physicians, staffing, standards, interpersonal problems, credentials, behavior, clinical compromise, decision making), nursing management is frequently, if not exclusively, responsible for "carrying the ball." True accountability, therefore, is only really exercised by those in nursing management. When the day-to-day activities of the nursing manager are closely examined, one can see that these matters and other activities fully occupy her time. Along with planning and providing leadership, then, the nurse manager must generally play caretaker of the nursing staff.

Building on the notion that nursing management activity places the nurse manager in a caretaker role, it becomes easier to see why the behaviors of nursing staff are not truly professional. Characteristics that identify behavior that can be called collaborative, knowledge based, or appropriately judgment rendering—based on standards with clear peer interdependence—have been notably absent from most professional practitioners of nursing. As a result, the professional nurse is a professional in title only. None of the descriptions that identify her role are clearly displayed in that role.

Organizational versus Professional Needs

Although the organization truly seeks professional behaviors from the registered nurse, its arrangements and relationships prevent her from exercising the kinds of responsibility that would demonstrate those behaviors. As a result, the staff nurse's role shows accommodation to the needs and bureaucratic context of the nursing system. These vocational or "blue collar" behaviors, while not required or requested by the organization or the nursing profession, are the only behaviors the institution finds acceptable and collaborative interactions would demand that an equal peer relationship exist between the professional health practitioners, including both nurses and physicians in the hospital structure.

Equality in Peer Relationships

Equality in peer relationships demands a different kind of organizational arrangement for its support. In the bureaucratic system, the physician has primacy in the clinical practice setting. True peer collaborative interactional arrangements between physicians and nurses cannot really be undertaken, however, without in some way jeopardizing the ascendant role of the physician and the organizationally dependent role of the nurse. Further, professional behaviors call for meaningful and ongoing dependence upon specific professional judgments made by the nurse. These judgments would relate to her clinical knowledge base and expertise in delivering appropriate nursing care. Her judgment would be trusted, valued, and protected by the organization. In reality, this is not generally the case. Nurses frequently are not validated for the judgments they make; nor are their judgments, in and of themselves, deemed significant enough to be validated within the context of nursing. The nurse's judgment in relation to practice is generally, if not always, subordinate and subject to what is considered the superior judgment of the physician. Physicians usually contest the validity of nurses' judgments as well as the value of nurses making judgments at all. The hospital supports this by preventing the nurse from making truly independent judgments by providing her with policy and procedural boundaries within which she is supposed to align her thinking and action.

The outcome of an independent nursing action not in concert with the physician's insight and wishes is not as dramatic as was once the case. When it is, the resulting conflict usually demeans the value of the nurses' judgment further in a situation where the physician is often the winner. Because of the possibility of this occurring frequently, the professional nurse retreats into accommodative, nonassertive, risk-free behavior that prevents anything from threatening her security in the practice environment. Such situations happen every day in hospitals in every community in America, continually reinforcing accommodating behaviors that are free of risks. They are, therefore, also free of the exercise of knowledge, independent judgment, and interdependent collaborative relationships with other professional practitioners.

Many nurses in management and clinical leadership in hospitals and other institutions work diligently to overcome these barriers to professional practice. These leaders constantly wage a battle against system barriers, trying to promote the growth of the professional nurse in the hospital's bureaucratic system. Even when newer strategies of interdependence in professional behavior do begin to develop in these settings, leadership frequently accommodates the bureaucratic framework, often at the expense of professional nursing practice. Trying to find ways within the bureaucratic organization to permit a glimmer of hope for professional practice for nurses is a challenging and, indeed, a full-time job. Because of constraints in the system and its inflexible response to alternative behaviors for the professional nurse, the battle between the system and the professional continues. This daily, ongoing conflict between structure and practice wearies the nurse leader. In the long term, it frequently reduces him or her to accommodating or defeated behavior within the organization.

The result is often an embittered, tired, apathetic, practitioner, working by rote, who no longer has the spirit or motivation to continue the struggle to create a coequal relationship between the bureaucratic structure and professional practice.

The history of this struggle has created for the nursing staff a clear picture of its true status in the hospital organization. Many decades of social and behavioral accommodation by nurses to the expectations of the bureaucratic system have reinforced their internalization that their contributions have not been valued. It is thus easy to see why the nurse who has practiced for any time either tires of the struggle and acquiesces to the demands of the structure, turning her interest in her work into a vocational pursuit; or rechannels her energy into a system that—if she is competent—will draw her away from the care-giving role and move her up the managerial ladder. The message to the nurse is loud and clear: Accommodate the demands of the system; "buy into" its values and mandates, and you will succeed and be rewarded. If not, at least do what the system asks of you. Do it well, and the system will take care of you to the extent it wishes. If you cannot do that, then the system has no place for you. Eventually, it will either ask you to seek opportunities elsewhere or penalize you in some other way.

Bureaucratic systems are replete with hidden messages; the politics of the organization are legendary. With others in the organization, nurses seem to be jockeying for positions of power and authority or ways to expand their personal influence. Often, others' positions in the structure are no barrier to the quest for dominance and control. The problem with this process is that everyone is aware that it is going on. Nurses also know that the locus of power in the organization rests somewhere other than in nurses' hands. Two things occur with this knowledge. The nurse senses the powerlessness in nursing and begins to look for the system's power centers that will get her what she wants. If that is unavailable, then opportunities to obtain some power of potential benefit will often be sought outside the organization, most often with unions. Even with this ultimate strategy, the nurse often fails to obtain the extent of power and control desired and merely adds another dimension to the bureaucratic relationship within the organization. For the most part, this adds to the "us–them" syndrome that lies at the very heart of the conflict. Thus we have gone full circle; the fundamental system and its internal relationships remain unchanged. The nurse remains frustrated, often overwhelmed, and impotent, with little evidence that much will change.

Per Diem Anonymity

Adding to the litany of problems between professionals and the bureaucracy is the chronic nursing condition we call per diem anonymity. Briefly, in this condition the nursing care service of the organization is not identified in financial terms that add value to the hospital. Nursing services have been and are still buried in the room rate of the hospital. For those who make financial decisions for the hospital, the issue becomes solely whether the bed is occupied or unoccupied. The issues of nursing service mix, care needs, intensity of service, differentiation of resource costs, and revenues attached to the rendering of specified nursing services are generally minimized. Addressing these issues in any way usually relates to the cost-generating psychology when thinking of nursing. Translating nurses and nursing into a revenue-generating service, which demands a change in thinking and operating, is not yet widely accepted even in the most progressive hospitals. One can try to imagine the effects of operating as a cost item in an industry that must value revenue generation in order to survive. As a cost center, the highest level to which nursing can rise on the priority list in a revenue-generating organization is fourth—behind laboratory, pharmacy, and radiology. Complicating this is the frequent cross-subsidization of these revenue services when nursing fills in the gaps in ordering, transcribing, and transportation to these services when such are not otherwise provided. Nurses not only perceive themselves as a major cost to the organization; they also know they must support the major revenue producers when the need arises. This does not help create a strong, positive self-image, nor does it lend any perception of autonomy and control over nursing destiny in the organization—both prerequisites to professional nursing practice in any setting.

The bureaucratic organization model clearly does not facilitate the development of a professional nursing organization and all that implies. Much of the struggle for growth and development in the nursing organization has been brought about with much pain. When positive change—change that upgrades professional nursing practice—occurs, the battle to maintain the advance becomes a cause célèbre in itself.

THE FUTURE OF THE HEALTH CARE BUREAUCRACY

No bureaucratic structure stands alone. It resides in a suprastructure that must deal with its constituents in a manner that can be understood and acted upon. In health care, a mammoth bureaucratic suprasystem exists that generates rules, regulations, and processes that tend to bureaucratize even further an already overburdened system. As the population becomes increasingly more dependent upon this system for meeting its health care needs, it appears that the system may become even more entrenched in bureaucracy.

The hope is that the system can begin to change from within. If nursing's part of that change is ever to take hold, there must be a systematic approach to creating organizational change in nursing in its primary settings and institutions, especially hospitals. To make the kind of impact on the health care system that is possible with almost 2 million nurses, it is necessary that we change our system of operation—first from within, then in the major political and social health care arenas. This process will occur in a variety of settings concurrently but can be facilitated by the professional development of nursing practice and professional relationships in the hospital setting.

The history of nursing demonstrates the need for changing the organizational design of most hospitals. The structure of the bureaucratic system simply cannot in any way facilitate the growth and development of professional nursing practice to the extent nurses envision. The constant antagonism between the professional practice needs of nurses and nursing and the tightly controlled hierarchic structure is a waste of energy and valuable human resources. It is time to admit that this tenuous relationship is neither valuable nor productive.

It is time to divert energy away from strategies aimed at accommodating the bureaucratic system. It is time to begin to explore those systems that encourage and support professional nursing practice internally. And it is time to show the external bureaucracy that nurses not only contribute to the success of the institution but are actually its leaders and most valuable resource. As in all efforts to build and grow, outcomes are always subject to proof. Therefore it is essential to begin such a transition carefully and from within the very center of the nursing organization, where the process of professionalizing the nursing staff will be the most challenging—and the most rewarding.

NOTES

1. R. T. Pascale and A. G. Athos, *The Art of Japanese Management Applications for American Executives* (New York: Simon & Schuster, 1981), p. 208.

2. R. Schrank, *Ten Thousand Working Days* (Cambridge, Mass.: MIT Press, 1978).

3. F. Taylor, *The Principles of Scientific Management* (New York: Harper & Brothers, 1911).

4. A. Maslow, *Motivation and Personalities* (New York: Harper & Row, 1954).

5. E. Mayo, *Human Problems of an Industrial Civilization* (New York: Macmillan Company, 1933).

6. D. McGregor, *The Human Side of Enterprise* (New York: McGraw-Hill, 1960).

7. C. Argyris, *Interpersonal Competence and Organizational Effectiveness* (Homewood, Ill.: Ervin Dorsey Press, 1962).

8. F. Herzberg, *Work and the Nature of Man* (New York: World Publishing Company, 1966).

9. R. Likert, *The Human Organization* (New York: McGraw-Hill, 1967).

10. E. Berne, *Games People Play* (New York: Grove Press, 1964).

11. D. Jongewood, *Everybody Wins: Transactional Analysis Applied to Organizations* (Reading, Mass.): Addison-Wesley Publishing Company, 1973).

12. P. Drucker, *Management* (New York: Harper & Row, 1974), pp. 130–158.

13. D. Cartwright and A. Sandler, eds., *Group Dynamics: Research and Theory* (Evanston, Ill.: Roe Peterson & Company, 1960).

14. R. Stogdell and A. Koons, eds., *Leader Behavior, Its Description and Measurement*, Research Monologue No. 88, (Columbus, Ohio: Ohio State University, Bureau of Business Research, 1957).

15. R. Blake and J. Mouton, *The Managerial Grid* (Houston: Gulf Publishing, 1960).

16. P. Hersey and K. Blanchard, *Management of Organizational Behavior Utilizing Human Resources* (Englewood Cliffs, N.J.: Prentice-Hall, 1982).

17. R. Likert, *New Patterns of Management* (New York: McGraw-Hill, 1961).

18. F. Fiedler, *Improving Leadership Effectiveness* (New York: McGraw-Hill, 1976).

19. F. Fiedler, E. D. Hutchins, and J. Dodge, *Psychological Monographs*, no. 473 (Chicago: University of Illinois, 1973).

20. A. Athos and R. Coffey, *Behavior in Organizations: A Multidimensional View* (Englewood Cliffs, N.J.: Prentice-Hall, 1968).

21. P. Hersey, K. Blanchard, and E. Lamonica, "A Situational Approach to Supervision," *Supervisor Nurse*, May 1976.

22. W. Ganong and J. Ganong, "Reducing Organizational Conflict through Working Committees," *Journal of Nursing Administration*, January/February 1972.

23. *Standards for Nursing Services* (Kansas City, Missouri: The American Nurses Association, 1974).

24. *Laws Regulating the Practice of Registered Nursing* (Olympia, Wash.: State of Washington, 1974).

25. M. Colton, "Nursing Leadership Vacuum," *Supervisor Nurse*, October 1976, pp. 29–37.

26. *Facts on Nursing* (Kansas City, Missouri: The American Nurses Association, 1983).

27. A. Ciancutti et al., "Creating Harmony Between Supervisor and Nurse," *Supervisor Nurse*, August 1976.

28. T. Porter-O'Grady, "The Organization of Nursing Services: A Model for the Future," *Supervisor Nurse*, July 1978, pp. 30–40.

Chapter 3

Times Are Changing

THE CONCEPT OF ORGANIZATIONAL STRUCTURE

Creating an organization that fits both the purposes of structure and those of function is a challenging task for any administrator. Making the nursing practice variable a part of the structural design further complicates the process of planning for organizational change. Many questions arise about which design best fits the function of the organization:

1. What is the work of nursing?
2. How does nursing practice effectively unfold in the hospital organization?
3. What are the control mechanisms in the organization that provide the structural "glue" that binds together both purpose and discipline?
4. What are the expectations and outcomes of the organization and how can they best be achieved by nurses?
5. What is the scope and value of nursing practice in the organization, and how do nursing practice dynamics influence interaction between the various disciplines?
6. How can the characteristics of a profession and all the responsibilities identified therein be actualized in the hospital operational environment?
7. How can the hospital organizational structure come together, to not only support professional nursing practice but also to survive, becoming less dependent on individuals and more so on the entire group?[1]

In assessing the organization for redesign, the nursing innovator must know that changes in organization and movement toward democratic and rational approaches to management of human resources and practice are common themes in today's management theory. Much work has been done to bring thinking about the management of the human group to a practical level, where alternative structures and decision-making processes can be brought into organizations. The fact that hospitals have been relatively slow to respond to these theories should in no way diminish interest in them or resources available to the nurse innovator who is seeking new alternatives for organizational structure and design.

The question of organizational structure and what it is supposed to accomplish is an important one for the innovator to ask. Organizational structure, of course, is more than the design in an organizational chart, with boxes and lines drawn from one spot to another. The structure relates the interaction and linkages that tie together the work of the organization, its tasks, all its human components, and its technology as it is expressed through the outcomes of work. Structure is the means by which the function and process of the organization accomplish its purposes. Organizational structure should facilitate information flow and decision making. It should be designed in such a way as to facilitate the generation and reception of all the information people in the organization need to perform their work. The system should be open and responsive not only to the needs of the product but also to those of the individuals responsible for ensuring a quality product. In nursing, the product is the patient, and the outcome is the patient's achievement of the highest possible level of functioning. The organizational structure, therefore, must provide opportunities for that to occur.

Organizational structure must also achieve effective coordination and integration of behavior and work. This is significant since all elements of the system are somewhat interdependent. In a hospital, no one individual can be totally accountable for the care and management of the patient. The hospital's organization is so complex and so interdependent that each piece of it interacts collectively; thus each component influences the outcome of the patient's care. This process, called reciprocal interdependence, is highly complex. Each unit depends on the other for the fulfillment of the goals of the whole. Also, since the hospital is a human organization, the relationships established between the elements of the system are key to the successful outcomes of the organization. Human-intensive environments have a special need for an organizational design that focuses specifically on the relationships established between the participants. It is this relationship and the interaction of all of the elements that become the basis for the productive and effective work of the organization.

The Human Service Element and High Technology

An additional component in hospital environments is the introduction of a high level of technology and all the implications that technology has for the organization. Those involved in delivering services, those who are dependent upon technology, must be highly skilled and well informed about specific parameters of practice, and how practice standards and technology interface. Therefore, most of the workers in this human-intensive environment have been prepared for highly specialized and complex roles in the delivery of patient services. The situation is no less true for nursing. As medical specialties have become more technical and complex, the delivery of nursing services has also become highly complex so as to provide the full range of required services. The theory base and practice parameters of nursing have all responded to the radical change in technology in the past two decades.

The increase of technology and dependence upon its mechanics have required that nurses assume an additional burden, adding another human element to the large number of variables with an impact on patient care. Much of the technology in service delivery is machine technology. Patients can get lost in the system and be depersonalized by the very technology designed to help their healing process. The interactional and human skills of nursing professionals have become more and more essential to service delivery since nurses have taken on more responsibility for assuring that the pieces of the human environment merge, providing a holistic approach to meeting patients' needs. This demand, along with that for management of new patient care technology, provides a complex environment for current nursing practice.

The organizational structure that provides the framework for nursing practice must include an understanding of the many variables involved in maintaining the human environment, not only for the patient, but also for the practitioner, who has a real need for support in organizational systems. These systems enable the nurse to fulfill both her needs as a human being and her role as a key provider of patient care.

The Need for Participation

This need for an organization and a structure that support interrelationships and interdependence is not new. Providing a working structure that goes beyond allowing participation in processes affecting the delivery of services, however, is a relatively new concept. It is just now being considered and discussed in a number of major national forums.

In his book *Megatrends* John Naisbitt indicates that a change in organizational structure is needed.[2] He believes that the people whose lives are affected by decisions must be a part of arriving at those decisions. Further, he believes that organizations are moving toward a participatory democracy. We will see more and more evidence of the democratic process unfolding in the business, corporate, and government structures of society.

Naisbitt points out the intensity of the human relations and interactions present in most companies and corporations, including hospitals. It is in our work environment that our abilities are most strongly used and our social ties with others are formed and solidified, he writes. It is in our work environment that self-esteem is imagined and perhaps actualized and where our economic basis for living has its source. Since the order of the American political and social scene is changing, people are becoming involved in new and participatory roles in government and other decision-making processes. The demands for participation spill over into the work environment, and they are becoming a part of the everyday rhetoric of the worker.

An interesting dichotomy occurs between the prevailing perception of people in the contexts of their social role and their work role. The social obligation of citizens in a democracy is to participate actively in exercising their franchise in the social institutions of which they are a part. Citizens are encouraged to act responsibly and to get involved in the processes that support their social and political institutions in a free society. However, citizens must usually spend at least eight hours a day, five days a week, in the work environment where the reverse is asked. In the work environment, people are expected to be essentially voiceless, to perform specific tasks, to defer to others in decision making and other involvement in decision processes, and to subjugate their personal interests, needs, desires, and personal accountability to those suggested by representatives of the larger organization. Thus, while they are asked to be responsible, participating, and active citizens in a free society while not in the work setting, they are not provided the opportunities to develop and exercise the required abilities in the workplace—where they will spend clearly half of their adult life. Viewing the individual in this context may give us insight into why there is not broader participation in the social forums and institutions of our society. It is no wonder that neither managers nor workers in the United States are culturally equipped to accept diffusion of responsibility and control in the workplace.[3]

Organizational Theory and Participatory Democracy

Much work has been done in the past two decades to provide a theoretical base for moving organizations to more rational participatory structures. Douglas McGregor provided some new thinking on human nature and its relationship to work in his theory of human motivation.[4] He believed that work is a natural part of the human condition and that, if all things are equal, people prefer to work and accomplish in a productive way. McGregor believed that self-control is an important component of achieving organizational goals and that individuals are able to exhibit self-control and to modify their behavior consistent with organizational needs. He also indicated that people have a tremendous capacity for creativity in assisting the organization to solve problems, and that this capacity is widely distributed among the worker population. McGregor theorized that motivation occurs at the social esteem and self-actualization levels, as well as at the physiological and security levels, building on Maslow's hierarchy of needs. Fundamentally, he indicated that people are self-directed and, if properly motivated, able to meet all of the conditions essential for high levels of productivity and positive responses to the needs of work in the organizational environment.

McGregor's approach was a radical change from the traditional belief systems that he called Theory X. It is Theory X upon which most bureaucratic expectations have been built, even though the worker behaviors predicted by that theory may not be a part of the belief system of today's managers. Those who operate in a bureaucratic system participate in a structure that assumes these behaviors to be part of the working environment. According to Theory X, work is inherently disagreeable for most people who have no interest in participating in work; in addition, ambition, the desire for responsibility, and the capacity for creativity are relatively remote influences on people's participation in the work process. In contrast, McGregor believed that motivation can be achieved through satisfaction of physiological and safety needs for most workers. He indicated further that workers need not be closely observed and frequently coerced into meeting organizational objectives, and that management's role is to assume responsibility for leading, organizing, controlling, and directing employees in a way consistent with the organization's goals and mandates. In attempting to provide alternatives to the traditional pyramidal bureaucratic structure that dominates most organizations today, Chris Argyris has devised a continuum on which employer expectations and employee behaviors can be assessed.[5,6] He calls this the immaturity-maturity continuum. On the continuum, immature behaviors include being passive, dependent, limited in expression, and very shallow and having erratic interests and having short-term perspective; accepting subordination and being unaware of the self are other immature behaviors. On the other end of the continuum, a mature individual is identified as being active, independent, and interdependent; capable of multiple behavior patterns; and having a deep and well-developed interest and an ability to view the long-term perspective, both past and future. Mature individuals are able to feel equal or superordinate in relation to others and have a strong self-awareness and the ability to develop self-control. In viewing workers in relation to this continuum, Argyris saw that in the bureaucratic framework, workers are expected to act in an immature way; as a result, immature behaviors are exhibited in most work settings. Argyris went so far as to say that bureaucratic organizations' very structure keeps people immature. The course of his argument went something like this: Organizations are generally created to achieve certain goals and objectives; these must be met collectively. After the leadership provides the goals and directions, the individual is then assigned a particular role. In the process of decision making, the goals and objectives of the organization come first and task specification comes second. Therefore, the bureaucratic system, using the scientific management processes previously outlined, uses tasks, authority, direction, and span of control as tools for accomplishing its prescribed objectives. In doing that, those responsible for carrying out the tasks in response to management authority do not undertake activity generally considered consistent with the maturity portion of Argyris's continuum.

Argyris showed that the formal bureaucratic organization leads to thinking about human activity and human nature that is inconsistent with mature human activity. Further, he believed that most organizations need to change their structure to permit mature behaviors to be exhibited in their work settings. He initiated many studies to support his theory, providing evidence of major improvements in both productivity and satisfaction when maturity-based frameworks were well established.

In his studies of human behavior in organizations, Frederick Herzberg developed an approach he called the motivation/hygiene theory.[7] Building on the work of Maslow, McGregor, and Argyris, he concluded that most workers have two unrelated levels of needs and that needs affect behavior in different ways. Studies revealed a frequent common pattern of response. When workers exhibited good attitudes regarding their work, they displayed satisfaction primarily with the work itself. When workers did not feel good about their work, they usually exhibited concern about the environment in which they worked.

In developing his theory, Herzberg called concerns about the work environment "hygiene factors" and concerns about satisfaction with the work itself "motivating factors." It is the motivating factors that seem to have an impact on performance and satisfaction. According to Herzberg, policy, procedure, administration processes, working conditions, relationships, money, security, and physiological satisfactions are the hygienic factors in most work settings. These are not necessarily intrinsic to the work, he stated, but are a corollary to the work setting. He found these conditions did not change productivity or work output in any way. He called them maintenance factors since they did nothing but maintain a specified level of work activity.

Herzberg listed the motivating factors intrinsic to the work itself as having the ability to grow, being satisfied with what one was doing, and having a feeling of achievement and recognition for work well done. The challenge and scope of responsibility and activity of the work were found to be strongly motivating and associated with worker satisfaction. Increased responsibility and satisfaction associated with recognition for excellence had an impact on workers' desire to grow and to contribute more fully.

The discrimination between dissatisfaction and satisfaction is a further key element of Herzberg's work. Herzberg believed that, when met, hygienic factors assist in the reduction of dissatisfaction in the work environment but do nothing to create essential satisfaction with the work itself. In his view, therefore, dissatisfaction does not indicate the absence of hygienic factors in the workplace. When motivating conditions are present and provided for by the structure, however, there is the possibility of achieving satisfaction. It is in this satisfaction that the individual finds growth and opportunity related to the work itself. Thus, satisfactory hygienic factors do not necessarily create a motivating urge in the worker that will improve her participation. But when motivating factors are present, Herzberg suggests, satisfaction is achieved. Satisfying the hygienic factors alone merely provides the starting place from which the opportunity can be created to motivate employees to more productive behavior.

PRACTICAL APPLICATION OF ORGANIZATIONAL THEORY

These theorists and others provide a basis upon which movement can unfold toward a participating and involved work force. In addition to the general, behavioral theoretic bases already described, there are certain implications unique to professional workers in the organization. Professional definitions and expectations have an additional set of criteria that impose additional obligations on professionals in the workplace.

Flexner, Bixler, and Blane identify seven basic criteria for a profession in a free society. According to those criteria, a profession:[8–10]

1. uses a well-defined and organized body of specialized knowledge that operates on a conceptual and intellectual level;
2. constantly enlarges a body of knowledge and improves the processes of education through use of scientific methods;
3. educates its practitioners in institutions of higher learning;
4. applies its knowledge and practice in areas that are vital to human and social welfare;

5. functions autonomously, formulates its own professional policy, and controls its own professional activity;
6. has a professionally based culture that attracts individuals with intellectual and personal qualities that further the interests of the profession and who see professional activity as a lifetime work; and
7. has some form of social and legal sanction.

It becomes clear that traditional bureaucratic approaches, when applied to the delivery of professional nursing services, must shift or give way to alternative designs if human potential is to be fully utilized in the hospital organization. To do that, a new way of thinking about organizational relationships, organizations, and the responsibility of their professional members must be undertaken. Organizations must provide a basis for creating a work design that responds to both the organization and those it serves. There has been some new and creative thinking that provides a conceptual basis for building an organizational model appropriate for professional workers and consistent with current thinking on human behavior in the workplace.

The Neoteric Model

L. L. Wade describes an appropriate model for hospitals: the neoteric model of organization.[11] According to Wade there should be a minimum of formal organizational structures to interfere with the individual worker's ability to participate in decisions directly related to the work itself. He indicates that productivity and internal functional autonomy come together when there are fewer "layers" in the formal organizational structure; he also mentions that output increases under these conditions. Traditional bureaucratic frameworks dissipate according to his organizational description. People limit their belief in the legitimacy of authority if that authority implies that there is submission of the individual and her work as in a traditional master/servant relationship. A rigid hierarchy does not fit into Wade's vision of the neoteric model. This model is especially meaningful for employed professionals because it depends upon the professional's knowledge and on scientific parameters to legitimize operation and function, rather than on arbitrary or organizationally defined parameters, which may not be sensitive to scientific or knowledge-based processes. Further, he states that facilitating interaction between professionals is essential to the work of the organization. Therefore, traditional human objectivity, a constituent of the bureaucratic organization, will not support the intensity consistent with the human relationships that are necessary for successful operation of a professional organization.

In addition, Wade points out that the traditional distinctions between governance and professional work activities diminish when related to the establishment of organizational policy and direction since both policy and planning are part of the very work of professional practice. Autonomy and accountability for establishing policy and participating in planning are fundamental to the professional's role. Professionalism, ethics, and practice processes should be incorporated into the policy and operational decision-making processes of organizations whose services are primarily professional in nature.

Wade identifies certain specific conditions as being necessary for the neoteric model to operate effectively in professional organizations. Internally, a general absence of rules and structured hierarchy is needed. There should be much latitude for judgment and variation in professional activity, with a high level of personal contact and relationship between professionals and their clients. Equity in the distribution of resource supports for activity and the work of the professional should be provided. Diminishing emphasis on conformity and rigidity of activity may frequently influence effectiveness and productivity. Finally, the neoteric model operates within the parameters of the professional's idea of role and responsibility. Mechanisms that support accountability derived from members' knowledge bases and the scientific process, as well as evaluation and implementation strategies, should be provided within the organization. Mechanisms for professional peer review and peer disciplinary processes need to be incorporated into the organizational structure.

According to Wade, the neoteric model requires outside acceptance by society as well as the expectation that professionals will conduct their activities in accord with clearly defined standards and social norms. Resources and social status are provided by society as a reward for, and an indication of the value placed on, the work of the specific professional. Political, social, and environmental conditions provide opportunities for the professional to continue to develop and to influence the society in positive and meaningful ways. It is this framework of accountability, autonomy, and a clearly defined knowledge base that provides the foundation for unfolding professional activity in the neoteric model. Self-governance, social, political, and legal support generate the environment for both internal and external consistency.

The Organizational Revolution

In his studies on hierarchy and democratic authority, Peter Abell, of the University of Birmingham, indicates that when the organizational revolution occurs, traditionally hierarchical organizational and social structures will disappear.[12] Newer structures with characteristics of a free society that represent democratic processes will replace traditional bureaucratic structures and behavior. In most industrialized countries, he states, the move is toward participation, power sharing, and self-management. He identifies this new emphasis as a move toward rational democratic authority, a theory he builds on the concepts of human behavior already reviewed in this chapter. Abell believes that people are self-directed and self-managing, and will assume responsibility for issues related to their own fulfillment. He also believes in group process and group decision making and asserts that higher-level goals can be achieved by groups than by individuals. Since information is central to the ability to make appropriate judgments and decisions, he states, appropriate and meaningful judgments can be rendered when people are provided sufficient information. Abell establishes as his a prior belief that only when all individuals in an organization have parallel voting rights can absolute political equality exist in the organization. Subordinate to that key idea is his support of representative decision making, as well as a need for unique, specialized knowledge in making informed decisions.

Based on his theory, Abell indicates some central characteristics of an organization that operates within the context of rational democratic authority. He sees the need to generate sufficient, appropriate information to allow members of the organization to make necessary decisions. When the organization and its people are in concert, the people will work to achieve the organization's goals. In a rational system if participating members are not committed to the goals and objectives of the organization, they are free to leave. By virtue of their membership, they must be committed to fulfilling their practice obligations in regard to the goals and purposes of the organization. Voting power in these organizations is available to all members, and it has a direct relationship to the decisions that are made. Representation in delegate assemblies is a part of the decision-making process in this kind of organization. Issues related to privacy, coordination, control functions, role clarification, and the democratic activities associated with delegate appointment are all parts of the rational democratic process.

Contracting for obligations that clearly delineate the expectations and responsibilities of members can also be considered a component of a rational democratic organization. Issues traditionally considered management prerogatives, such as the quality of work life, salary or wages, benefits, and other economic considerations, become part of the framework of a rational democratic organization. Granting credentials and implementing disciplinary processes become responsibilities of members of the organization rather than of its management. Mandates for these processes are provided within the staff structure of a rational democratic system.

The rational democratic authority structure provides an appropriate framework for the support of professional nursing activities within a hospital organization. Because of nursing's consistency with professional descriptors, a close parallel appears between nursing and the characteristics of a rational democratic authority structure. Democratic authority humanizes the work environment and establishes an organizational framework based on human values that reflect beliefs and practices that are consistent with the nursing profession. Creating a democratic framework for the professional work environment helps reduce the traditional intervening variables whose placement in the bureaucratic organization actively hinders the flow of relationships and behaviors necessary to professional nursing practice.

Oscar Mink and his associates have done much to provide a balanced view of the new organizational framework that puts the complex organization within the context of a changing environment.[13] They believe that classic bureaucratic theories supported a relatively stable, predictable environment. Therefore bureaucracy supported order, fairness, control, and norms of personal conduct that represented a relatively predictable environment. However, accelerating complexity and change in the world have created a work environment and a world order that are unpredictable. No longer can organizational stability be assumed through standard operating procedures, nor can control be concentrated at the top. Internal rigidity consistent with bureaucratic organizations creates procedural buildup, departmental territoriality, and stalemates among vested interests in broad organizational environments.

The organization of the future will depend upon adaptability rather than predictability. An open organization will consider process more vital than structure; it will create opportunities for free interaction and communication and reduce the impact of utilizing chain-of-command hierarchies. Organizational philosophies of the future will depend on viewing human life as organic and fluid, not mechanistic; they will be dependent upon personal and group relations, rather than on cause-and-effect relationships. These organizations will be intuitive as well as rational. Systems theoretical approaches will deemphasize structure as a basis of organization and focus more on function, process, self-organization, and self-governance. Open systems being developed for the future will freely exchange information, energy, and material in relation to their environment. Social systems will be open and responsive. The ultimate measure of an organization's ability to adapt will be its capacity to respond to the environment. Closed organizations, such as bureaucratic structures, respond to environmental changes and influences very slowly. Open organizations, neither hierarchic nor structurally rigid, will become more responsive. They will depend more on information and feedback mechanism and will adapt their responses to changes in the environment quickly and freely. Members of the organization itself will participate fully in its direction, policy, goals, and activities. Those vested with accountability for carrying out the work and fulfilling major functions will be central to the establishment of direction and objectives for the organization.

It is upon these theoretical bases that the concept of shared governance in nursing is based. In an effort to restructure the organization to make it supportive of professional nursing activities, it is necessary to have some legitimate theoretical underpinning for providing a unique thinking process for unfolding professional nursing practice. It must be different from what has been experienced in the past. Neoteric, rational democratic authority, and open organizational approaches all provide a general base for moving toward a more humanistic structure that operates more effectively in human-intensive settings such as hospitals. However, these approaches include obligations. They require that the professional worker be a full participant in the organization and the work environment. The individual's commitment to the organization and its goals holds additional obligations and responsibilities. A continuum of relationships operate at different levels of intensity and in different directions between the organization and its professional members, with each providing support for the other. The dynamic nature of this relationship is facilitated when both the individual and the collective, which is the organization, fulfill their obligations to each other.

The translation from knowledge and theory to implementation is often slow and frequently difficult. Many risks are involved in making significant changes in organizational structure, especially structure that has been in place for many decades. Such change requires whole new ways of looking at one's relationship with the workplace and with the worker. The nurse has not only the traditional employee characteristics of most workers; she also has additional obligations that emerge from the expression of professional nursing values. In becoming a participant in the profession of nursing, the nurse commits herself to the values of that profession. Such values are reflected in how professionals view their work and in the relationships they establish with one another. Professional nurses require a high degree of collaboration and many collegial relationships. Much of the communication between members of the profession is lateral. These inherent characteristics and values of the profession are added to the motivational needs of workers. As previously mentioned, this additional professional overlay further complicates an already complex situation in the hospital workplace.

IMPLEMENTING CHANGE IN THE NURSING PROFESSION

With all these high-risk, human-intensive factors affecting one another, the first question that arises is where one can begin to make changes. For nursing, the first step is to define basic beliefs upon which professional practice in an open organization might unfold. Developing these basic beliefs within the hospital or health care institution must be done at all organizational levels of the nursing service. Those most directly involved in establishing policy direction for nursing must also be involved in establishing the belief system that will be the basis for initiating change in the organization. Beliefs must be defined not only conceptually but also practically, so that they can be implemented to provide the framework for all subsequent activities.

Consistent with the move toward a shared governance organization, there are essential beliefs in nursing that must be characteristic of professional nursing practice in institutions. Simply stated, these beliefs are as follows:

1. Nursing is a professional practice and, as such, exhibits the behaviors and characteristics consistent with professional practice.
2. All human beings are intrinsically motivated, have a desire to accomplish, and seek the opportunity to reach their maximum potential.
3. The organizational structure of the institution should be designed in a manner that supports and upholds the characteristics essential for delivering professional nursing services.
4. The hospital is essentially a human service organization and therefore must reflect all the characteristics of human interaction and behavior that are essential to fulfilling the needs of the clients it serves.
5. Bureaucratic and professional behaviors do not mix. One must either operate within the bureaucratic framework or reject that framework and accept a professional model of behavior.
6. The registered nurse currently is the primary practitioner of professional nursing and is a key element in the delivery of health care services: therefore, nursing plays a pivotal role in delivering health care services in the hospital and other health care settings.
7. Provided the opportunity, the environment, and the framework, registered nurses will make appropriate and meaningful judgments about

professional nursing practice and the direction and operation of the nursing organization.

8. Provided the opportunity, the environment, and the framework, professional nurses will seek to render the highest level of patient care; further they will seek unique and creative opportunities to improve the profession that will result in rendering effective patient care services.

These basic beliefs are essential for initiating meaningful movement from a bureaucratic structure to a professional model in the hospital organization. These beliefs, formulated in conjunction with the standards defining professional activity, provide a philosophical base for moving toward a structure and system that will support and promulgate professional nursing behaviors. As in any meaningful and valuable change, much of what occurs in this change process must be based on a firm foundation of understanding and belief. The concept of shared governance in nursing will have difficulty evolving without understanding the organizational theoretical base, undertaking commitment to professional nursing practice, and incorporating basic nursing beliefs as described herein.

Notes

1. R. Duncan, "What Is the Right Organizational Structure?" *Organizational Dynamics*, Winter 1979, pp. 59–79.
2. J. Naisbitt, *Megatrends* (New York: Warner Communications, 1982).
3. J. R. Witte, *Democratic Authority and Alienation in Work* (Chicago: University of Chicago Press, 1980), pp. 1–10.
4. D. McGregor, *The Human Side of Enterprise* (New York: McGraw-Hill, 1960).
5. C. Argyris, *Integrating the Individual and the Organization* (New York: John Wiley & Sons, 1964).
6. C. Argyris, *Interpersonal Competence and Organizational Effectiveness* (Homewood, Ill.: Ervin Dorsey Press, 1962).
7. F. Herzberg, *Work and the Nature of Man* (New York: World Publishing Company, 1966).
8. A. Flexner, "Is Social Work a Profession?" *Report of the New York School of Philanthropy*, 1915.
9. G. Bixler and R. Bixler, "The Professional Status of Nursing," *American Journal of Nursing*, August 1959, p. 1142.
10. D. Blane, *The Hospital as a Professional Bureaucracy Trustee* (American Hospital Association, 1975) pp. 13–16.
11. L. L. Wade, "The Neoteric Model" *Human Organization*, no. 26 (Chicago Ill.: Spring/ Summer 1967): 40–46.
12. P. Abell, "Hierarchy and Democratic Authority," in *Work and Power*, ed. T. R. Burns, L. E. Karlsson, and V. Rus (Beverly Hills, Calif.: Sage Publications, 1979) pp. 141–171.
13. O. Mink, James Shultz, and B. Mink, *Open Organizations* (Austin, Texas: Learning Concepts, 1979).

Chapter 4

Nurses at Work: What Do We Do?

Before discussing the initiation and development of the concept of shared governance, let us examine the work of nursing in the hospital to gain a clear idea of the essential activities that require organizational and structural support. Through examining these various components, we begin to gain a functional view of the scope of nursing activities within an organizational context. By looking at the work of nursing and examining its elements, we can begin to conceptualize an organizational framework that will support the profession's activities. We thus provide an organizational overlay that facilitates the practice of nursing within a professional model.

THE PHYSICIAN–NURSE–PATIENT TRIAD

The first step in discussing nursing's work is to examine the key to relationships begun when the patient first uses the hospital's services. It is at this point that the essential patient care triad is established. The patient is admitted by the physician for specific care needs. When admitted, the patient moves into a relationship first with the nurse. The patient identifies for the nurse specific matters essential to his care. The physician also identifies specific procedural necessities for resolving medical care problems. With the physician and the nurse, the patient becomes the third component of the triad. The patient becomes involved in medical care, which will either return him to an acceptable level of wellness or help him adjust to limitations or illness. It is this relationship—the physician, the nurse, the patient—that is fundamental to the patient's process and progress throughout the hospitalization period (see Figure 4-1).

When the relationships in the patient care triad are begun, particular actions are taken consistent with those relationships. The physician usually makes a diagnosis based on medical information and prescribes care

Figure 4-1 Conceptual Framework for Professional Practice

CONCEPTUAL FRAMEWORK FOR PROFESSIONAL PRACTICE

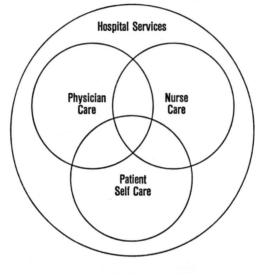

Hospital Patient Care Triad

essential to addressing the medical problems that have made hospitalization necessary. After that prescription has been provided, certain medically related activities are undertaken to treat the patient. Those activities may relate to any or all of the service functions of the hospital.

Corollary to the medical prescription and regimen of care upon admission, nursing activity begins. Based upon a thorough nursing assessment and problem identification, resulting in specific nursing diagnoses, a plan of care tailored to the patient's needs may be undertaken. Like the medical plan, the nursing plan, if properly drawn, includes inputs provided by the patient. With the patient, the physician, and the nurse, a treatment program and the nursing plan of care ideally are undertaken to address the patient care needs. Activities directed toward discharge planning, returning the patient to a level of wellness, or helping the patient to deal with limitations in health are undertaken in the context of the patient care triad. This nurse–physician–patient interaction becomes essential to the patient's treatment and recovery. This combination of interactions is the basis for the patient's movement through the hospital stay (see Figure 4-2).

The primary interaction between the patient and the institution is often displayed in the nurse–patient relationship. This key relationship exists

Figure 4-2 Nurse–Physician–Patient Interaction

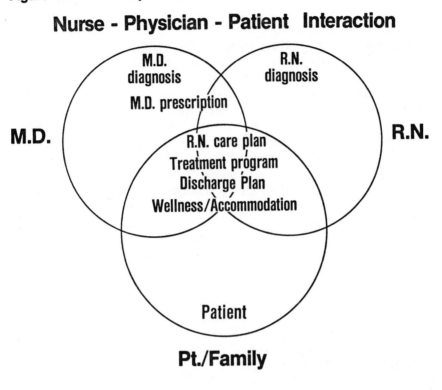

Nurse - Physician - Patient Interaction

M.D.

R.N.

M.D. diagnosis

R.N. diagnosis

M.D. prescription

R.N. care plan
Treatment program
Discharge Plan
Wellness/Accommodation

Patient

Pt./Family

throughout the patient's entire hospital stay. It is central to the successful coordination of health care activities directed to meeting the patient's needs. An appropriate nursing relationship reflects the caring components of nursing practice as they are applied to the patient's expressed and unexpressed needs. Through the interaction between the nurse and the patient, these needs are identified and addressed, and the patient's adjustment to illness and adaptation to changes in health status are actualized for his benefit. Both the nurse and the patient bring to the relationship skills and abilities consistent with their positions, roles, and responsibilities. Patients bring with them values, perceptions, practices, a social role in the organization, and their supports, which may be social, economic, or emotional. The nurse brings her clinical understanding and knowledge base, her ability to collaborate and communicate effectively, perceptions based on the scientific knowledge she applies to interaction with the patient, and her values, roles, supports, and resources. The nurse reflects care standards applied to the specific patient's needs and her ability to interact in a holistic and positive way, facilitating the patient's understanding of his illness and encouraging self-directed activity to address that illness.

Both the patient's and the nurse's skills, abilities, and resources converge on the health problems as they develop a shared knowledge base. Supports, either familial or from significant others, provide encouragement and perhaps even direct care to assist the patient to some extent. Also, care skills and clinical interaction, understanding, and trust develop between patient and nurse. All these are articulated in the care plan that emerges from the sharing of information and collaborative activity between patient and nurse. Through this relationship, an integrated, systematic approach to addressing the patient's needs unfolds. Through continual dialogue, the relationship is facilitated. The care plan continues to be adapted as the condition, situation, and needs of the patient change throughout the hospitalization process.

This dynamic process is begun first between nurse, patient, and physician, and then specifically between the nurse and the patient whenever a patient is admitted to a hospital. It is the basic element of hospital nursing practice and provides the functional base from which all nursing practice evolves. This functional nurse–patient interrelationship must be maintained and facilitated by the professional nurse in the hospital framework. The nursing profession in the hospital provides mechanisms and processes that continually support this relationship and its subsequent daily activity. (see Figure 4-3).

Organizational Support of Physician–Nurse–Patient Relationships

That fundamental basic interaction between nurse, patient, and physician is key to the human activity associated with delivering patient care. The organization should be structured to support that activity. It is important to define the specific activities of a hospital nursing service that offer the framework that supports professional practice. In nursing organizations there are essential corollary functions that are carried out primarily to facilitate the nurse's patient care activities. Although these functions may not be directly related to hands-on practice of professional nursing, they do provide some of the integrated and coordinating activities that assure that supporting structures are in place. This encourages effective nursing practice.

Over the years the nursing profession has described basic characteristics of professional practice in the hospital, where functional areas of account-

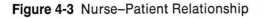

Figure 4-3 Nurse–Patient Relationship

Nurse & Patient Relationship

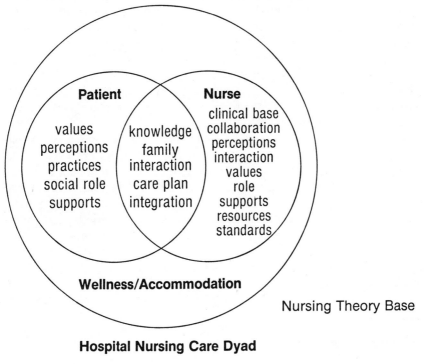

Hospital Nursing Care Dyad

ability ensure appropriate and meaningful nursing care delivery. Broken down into specific areas of accountability in nursing, these areas are:

- nursing practice
- nursing staff development
- nursing quality assurance
- nursing peer relations
- nursing governance (see Figure 4-4)

These five elements are intended to help nursing practice evolve appropriately. The nursing service organization is responsible for assuring that nursing care that meets the institution's standards is rendered. The five basic components not only serve as the framework that supports nursing practice but are necessarily incorporated into that practice. For example, no nurse can deliver full nursing care without some element of applying the standards of practice, as well as maintaining a specified level of quality for which the institution holds her accountable.

The governance framework provides direction and support to the nursing organization that is directed toward providing services. Nurses, of course, cannot work in isolation; therefore, peer relations and all their requirements must be incorporated into the practice environment. Since nursing is a science-based practice, changes in technology and science have impact on nursing care. Mechanisms that assist in educating the professional nurse in her effort to maintain competence are incorporated into the work environment.

All these elements have varying degrees of impact on one another. No one component can operate apart from the others; all are essential to appropriate delivery of nursing care services. Each component becomes a constituent of the hospital nursing care delivery system. The nursing care system, like any other system, has not only its major components, such as practice, education, quality assurance, peer relations, and governance, but also necessary subcomponents in each major component that focus on specific operational areas. Each subcomponent addresses a specific process or factor that is a piece of its major component; each one has an impact on nursing practice. A more detailed examination of the components and their subcomponents will help clarify their relation to one another.

NURSING PRACTICE

Practice is a basic component of all nursing activity. Without this component, all supporting structures and associated activity would be meaningless. Because nursing practice is at the heart of the organization, it must be considered central when developing any conceptual framework for a nursing organization. When a consumer uses the hospital or health care agency, especially nursing care services, it is through nursing practice that those services are generated. Therefore, the relationship between patient and nurse is central to any consideration in designing an organization that supports professional nursing practice.

To address this essential relationship specifically, some basic articulation of the nurse–patient relationship and its parts is vital to understanding the organization that will support it. A patient being admitted to a health care institution brings a set of behaviors, values, perceptions, practices, and an assumed social role in the community. These form the patient's support systems. When entering the nursing care frame of reference, the patient has a new experience with a unique set of variables that will have an impact on what happens to him. The nurse, too, brings to the situation her own values, perceptions, practices, and nursing's social frame of reference, as well as a tremendous amount of internal support systems for delivering care. In addition, the nurse brings an area of expertise, a clinical base, her ability to collaborate with other experts in the organization, and skills related to appropriate interaction with the patient and the scientific base of practice. While developing their relationship, the two participants in this interaction combine their skills, abilities, insights, and special references. With this accumulation, they work to develop a process that will ultimately result in the patient's movement toward wellness or accommodation to illness.

Through use of family and significant supports and constant interaction, the two can devise a care plan that reflects both the needs of the patient and the nature of the relationship between patient and nurse. Thus the skills, abilities, and resources of both nurse and patient are directed together toward fulfilling essential processes.

Although there are many ways to describe the factors, components, and processes involved in this relationship, the fundamental interaction usually contains all the elements previously described. The organizational design that will support nursing practice should—in its structure, purposes, and processes—facilitate the relationship between nurse and patient. It should also include consideration of the relationship of all those who have an impact on the patient's movement toward wellness or health care accommodation. The key thought in organizational structure should be to prevent any part of the structure from diminishing or interfering with the patient care process. Organizational structure therefore should optimize practice and the relationship between nurse and patient upon which practice depends.

Because nursing practice is based on professional determinations of what it is, it is important to seek evidence in the organization that the nursing service operates in accord with professionally defined standards. It is from these standards, the building blocks of professional behavior, that appropriate and meaningful nursing care emerges. Standards provide a point of reference for the organization against which all practice activities can be measured. Standards also give patients an opportunity to understand the basis upon which expectations for care can be entertained. Standards provide an opportunity for both the institution and the profession to measure the basic processes to which they are committed in rendering nursing care. Nursing care standards help other professions recognize which activities are specific to nursing practice and thus will be the focal point for all its subsequent activities. Standards can easily be iden-

Figure 4-4 Structural Integration for the Nursing Organization

STRUCTURAL INTEGRATION FOR THE
NURSING ORGANIZATION

---

tified in the nursing organization's policy framework. Standards allow those inside and outside the nursing organization to understand what its decision mandates will be when they are applied to the delivery of nursing care. The policy and procedural elements within the standards framework are usually described somewhere in the nursing organization. The description of these standards is usually present on the clinical unit and is available to both the nursing professionals practicing within the context of those standards and to all interested individuals who want access to them. It is important to consider that all service standards related to delivering nursing care within the institution are based on national practice standards that provide an overall framework for such activities. This national standards framework provides some continuity to the professional—nationally, regionally, and locally—in the delivery of nursing care services. Through this continuity, nurses in all parts of the country can subscribe and adhere to established norms and expectations for practice that can be articulated, monitored, and evaluated within the institution's nursing system.

THE MECHANICS OF DELIVERING NURSING CARE

Central to the exercise of practice are the tools of the nursing process; that process adapts to practice the scientific bases of all nursing activity. Virtually all nurses have been exposed to the nursing process: assessment, planning, intervention, and evaluation as the constructs of the delivery of all clinical nursing care services. Through the nursing process, total patient care needs are addressed with the needed continuity of care. The nursing process "umbrella" assures patients that the full range of options and opportunities for meeting their needs will be addressed and evaluated. This central process maintains for patients a standard of performance for which nurses can be held accountable. The organizational structure must be devised in such a manner that nursing activities and the time necessary to perform them are a part of the delivery system. Undertaking nursing activity without supporting the processes essential to the exercise of its full scope is like constructing a building on sand. Without the bedrock of nursing process as the cognitive and activity framework for delivering care, standards cannot be defined nor performance evaluated to assess nursing care standards.

A considerable segment of the professional nurse's role relates specifically to helping the patient understand both his wellness and illness. An important part of the nurse's role, therefore, involves educating the patient in developing skills and strategies not only for responding to illness but also for undertaking processes that focus on preventing illness and maintaining wellness. Since health is the central concern of the nursing profession, strategies, processes, skills, and abilities directed at maintaining health are an essential part of the activities of nurses. Institutions need to provide for the actualization of this role in nursing practice. Too often, nurses are caught up in the medical model of delivering care, where the focus is on the specific illness for which the patient has been admitted. No thought is given to preventive strategies that might assist the patient in maintaining a level of wellness. This wellness or health focus demands a response different from that normally made in the illness/wellness continuum. Thus the organizational structure must reflect the philosophy that a satisfactory level of wellness is expected for all and that all activities, energies, and strategies in the nursing organization must be directed toward achieving that outcome.

Within the context of nursing practice, the framework for providing nursing services is an important consideration. The system used to deliver nursing care gives the objective observer some idea of the context of care delivery and the philosophy of the organization. Whether it be functional, team, primary, or some modification of one of these, each system reflects a particular philosophy and the way that professional practice of nursing unfolds. The organization must commit itself to a delivery system that will articulate in practice the philosophy, beliefs, and standards that are applied to nursing care and that are acceptable to the institution. While it is argued that some nursing care delivery systems reflect a higher level of professional nursing practice than others, the decision about which system is most effective and most representative of the resources, skills, and abilities of a particular institution's nursing professionals must be made realistically.[1] Appropriate structural and practice strategies can be undertaken within any nursing care system that preserves and promotes high standards of practice. With an understanding of all constraints and pursuing all possibilities available to the nursing organization, the highest level of practice effectiveness must be demanded by the practitioners themselves. It is in that context that any choice of an appropriate nursing care system should be addressed (see Figure 4-5).

NURSING QUALITY ASSURANCE

The role of quality assurance in the nursing organization is to address standards of practice and to assess nurse compliance with those standards. All the organization's elements and activities that are involved in patient care are within the purview of the quality assurance function. Since nursing practice and, ultimately, patient outcomes are the central concerns of the nursing organization, quality assurance should be directed at addressing matters that are essential to maintaining that practice at the highest possible levels. Therefore, not only should nursing activity be reviewed in process; patient outcome should also be assessed.

Structure is also an important component of quality assurance because the organizational structure and all its elements may facilitate or constrain the appropriate delivery of nursing practice. All the factors that have an impact on the outcome of nursing care should be subject to the quality assurance function of the organization. Therefore, quality assurance assumes a status and importance equal to those of the nursing practice delivered. This equality requires that the quality assurance function be provided parallel to the delivery of nursing care; it should be incorporated, as much as possible, into the ongoing activity of delivering nursing services.

All activity within the nursing organization should be subject to review and evaluation by the quality assurance function because all activities in the organization have some impact on patient outcome. All nursing activity is affected by the systems and services that are provided to support nursing care. All these processes and functions—both nursing activities and sup-

Figure 4-5 Nursing Practice

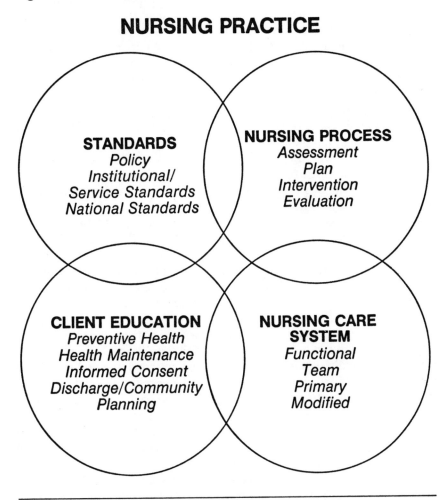

NURSING PRACTICE

STANDARDS
Policy
Institutional/
Service Standards
National Standards

NURSING PROCESS
Assessment
Plan
Intervention
Evaluation

CLIENT EDUCATION
Preventive Health
Health Maintenance
Informed Consent
Discharge/Community
Planning

NURSING CARE
SYSTEM
Functional
Team
Primary
Modified

port systems—must be incorporated into the nursing quality assurance function; therefore, review of the structure, care process, and nursing outcomes is just as important to the organization as the care delivery process itself.

Nursing structure should always be directed at supporting practice in the organization. The quality assurance function must include review of staffing practices and processes, staffing levels, and staff distribution between professional and auxiliary personnel. Distribution of staffing ratios over the 24-hour period, levels of staffing, hours of care, and mix of staffing in relation to patients' disease severity—all are appropriate topics for quality assurance review. Issues related to organizational structure, to the decision-making process, and to the leadership function—as well as to support systems, both material and fiscal—fall within the purview of nursing quality assurance. These activities are not traditionally considered part of nursing quality assurance. However, they clearly have an impact on appropriate delivery of nursing care services and thus have direct implications for quality assurance.

The actual delivery of nursing care is a vital component of the quality assurance program. Inpatient nursing care, the documentation process, the hands-on delivery of care, and the assessment of mechanisms, strategies, and procedures for that delivery, as well as patient interactional processes and nursing knowledge, skill, and ability are appropriate components of quality assurance. Assessment and evaluation of these activities take on special significance in terms of how important activities are to the patient's progress to the highest level of wellness. Consistent with these direct care delivery activities is an assessment of the environment within which the care is delivered. If the environment has structural considerations as well as functional processes that interfere with the delivery of nursing care, those considerations and processes also have an impact on outcome and are appropriate elements for review.

Nursing care has little value or meaning if the patient's condition is not significantly different after care is provided than it was before. While it can be expected that some alteration in patient condition and status will occur after hospitalization, it is vital to know specifically what was influenced by nursing activity and what the specific impact of nursing care was. The nursing quality assurance process includes: application of standards to outcomes as well as to patient and staff expectations and goals; reviewing the discharge process and patient status upon discharge; assessing continuity of care and results of care; and assessing the patient's perception of care and response to the delivery of care services. Looking at outcome is a vital part of assessing the effectiveness of nursing services. Effectiveness is essential to meaningful care and is an appropriate adjunct to evaluating correlations that relate outcome to process. Quality assurance allows nurses to depict the kind and qualities of activity that are appropriate and meaningful in delivering nursing care that creates a desirable outcome. The quality assurance mechanism is a major contributor to this process.

The ability to correct practice, change behaviors, and apply new knowledge and research is essential to ongoing improvement in clinical practice and to assure that the basic components of nursing are consistent with approved standards. Assessment and evaluation of nursing care have no meaning if no change in performance occurs when evaluation reveals inadequacies. The ability to integrate quality assurance activity into care delivery and to remedy discrepancies between practice and standards must always be part of the nursing organization's commitment. Also, those structures that intervene in the delivery of nursing care services—whether related to positions, persons, or staffing—must receive the necessary follow-through if quality assurance is to have a meaningful impact on the delivery of nursing services. The ability of the nursing organization to respond to the discrepancies between the system and its outcome is important to the viability of the nursing care service in the institution. Perhaps one of the greatest constraints on nursing in many hospitals is the organization's inability or unwillingness to respond in accord with a clearly identified need often determined through the quality assurance mechanism. The risk inherent in nursing quality assurance is offset by the opportunity for gain that emerges from confronting the risk to achieve the highest level of nursing practice. The ability to undertake a broad range of corrective actions to assure compliance of practice with standards is obviously vital to the evolution of professional nursing care (see Figure 4-6).

NURSING PROFESSIONAL DEVELOPMENT

Growth and change in the dynamic nursing organization are natural corollaries to professional practice. Because nursing is both a scientific and a human activity, it must respond to both technological and human changes that occur in theory and practice. Thus, an ongoing development program for professional staff is a core constituent of most nursing organizations. Traditionally, nursing education and development have been ongoing activities in the nursing organization.

Nursing staff cannot be sensitive to the development and application of standards without knowing something about how to incorporate those standards into practice. Apply the educational and developmental resources of the institution to the learning process that defines standards and practice behaviors consistent with those standards is an important part of delivering nursing care. Using information obtained in the educational process, nurses can integrate specific behavioral and performance standards into their daily practice. Continuing review of practice standards and their applications keeps the individual nurse up-to-date and provides her opportunities for new and creative mechanisms for incorporating standards into practice.

When discrepancies arise between standards and practice, as well as between expectations and behaviors, the educational component of the nursing organization can be directed toward corrective education. Elimi-

Figure 4-6 Nursing Quality Assurance

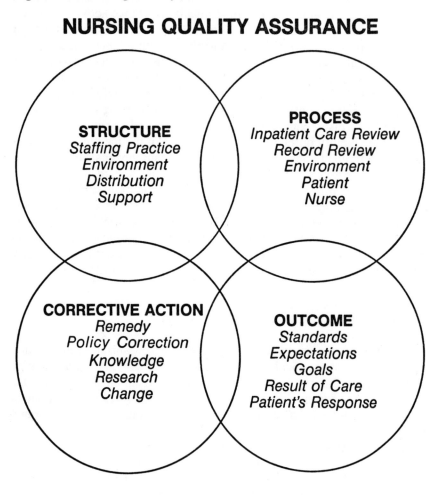

NURSING QUALITY ASSURANCE

STRUCTURE
*Staffing Practice
Environment
Distribution
Support*

PROCESS
*Inpatient Care Review
Record Review
Environment
Patient
Nurse*

CORRECTIVE ACTION
*Remedy
Policy Correction
Knowledge
Research
Change*

OUTCOME
*Standards
Expectations
Goals
Result of Care
Patient's Response*

nating discrepancies and deficiencies and finding newer, more creative ways of assuring consistency with practice standards can dramatically increase the staff's sensitivity to the value the organization puts on consistency between practice and standards. Developing that consistency integrates the two processes of professional development and quality assurance; this indicates the dependency of each of these components on the other. Further, it indicates the necessity for the nursing organization to serve the purposes of practice in delivering nursing care services.

Education about new concepts in the development of clinical skills occurs through the professional nursing development function. The continuing application of new technology assures implementation of the most current nursing knowledge and skills in the patient care environment. Introducing new equipment, materials, and supplies that improve patient care is also appropriate in the professional development process. Since medical and nursing practice is always subject to the dramatic pace of health care technology development, educating for new concepts and developing applicable clinical skills are activities consistent with the education role of the nursing service. For these reasons, education is central to the success of patient care delivery (see Figure 4-7).

PEER RELATIONS

The relationship between peers in any professional organization is central to their activities; it is key to the evolution of nursing services. The

Figure 4-7 Nursing Professional Development

NURSING PROFESSIONAL DEVELOPMENT

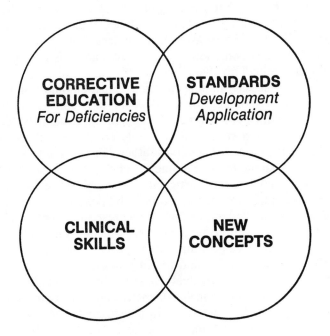

nurse must be able to relate first to her own practice and then to the practice of, and interaction with, other professionals in the organization. Peer relations speak not only to the interaction between professional peers but also to the compatibility of one nurse's experiences with those of another. Minimum standards are applied to competency and to the nurse's ability to fulfill consistently the obligations of the institution and its nursing service. Therefore, through its hiring standards, the institution provides a baseline not only for the delivery of nursing care but also for the peer relations of nurses as they assume corporate responsibility for delivering care services. Where there is incompetence, inadequate orientation to role, position descriptions that do not accurately reflect expectations and responsibilities, or an evaluation process that is inadequate or inappropriate, patient care is ultimately endangered.

Minimum standards of competency must be determined and maintained in the application of nursing skills and abilities in the organization. Determining expectations for practice and standards in relation to education and previous experience, along with the role and behavior of the professional nurse in the organization, all provide a framework for the patient's expectations of nursing services. Competency addresses both skills and the application of nursing techniques, as well as the ability to assess, to plan, to implement, and to evaluate nursing interventions as an ongoing part of delivering care. Expectations of the nursing process, the nurse's competency in articulating and demonstrating that process, and documentation through one of the measurement devices that determine whether individual practice is consistent with overall standards and practices of the organization are all involved.

An outline of necessary nursing practice obligations and responsibilities through a position statement or job description is considered relatively elementary to defining competency. It is important to acknowledge, however, that the position statement or job description should be accountability based, delineating expectations rather than specific tasks and activities of the professional nurse. Parameters of expectation and appropriate performance behaviors are articulated through criterion-referenced descriptors that refer to specific accountabilities. Thus, the individual nurse gains a basic understanding of the responses and expectations demanded by the institution and the nursing organization. And through an appropriately descriptive position statement, the basic standards of care to which the nursing service and the institution ascribe can be applied within the context of the individual's practice. By articulating competencies in a clearly defined position statement, the nursing organization begins to establish a baseline from which performance can be measured. Without having specifically defined competencies and accountabilities, the practitioner's contribution to the delivery of nursing services and to the profession within the institution cannot be clearly evaluated. Also, the practitioner cannot determine his or her relationship to the institution or its expectations for performance in order to meet satisfactorily the demands of the organization and its standards of nursing.

Since institutions and nursing organizations recognize the importance of each nurse's professional competence, much effort is directed to ensuring high-quality position statements that accurately reflect the expectations and obligations of the organization (see Figure 4-8). Practice and competence are only two components in the nursing organization's range of activities, but they represent basic expectations and standards for evaluating nursing performance.

Figure 4-8 Peer Relations

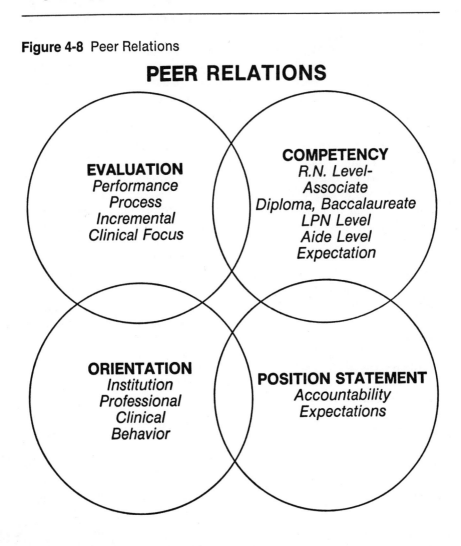

PEER RELATIONS

EVALUATION
Performance
Process
Incremental
Clinical Focus

COMPETENCY
R.N. Level-
Associate
Diploma, Baccalaureate
LPN Level
Aide Level
Expectation

ORIENTATION
Institution
Professional
Clinical
Behavior

POSITION STATEMENT
Accountability
Expectations

Nursing performance evaluation lies at the heart of determining an individual nurse's success in applying skills and abilities to meet the patient's needs within the context of the organization's values. Performance evaluation is usually accompanied by a great deal of anxiety and stress related to the assessment of one individual by another or, within a peer-related organization, by several of the individual's peers. Through the assessment process, the individual comes to know others' perceptions of her skills and abilities. Further, the assessment provides an opportunity for the individual to reflect on her practice skills and abilities. It involves her in a self-assessment of her contribution to the organization's strengths and needs, and a search for opportunities for practice changes that would yield individual growth. The evaluation process must be an objective one, reflecting the organization's expectations in relation to practice standards and as articulated in the position statement.

Through an understanding of the values expressed within the context of governance activities, disciplinary processes and appropriate provision of resource supports clearly unfold. The disciplinary processes attempt to maintain the professional mandate and desires of the organization, assuring control of those accountabilities through peer activities of the organization. Assurance of compliance with expectations, minimum levels of competency, and evaluation of individuals, systems, and activities with each unit level of operation all fit inside the controlling framework of the organization's governance structure (see Figure 4-9). Through adjusting and adapting alterations to facilitate patient care outcomes, the organization maintains its responsiveness to the requirements of both the professional and the patient to whom the professional directs her services. The governance activity of control, it is emphasized, is a responsibility of the profession, and mechanisms designed to incorporate all professional members into the controlling function facilitate the accountability and the ownership of the organization by the professional nurse. Thus, each member of the organization shares the responsibility for success, as well as for limitations; each member is accountable for reducing constraints and encouraging potential.

GOVERNANCE

Finally, and perhaps most controversial, is the need for participation by each professional member in delineating and determining economic factors to support maintenance of the organization's highest standards. Involvement in a participatory, advisory, and direct decision-making role in regard to wage and salary concerns, working conditions, and benefits programs is very much a part of the individual practitioner's obligation. The nurse plays a key role in establishing standards, integrating control mechanisms,

Figure 4-9 Governance

GOVERNANCE

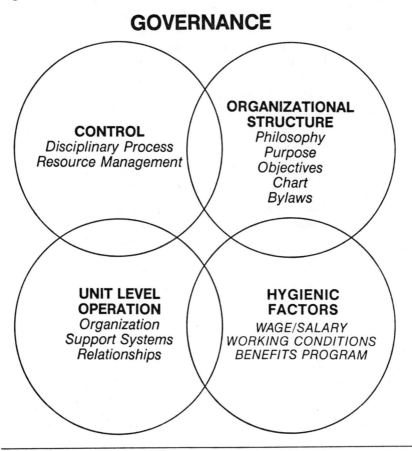

providing organizational structure, maintaining discipline, determining competencies, and the whole range of other professional behaviors that make up the practice of nursing in the organization. Thus a structure or mechanism for addressing economic factors is necessary to the framework of the governance activity of the professional nurse. Structuring that opportunity within the organization, rather than through a third party, is a key element in involving the nurse in the full range of activities directed at meeting the organization's need to support itself and achieve rewards for high levels of performance. It should be clear that the same high expectations for professional behavior in motivational factors also apply to economic factors. It is only natural that professional nurses who deliver patient care would play an important role in making decisions on matters pertaining to economics and social influences. The key here, as in all areas of the organization, is expectation of professional performance. When such behaviors are expected and valued, they will be displayed. While this expectation creates new obligations and new relationships, it also provides new opportunities to incorporate the nurse fully into decisions having an impact on the organization's operation.

The functional components of the nursing organization provide the stage for all nursing practice. To assure that patient care outcomes—from the nursing perspective—are facilitated, the structure must be integrated and coordinated so that each piece of the organization interacts positively to influence appropriate nursing activity. In many organizations, some pieces of the structure often work more successfully than others. Yet the approach to nursing management in hospitals frequently fails to consider the need for integrating functions of the nursing structure. Thus those pieces not strongly developed and encouraged tend negatively to affect other portions of the organizational structure that struggle to operate effectively. Frequently the problem is incomplete development by nursing leadership of a holistic or integrated view of structure and the supporting activities involved in maintaining that structure. At the care point of any operation is the "fit" between the components that work to fulfill the organization's objectives. Thus, if one piece of the organization is not adequately developed and does not provide the supports necessary for other components, then all structural elements are adversely affected.

The design, therefore, should reflect integration of the component parts supporting the organization's activity. Goals, objectives, purposes, and processes must be pursued to fulfill the mandates of the organization. In undertaking those activities, however, nursing leadership should remember that failure to be sensitive to each of the elements supporting the organization's work can create significant dissonance. Considering the organization and its design in relation to supporting the activity of nursing is the major concern of the nurse innovator. Changing the organizational structure from the traditional bureaucratic framework to one more accurately reflecting the professional work of nursing now becomes an essential focus for the innovator. Without having clearly outlined each of the components and its elements, the organizational change agent would be insufficiently prepared to address development of an appropriate structure. After reviewing the work components of nursing—identifying and articulating their characteristics—suggesting a design for an appropriate governance structure could then be undertaken.

NOTE

1. G. Marram, M. Schlegel, and E. Bevis, *Primary Nursing* (St. Louis, Mo.: C.V. Mosby Company, 1974).

Chapter 5

Smashing the Pyramid . . . Creating a Network

ACCOUNTABILITY IN DELIVERING NURSING CARE

When the functional determination of the five specific areas of accountability in nursing delivery is made, an organizational structure must be established to integrate these areas into the operation of the nursing division. Since these five components—practice, quality assurance, professional development, peer relations, and governance—are essential to the organization's success, it must be designed to support these five structures. Such support is not difficult in the bureaucratic framework. In the traditional organization the management team usually provides the impetus and generally accepts accountability for ensuring that the functional activities outlined in these components are carried out in the nursing organization. In this setting, management becomes the organization's accountable entity for fulfilling the objectives of the nursing service within the five functional areas of nursing activity.

The problem with management accountability, however, is that management generally becomes responsible for all the activities of the organization and owns those activities on behalf of all the organization's members. Yet the professional staff members who are responsible for carrying out the activities and ensuring their compliance usually are not accountable for them because ownership of these activities does not rest within their roles. While they must perform the activities of the nursing operation, they are not vested with accountability for their undertakings. Outcomes, although important, do not appear to be invested in the staff member who is responsible for all of the actions associated with the delivery of nursing care.

In the bureaucracy, the management team—because of its centrality to the organization's objectives—assumes accountability on behalf of the practicing nurse. Management ensures that all the supports and activities essential to successful nursing practice are in place, then puts the responsibility for implementing that practice on the nurse. This creates significant problems rooted in obtaining compliance from the professional staff who must carry out these actions. There is constant conflict between the management structure responsible for implementing the functions of nursing and the staff nurses who have the responsibility for carrying out those functions. Within the bureaucratic structure, the organization constantly lives in a *Catch-22* situation. On one hand, nursing management is responsible for ensuring that nursing services are satisfactorily performed. On the other hand, staff nurses are charged with actually performing those activities. Management has the accountability, and staff has the responsibility. The conflict between the two is exacerbated by the fact that one owns no significant part of the obligation of the other.

SHARED GOVERNANCE ACCOUNTABILITY

In a shared governance framework, accountability and responsibility for both process and outcome are placed on the same individual. Thus, accountability is transferred to the person most logically and appropriately equipped to fulfill the requirements of a specific function. The individual is both responsible and accountable for fulfilling the obligation; she also has the authority to make sure that the activities are appropriately handled. Within the professional context, then, the statement that the professional is accountable for her practice has meaning only when the necessary authority, which is part of that accountability, is transferred to the individual who assures compliance and who is capable of taking corrective action in the absence of compliance. When that authority is given to accountable personnel, however, especially at the practice level, it must be provided within the organizational context, or chaos may result. That context, of course, provides opportunities to avoid chaos, and shifts in organization must be made very carefully to ensure that there are some internal controls demanding a discipline associated with real accountability. Operating integrity is provided through the overall organizational structure. The functional components of nursing care must be incorporated into the governance activity that is integral to the service that renders this care. Thus, there must be movement away from the traditional accountability invested in the management track for the broad range of nursing activities. Those activities most closely associated with the delivery of clinical services must be the work of accountable clinical individuals, who also assume responsibility for the delivery of those services. Therefore, the elements of the organizational design that are clinically mandated and that have a clinical frame of reference must operate under the authority of the clinical individuals, and an organizational structure must be designed to make those people accountable for the activities for which practicing nurses are responsible.

Collaterally, a new entity must be conceived outlining both the responsibility of the nurse and the constraints of the nurse manager's role in a professional organization. Management must then evolve within a new context limited to those areas over which it has direct control; in turn, it must support the role, decisions, and accountabilities of the clinical nursing practitioner.

In hospital organizations, this transitional concept is a radical departure from the traditional "lines of authority" theory. Lines of authority are effective within bureaucratic organizations when accountability can be centralized in a specific function, person, or activity, such as management process or the individual manager. In a professional organization where accountability is spread over a broad base and many elements are involved in delivering a service, accountability for parts of the service must be conferred upon the nurse, with attendant expectations as part of her role in delivering professional nursing practice. It is within this nurse that the demands of the profession and the accountability of the individual converge. The profession is accountable for the delineation, the delivery, and the evaluation of professional services. Accountability for the delivery of those services and its associated processes must obviously be invested in the representative of the profession, the nurse. As a result, the structure supporting those activities must align the functional components in such a way that they not only support the individual nurse in performing her obligations but also transfer accountability from her to the institution, and to the profession represented within the context of her role. Therefore, the old traditional lines and divisions on the organizational chart are inadequate to describe this relationship in a truly dynamic, professional nursing organization.

Shared Governance and Organizational Theory

Building on the previous chapters' discussion of newer theoretical frameworks, especially the neoteric organizational model and the democratic rational approach, it becomes clear that a different kind of relationship must be established in the nursing organization. In terms of neoteric and democratic rational thinking, traditional organizational design must give way to a new kind of organizational diagram. The design adequate to professional practice encourages and facilitates a structure supporting behaviors associated with peer and professional relationships. The appropriate design will support consultation, collaboration, exercise of judgment, a high degree of lateral communication based on the quality of the individual's judgment, and the exercise of nursing practice according to professional standards. Appropriate measurement of nursing practice and patient outcomes through assessment and evaluation plays a highly interdependent role, both intradisciplinary and interdisciplinary. This role is considered part of the functional process of professional nursing and must be supported in the system. The organizational structure that facilitates these kinds of behaviors cannot be envisioned within the context of the traditional bureaucratic structure. The lines of organizational control, the reporting mechanisms, the authority, and the responsibility relationships all must be far more loosely structured in the open clinical environment. The organization's integrating elements must be based on characteristics other than those traditionally found in line/staff relationships. Further, because democratic rational approaches to governing and operating the nursing organization are more consistent with behaviors of the professional practice framework, the organizational design should reflect that theory base. It is within this context that a new design for the nursing organization, reflecting both its action and activity and all the professional delineations associated with it, must be conceived. Within this context, the functional components of practice, quality assurance, peer relations, professional development, and governance can be incorporated and structured to facilitate activities essential to nursing care.

Shared Governance—From Theory to Practice

While accountability for fulfilling the obligations of nursing practice in the traditional organization rests with management, nursing managers in the participatory system recognize the need to be assisted in that process and to incorporate staffing input into the system in a somewhat formalized way. To provide professional staff with the opportunity to participate in the system, the traditional nursing administrator devises mechanisms through group process to incorporate their input, advice, recommendations, and feedback for the nursing administrator and other nursing managers. These formal work groups are generally called committees. By definition, committees are groups of individuals operating under specific directions for a task or purpose to give advice, make suggestions and recommendations, and outline alternatives to a decision-making entity.[1] Committees are granted certain levels of authority to investigate and make use of appropriate resources in order to collect sufficient information to make appropriate recommendations. The committee is rarely given authority to take action independent of the authority-granting body, however.

Because of those significant limitations, committees are not themselves the decision-making authority for the organization. The committee's responsibility ends where the manager's responsibility begins. While committees permit the professional staff to participate in part of the decision-making process, committees by their very structure do not permit the decision-making process to remain a part of their activity in the organization. By definition, the bureaucratic structure places decision-making power in the individuals identified as the leadership (managers) of the system. Those leaders use whatever resources are available to assist them in rendering decisions. The committee structure in the traditional organizational system is generally regarded as one of those resources.

Therefore, using committees in making decisions in the traditional bureaucratic structure, while improving the effectiveness of more centralized, individualized decision making, does not fully invest accountability in the practicing nurse. Even if the professional nurse participates fully in arriving at decisions, and even if the committee's recommendations are universally accepted by nursing management, that relationship sends a clear message that nursing management is finally accountable for decision-rendering activity. In a truly professional organization, however, final accountability is invested in the practitioners of the profession, and a structure is designed to support them. Committee action and managerial function, therefore, are not fully adequate to meet the profession's need.

THE DEMOCRATIC FRAMEWORK

Corollary to moving the organization to professional accountability within a rational democratic framework, a concrete democratic structure must be provided to support broad-based decision-making processes in the nursing organization. To do that in a large, complex, highly diverse functional nursing operation, a representational framework appears most appropriate. Representational systems, however, must be carefully structured to prevent the organization from removing the obligation for making necessary decisions from the individual nurse. The representational structure must invest in representative professionals the obligation both to make decisions and to be accountable for their impact on the organization as a whole. These corporate responsibilities, and the decisions associated with them, should be consolidated within the representational framework. This framework, however, must be flexible enough to assume corporate responsibility for the functional components of the delivery of nursing services while returning to the individual the professional accountability for the delivery of those services. Therefore, the representational framework for organization must flow in two directions—to meet the needs of the profession delivering the service, and to meet the needs of the individual accountable for her nursing practice. In this case, structure meets two sets of needs: those of the institution in addressing patient care, those of the individual in rendering nursing care. Through the representational structure, a two-way bridge is provided between the organization and the nurse.

Status in Management

In forming a rational democratic professional organization, the issue of status must be addressed. Status needs will always be with us in human groups. Because of this, attempts to eliminate status and all the energies associated with those attempts will generally fail. In the bureaucratic organization, issues of status are generally related to position and to the power associated with that position. In a rational democratic organization, issues of status move from position to role. Thus, roles are invested with specific levels of status, consistent with the individual's participation in the collective activity of fulfilling the organization's responsibility. Status, therefore, should be invested in the functional components that are directed toward fulfilling that responsibility. Those involved in exercising responsibility for practice, quality assurance, development, peer relations, and governance will be invested with the status and power associated with that responsibility. Power will not be held exclusively by individuals, however; individual power in a rational democratic organization will be limited to the extent of the person's participation in the group's governance activity. Since most functional power and status will be invested in the work group, association with the work group will be the primary source of status. While investing power and accountability in the professional staff may arouse some concern from the traditional nursing administrator, this leader will be relieved to know that the exercise of individual power in a shared framework is limited at best. The real power in the organization will rest with the constituent responsible groups.

Councils and Accountability

In the traditional bureaucratic organization, the committee structure primarily serves to render advice and guidance to management's decision-making process. In a representational context, a group structure must be developed that will permit the investment of power and accountability for decision making. Within this group, power, authority, accountability, and final decision-making capacity will be invested in the membership. Since the group will be a functional responsible unit of the operation of the nursing division, incorporation of appropriate authority will be necessary. Perhaps one of the most effective ways of engendering this authority and responsibility is within the council framework. Councils differ from committees in that they are invested with specific functional responsibilities, all the accountability for decision making, and responsibility for undertaking action consistent with its own functional delineation.[2] A council is ultimately accountable for its activities and the activities of those it chooses to fulfill portions of its work. With this form of operation, accountability and evaluation of outcomes rest exclusively with the council mandated to perform specific functions. It is in this framework that new thinking about the organization of nursing activities and operations can be incorporated in the hospital's nursing division. Within the context of council structures, each accountable for specific activities in the division of nursing, a new kind of responsibility relationship is established, one that no longer parallels the traditional bureaucratic management line/staff setup. In the council framework, a new set of relationships and obligations are undertaken in a unique way. They involve a different grouping of decision makers in a complex of relationships that interact, supplement, and interrelate with one another. The seeds of shared governance in nursing are nurtured in this context. From this basis, we begin to define and develop a nursing organization that pulls together all of its elements and far-flung pieces and provides an integrative framework that shares opportunities for involvement in the processes affecting each of those pieces. In this process the professional staff becomes involved, not only in providing support and resources for decision making but also in actually making decisions. Accountability for decision making is thus no longer transferred to third parties through the management structure; rather, it is incorporated into the operational processes of the staff in delivering their services. It becomes an expected part of their role. The nursing professional is therefore no longer accountable for merely delivering nursing care but also for all the activities supporting and facilitating the delivery of that care. Through this process, accountability is internalized, not only into practice but also into the practitioner. By maintaining membership on such a nursing staff, the professional nurse assumes obligations beyond the hands-on delivery of nursing care; she also assumes obligation for activities that support current means of care and that provide a basis for the expansion of those means. The staff becomes involved in confronting health issues as they become more complex and more diverse, and as nursing practice expands to cover a broader base of consumer services. In this context, the professional nurse becomes truly professional.

The Network Organization

As John Naisbitt so clearly points out, the failure of the hierarchy and its inadequacy to meet people's needs have resulted in the need for a structure that permits people to talk to one another.[3] This diminution in the value of the hierarchy has built a more equalitarian framework for interaction and has created, in place of hierarchies, a need to build systems and structures that permit lateral networking. A network organizational structure provides an unfettered opportunity for people, especially professionals, to share ideas, information, and resources and to direct that sharing to a common goal or purpose. In health care, the common goal or purpose is to meet the needs of the client and the delivery system that serves the client.

The network provides an opportunity not found in the bureaucratic structure; Naisbitt calls this the horizontal link. We are living at a time when all traditional structures and forms are in question. Traditional structures have not been adequate to support the major transitions in technology, innovation, and society. Therefore, the facilitation of networking in organizational structures permits people to communicate effectively horizontally; this fills their need for belonging, participation, and ownership.

Because of the hierarchy's long failure to resolve human problems, people have sought opportunities outside traditional structures to resolve problems and to create relationships that more adequately fill their needs. The shared governance structure provides a framework of opportunity that attempts consciously to reduce the barriers to the collateral communication and interaction that are so essential to professional service. The nursing organization in a shared governance structure creates relationships and communication networks that facilitate the nurses' ability to identify, plan, resolve, and evaluate all the processes associated with the delivery of nursing care. The shared governance structure will therefore use the broadly based resources available in the nursing organization—across departmental and divisional lines—so that all individuals in the organization have access to one another and can address and facilitate problem solving, strategy development, and planning activities and processes directed to meeting the profession's needs and objectives.

NURSING PRACTICE

Nursing practice, which is the first area of accountability in nursing delivery, is at the heart of nursing activity in the organization. It is therefore appropriate for transition first to address a governance framework that deals most directly with nursing practice issues. In traditional structures, all matters of policy and practice, while determined in collaboration with the staff, were finally decided, determined, and policed by the management team. As a result, practice became narrow, rigidly defined, and policy oriented; it fell within constraining parameters consistent with the demands and needs of the management structure. Further, all the governance issues related to influencing practice, both directly and indirectly, centered on those tasks and activities that established policy, procedure, directives, permissions, and parameters for nursing practice. Within this context, practitioners were required to fulfill the multiple, varied obligations of nursing practice. In the nursing delivery system, practice became considered a series of prescribed, narrowly defined, procedural tasks that fell within the area of activities considered appropriate by both the hopsital and the physician.

The nurses' role in the governance and delineation of practice has been limited to participation in policy and procedure committees. That role was focused on making sure that policy and procedure documents were appropriately defined—precisely those items and procedures considered appropriate for nursing practice within the purview of a particular institution. The indirect intent of this process was essentially to provide protection for the institution against possible noncompliance by individual nurses and conversely to ensure protection to the patient that safe care was being rendered. Because safety depended upon consistent performance, the opportunity for independent judgment was narrowed and the expectation that predescribed activity would be fulfilled was facilitated. The hidden message for the practicing nurse has been the organizational devaluing of independent judgment in clinical situations and support for those who comply with the parameters of care prescribed by the institution.

In the traditional organization, upon completion of manuals and texts used to define and document, these manuals were generally moved on through the management track for the review and approval of the nursing administrative officer ultimately accountable for all nursing activity within the organization's division of nursing. Clearly, all these behaviors represent the classic bureaucratic expectations. In a shared governance organization, different sets of expectations are outlined within the practice framework. The practice group responsible for setting nursing practice standards (as opposed to policy or procedure) may have management representation. The focus, goal, and thrust of the group, however, is directed toward addressing nursing practice and providing for the determination of standards against which practice, nursing judgments, and activities may be measured. Standards differ from policy and procedures in that they define basic expectations for performance against which appropriate judgment, activities, and processes will unfold. Unlike policy and procedure, standards have no constraining characteristic but provide an opportunity for a wide variability of judgment and action; the variability, however, always reflects those basic standards of practice.

Providing the organizational framework for this responsibility within the council or democratic rational approach to organizational integrity requires a different view of the mandate and the relationship of the group. Since the thrust of nursing practice is primarily clinical, the primary responsibility for the group's actions must also be clinical. The translation to shared governance in the organization begins to take fundamental form here. The definitive establishment of standards of practice, the delineation of those standards, and the determination of the expectations based on the standards are invested in the accountabilities and responsibilities of the professional nurse. In shared governance the accountability for that process does not transfer to others not directly involved in actually delivering clinical services. In other words, clinical practitioners are responsible for the delivery of hands-on nursing care to patient or client; therefore, they are accountable for the standards that describe what that nursing care will be. In the shared governance organization, accountability is invested in those who represent, in a councilar framework, the clinical practice of nursing. Decisions related to appropriate clinical practice rendered by this group become the mandates of the organization for all professional nurses. At this point three fundamental statements are made within the organization:

1. The clinical professional nurse has a responsibility for all clinical nursing activity.
2. The clinical professional nurse shall define, delineate, approve, and evaluate the acceptable basis for clinical nursing practice within the institution.
3. The process and responsibility for managing practice do not transfer to some disassociated second-level individual or group traditionally recognized within a management context.

This representative group of clinical practicing professional nurses is described as a council on nursing practice. Within the council's role, and in keeping with shared responsibility for decision making in the clinical arena, multiple traditional management responsibilities become an accountability of the council on nursing practice. Because of this transfer of accountability and investment of key decision-making powers within the council, selection for membership should be considered very carefully. The council would be expected to represent the major clinical services within an institution, chosen either by division or service. The major choice of members should obviously reside with the practicing nursing staff. Practicing nursing staff should be defined as that group who consistently renders direct nursing care as its main function and responsibility in the organization. Representation by clinical specialists and other advanced practitioners would have to be carefully delineated by the council's primary staff nurse members. Caution is advised in assembling the members so that the council represents the interests of the nurses most broadly distributed in the clinical setting. This caution provides that no special interest group at advanced levels of practice would be able to influence the council unduly and provide for decision making that may be favorable to some special interest group. Thus, choosing members must be an extremely well thought out process managed within the clinical context. Whatever representation occurs from other groups, including clinical specialists, clinical support people, coordinators of clinical care, and management representatives, should never exceed a minority on the council. Should issues be rendered to vote, the collective vote of professional nursing staff in nonpatient care should, in aggregate, always constitute a minority vote.

The functional responsibilities of the council must include, but not necessarily be limited to, the following:

- delineation, development, approval, and implementation of all clinical standards of nursing practice within the institution;
- review, discussion, and approval of all issues related to the development of policy as applied to the clinical practice of nursing in the institution;
- determination, definition, and articulation of roles, responsibilities, and functions of all levels of nursing care givers;
- determination and resolution of all conflicts, controversies, and issues related to the appropriate delivery of clinical nursing care;
- research, discussion, determination, and implementation of the selected, appropriate nursing care delivery system;
- representation on all forums, committees, task forces, or other decision-making bodies, a portion of the function of which is to influence the delivery of clinical nursing care services;
- representation by a chairperson to the governing administrative forums or management processes with broad decision-making authority for the institution's division of nursing;
- generation of all communication, both oral and written, to all governing bodies within the nursing organization about all issues of nursing practice and compliance with them;

- determination and evaluation of all functions, processes, and relationships within the council on nursing practice in consideration of its roles, responsibilities, and operation; and
- delineation, determination, and implementation of all corrective and disciplinary processes directed toward augmenting the effectiveness of both the membership and the work of the council on nursing practice.

The council's major role is obviously directly related to the establishment of professional nursing standards using all available resources—especially those articulated through the professional organizations. A framework for practice is provided that allows practitioners to understand fully the basis upon which their practice in the institution will develop. Institutions using nationally acceptable standards of practice as a basis for their own nursing standards assures a concerted effort in addressing consistency. It is understandable that standards must be adjusted to the needs of each organization, but it is also important to recognize that professional nursing practice is built on certain common beliefs and processes. What the council does, then, is adopt these standards and articulate the development of nursing practice upon that firm basis. If most institutions did this in a consistent manner, the application and evaluation of nursing standards of practice could be measurably facilitated. The question of what nursing practice is and how it is developed would be more easily answered if a consistent basis for measuring and evaluating the standards of that practice were established.

Using this approach, the council has already established a strong basis for legitimate action. Standards are not identified in isolation, and all resources that address the issue of standards of practice are incorporated into the council's authority. Therefore, a formal undergirding is provided for the organization's work in establishing and maintaining professional nursing standards. The legitimacy of the process is facilitated through a uniform approach to the establishment of standards. The investment in the clinical practitioner is also a reaffirmation of the legitimacy and liability of the application of standards to nursing practice. Through moving accountability and authority for clinical nursing standards to the nursing staff, a clear statement is made on the key role of professional staff in self-determination on issues of practice. When the management structure clearly divests itself of accountability for clinical practice decisions and all related matters, and when the responsibilities associated with clinical practice rest with the clinical nurse, a strong statement about the value of the clinical nurse in regard to nursing practice is made by the institution. The key to success, of course, is the organization's ability to design the structure in such a way that management personnel traditionally responsible for these issues no longer assume the function and can formally transfer accountability to professional staff.

It is important to note that the responsibility of a council on nursing practice is to govern both standards of practice and the behaviors related to those standards. The council is charged with the responsibility for delineating the practice in an appropriate and meaningful way. Practice is not only a set of criteria that determine performance but also the performance itself. Behavioral delineations are a key part of the development of nursing practice. Issues related to job descriptions, performance evaluations, minimum expectations for nursing practice—all these become key parts of the role of the council on nursing practice. Transferring responsibility for delineating these behavioral expectations and functional elements to the practice council makes an additional statement within the nursing organization. It becomes clear that peer relationships and peer involvement in determining essential practice behaviors and relationships are central if the profession is to assume responsibility for professional nursing practice. Moving accountability for delineating practice standards and behaviors to the clinical council creates a significant shift in the organization; that shift requires an entirely different approach to the involvement of nursing staff in ongoing governance activities. The statement to both the nurse manager and the practicing nurse is fundamentally the same: accountability for clinical nursing practice cannot legitimately be transferred out of the hands of the clinical practicing professional nurse. To the extent that this accountability is so transferred, it loses its effectiveness in giving control for nursing practice to those most responsible for its development—clinical nursing staff.

QUALITY ASSURANCE

The second major function of delineation for which nurses have accountability is the quality control of nursing practice. Where a full range of quality assurance activities take place, such as in a hospital, nursing plays a major role in the application processes that define and evaluate the delivery of patient care. As part of the hospital's quality assurance obligation, the nursing staff needs to be actively involved in mechanisms that review, and take corrective action on, the kind of nursing care delivered. As a result, quality assurance is a major component of the clinical practice structure that must be facilitated in a shared governance framework.

The council on quality assurance, like the one on nursing practice, should represent the broad range of practicing, direct-care professional nurses. Therefore, the majority of this council should represent the broad-based, direct-care nurses. The basic major clinical areas within the hospital structure must obviously be adequately represented in such a council. The council's quality assurance activities must also be facilitated by people clinically prepared enough in advanced nursing practice to provide resources for determining care definers and undertake measurement strategies and processes that will accurately and adequately measure nursing care against agreed-upon standards.

The council on nursing practice must articulate and provide standards of practice upon which nursing care will be based. Accountability for monitoring compliance with those standards and determining whether nurses practice according to approved and acceptable standards is the obligation of the council on nursing quality assurance. Thus, the council on nursing quality assurance must be involved in reviewing all clinical nursing practices in the institution. The council's objective is to determine whether compliance with standards has been achieved. The council must also assess whether the standards themselves are adequate or whether new care processes need to be initiated, or standards developed, in areas where a change or innovation may be at hand. Since nursing quality assurance activities must integrate with the activities of the entire institution, the quality assurance council should be responsible for assuring that quality assurance processes and practices are consistent with the hospital's quality assurance plan.

As part of its role in assuring high levels of practice, the quality assurance council will be involved in devising appropriate assessment and evaluation tools to monitor ongoing nursing care activities. By using these tools, the council can review and compile the data necessary to reflect the outcome of processes, studies, and activities in patient care. Upon determining the need for further action or corrective measures, the council on nursing quality assurance must be responsible for decisions related to taking corrective action or recommending altered practice processes.

The quality assurance council is accountable for deciding what specific actions shall be undertaken as corrective action or in support of nursing standards where such compliance does not exist. The council must, to the fullest extent possible, direct all actions that assist the nursing organization in maintaining practice at the highest possible level. Where acceptable limits of practice are compromised, the quality assurance council is obligated to direct the organization to take appropriate corrective action or to recommend appropriate discipline when such action is not taken or negligence continues. The council is also accountable for defining appropriate disciplinary processes in such matters. Such action is undertaken by the organization when it is deemed necessary by the council in the normal conduct of its business.

The council on nursing quality assurance must also have some control over the acceptance and approval of new members to the nursing staff. To ensure that standards of practice operate at the highest levels, those who render nursing care must meet set standards. The quality assurance council, therefore, should have a major role in the process of granting credentials. This may be undertaken by a subunit, committee, or other body within the quality assurance council. Membership applications should be directed to an appropriate credentials review process, so that the staff plays a strong role, both in granting credentials appropriately and accepting those who fulfill professional nursing responsibilities. Through control of all nursing membership activities, elements, and processes that have a direct impact on nursing care, the quality assurance council provides a broad base of responsibility for taking action that can maintain clear nursing practice strengths. Through this process, the council provides accountability for nursing practice and all the portions of both organization and practice that influence the level of care and its outcomes. It is not inappropriate, then, to expect there to be a somewhat "policing" character to the activity of the quality assurance council. It is hoped that that policing role may rarely require the council to make difficult disciplinary decisions regarding the action of peers in order to bring such action into compliance with acceptable practice standards.

From the work of the council, a nursing quality assurance program develops in order to coordinate and integrate quality assurance activities within the whole organization. Where possible, it should reduce duplication of efforts within the nursing service. The council will, therefore, be responsible for the flow of activity intended to fulfill obligations for an appropriate, organized, and integrated quality assurance program. Activities that must be undertaken by the quality assurance council are as follows:

1. The problem must be identified. All data sources need to be used and should be forwarded to the council on nursing quality assurance for its discussion and review. Time frames need to be established for undertaking the quality assurance program.
2. The nursing quality assurance council will collaborate with all appropriate people who are identifying problems and seeking solutions. The council will undertake objective assessment processes to determine cause, scope of problems, and concerns and will establish priorities for investigation and solving problems.
3. All nursing quality assurance problems will be given priority according to their degree of adverse impact on patient care.
4. After establishing priorities, the council will collaborate with appro-

priate membership and nursing departments to evaluate problems for recommended corrective action.

5. Criteria will be developed by the council through the advice and service of the appropriate clinical specialty. Criteria will be pre-established in an objective, measurable format according to applicable standards; these criteria may require examination and evaluation of structure, process, and outcome.
6. Performance is an appropriate matter to be evaluated and compared with established criteria by the quality assurance council.
7. Deficiencies, when identified, will be clearly described and compared to appropriate standards.
8. Action, recommendation, or discipline will be determined and taken, as appropriate, by the membership of the quality assurance council. Action should be consistent with the severity, impact, and needs of the problem situation.
9. The nursing council on quality assurance will take appropriate follow-up action so that the action, recommendation, or determination is implemented as described within the quality assurance plan.
10. The quality assurance council may restudy areas where there are dynamic processes that may indicate a need for follow-up studies over a long period of time. The council may describe those areas that are appropriate for restudy and may take disciplinary action where restudy indicates noncompliance with previous recommendations.
11. An ongoing mechanism for granting credentials, run by professional nursing staff, will be undertaken by the council on nursing quality assurance. All activities associated with approval of applications and evaluation of credentials fall within the scope of the quality assurance council.
12. Approval of all research activity in the nursing division will be rendered by the quality assurance council. Appropriate protective human rights' standards are promulgated and research outcomes are disseminated to improve nursing practice.

Quality assurance activity in nursing is a primary organizational activity for which the staff can have major responsibility; this should be facilitated and encouraged. The governance structure that gives significant decision-making authority to the quality assurance council is appropriate and necessary. Having quality assurance decisions, activities, corrective action, and evaluation processes assumed by practicing professional nurses spreads a sense of peer responsibility for the quality of professional nursing practice. This professional, collaborative, interactional process of ensuring quality through staff surveillance removes responsibility for quality assurance from an objective, third-party management role and places it squarely within the realm and responsibility of the clinical practitioner. Establishing the authority to make decisions, take corrective action, and undertake disciplinary processes within the staff governance framework provides an organizational mandate and the subsequent staff nurse clout that are essential to the success of the process. A strong, effective quality assurance program, structured at the staff level, can facilitate and support the full range of nursing activities essential for delivering appropriate and meaningful patient care.

NURSING EDUCATION

The work of nursing development is vital to the growth of nursing practice because of current technology and innovations in nursing and medicine. Thus, it is important that education and professional development be facilitated to maintain high levels of competency in this highly complex clinical environment. Education has traditionally been an interruptive process within the hospital structure. Nurses who seek opportunities to grow must stop their direct delivery of care in the hospital to participate in a learning experience for between 15 minutes and 2 hours. In most such circumstances, the quality of the education process is diminished because the nurse is preoccupied with the patient she has left and the clinical activities left undone. It is thus difficult to actually incorporate newly learned skills immediately into practice to effect an improvement.

Further impact of nursing education relates to ensuring that compliance with standards, improvement in standards, and new skills and clinical concepts are integrated into ongoing nursing care activity. This whole process assures the organization that the most current concepts of practice are being followed in the delivery of clinical nursing care. Also, the nursing organization is assured that compliance with existing standards—validated and monitored through the quality assurance process—is being supported through appropriate educational mechanisms.

The council on nursing education must make sure that the design, structure, and delivery of educational services within the division of nursing are directed specifically to meeting the needs of the clinical practitioner and the standards needs of the organization; the educational services should also integrate appropriate new concepts into practice.

The council's responsibility is to ensure that mechanisms to maintain high levels of competence are in place and to provide the supports necessary to the meaningful delivery of clinical nursing services. Thus, the council ensures that both the most modern principles of adult education and the application of clinical knowledge are incorporated into its operational framework and are parts of its consideration of all educational processes.

Membership on the education council represents all the unit level services. Although this may broaden membership on the council, usually beyond that of the other councils, it indicates that nursing education cannot generally be met solely on a division-wide basis. While there are general programs appropriate to the corporate nursing body, most educational processes need to be directed to specific clinical activities that are unique to individual clinical units. Education appropriate for a neurological nurse may not necessarily be so for a renal nurse, and so forth. Those institutions that attempt to meet specific educational needs through a division-wide program not modulated to address unique clinical needs really do not fulfill the obligation to develop the individual practitioner of professional nursing. In representing specific clinical divisions within the nursing service, the council can more clearly and adequately address specific needs for learning consistent with new clinical skills, new concepts, corrective action, and developmental education.

Through these processes, the council on nursing education becomes accountable at the unit and corporate levels for all educational activities within the division of nursing. Since the unit representatives are responsible for translating educational requirements to the council and their respective units, each area of focus for clinical practice is addressed by the entire council. Since accountability is invested in these representatives, the educational calendar, its variations, and the finances set aside to support education can be developed, reviewed, and approved by the council. It is to be emphasized, therefore, that the council takes on the burden of operational accountability through its authority in approving essential financial and support resources. Further, the department of nursing education, which operates fundamentally as the educational unit of the nursing division, reports to the council on nursing education in the shared governance approach. Through its relationship with the chairperson of that council, in collaboration with the department head, the educational department takes its direction for developing appropriate educational facilities, services, and programs from the council on nursing education. Here, too, the entire organization receives evidence that the professional staff, in being accountable for its own professional growth and development, exercises that accountability and associated authority toward those who ultimately will be responsible for carrying out the mandate of the nursing education council.

Consistent with the authority invested in the nursing education council, the following goals, responsibilities, and standards provide the framework for its activity:

1. ensuring the promotion of nurses' individual accountability for continued learning consistent with the needs of the institution, applying what is learned to the practice environment;
2. continuously assessing, identifying, and defining immediate as well as long-term educational needs for nurses within the nursing division;
3. seeking opportunities for learning directed toward increasing competence appropriate to the roles of specific specialty nurses;
4. identifying a program that maintains flexibility and responds to nurses' learning needs, using all available educational resources and supports;
5. using nursing research and the outcomes of nursing science, and incorporating those outcomes into the establishment of nursing practice consistent with appropriate standards;
6. identifying clearly changes in health technology, health care delivery, and nursing care emerging from growth and development in the health care field;
7. developing a system for the ongoing evaluation of the effectiveness of the nursing education council and educational programs, for both the long and short terms;
8. collaborating closely with the councils on nursing quality assurance and nursing practice in instituting new standards of practice; undertaking corrective education to do away with compromises or conflicts between standards and nursing practice; working with all governance councils to monitor and test nurses' knowledge and competence related to nursing practice;
9. providing opportunities for auxiliary nursing personnel to provide appropriate support to professional nurses in delivering nursing care;
10. developing specified consistent program formats for designing, implementing, and evaluating all nursing programs within the division of nursing;
11. determining the appropriate number of contact hours to be attached to program offerings and the appropriate approval mechanisms for awarding contact hours;
12. determining the access, availability, and time limits associated with delivering educational services so that education can be incorporated into the ongoing activities of individual nurses;
13. designing appropriate mechanisms for disseminating educational information, support, resources, and notification regarding continuing education programs;
14. specifically determining the required number of continuing education hours necessary for maintaining privileges for nursing staff

membership consistent with the appropriate clinical level's program for the individual nurse;

15. taking corrective action in regard to the program, the planning, the department of nursing education, and individual staff members when compliance with acceptable parameters has not been obtained; and

16. defining, reviewing, approving, and budgeting appropriately for the annual unit and divisional continuing educational calendar annually, with appropriate quarterly reviews of all program offerings.

Clearly, the role of the council on nursing education is directed toward supporting the self-development of the professional nursing practitioner. Planning and defining goals, as well as implementing and evaluating programs for the units in the division of nursing, are necessary for that self-development to occur. It is important to recognize, however, that the education council cannot be fully responsible for integrating education into the role of the individual nurse. Assisting nurses with materials, resources, supports, references, and other material, as well as designing a program that meets the specific needs of units and nurses, is a central activity of the council on nursing quality assurance. The obligation to pursue continued education rests, however, with the individual professional. Working together closely, the individual nurse and the nursing education council can meet accelerating needs of patients and incorporate new technology and new behaviors into practice. Devising mechanisms and processes that will facilitate this is clearly a challenge to the council on nursing education. Thus, all the growth and development strategies previously discussed become the central role and obligation of the council on nursing education.

NURSING MANAGEMENT

Structurally, the council on nursing management does not differ specifically from most nursing management committees, congresses, executive committees, or boards. It is formalized as a component of the integrated nursing organization in a shared governance framework. The activities, deliberations, and undertakings of the council do not fundamentally change as one moves to the council format. It must be emphasized, however, that the council's focus may change considerably. In the bureaucratic or hierarchic organization, the nursing management group is responsible for the full range of nursing activities, and its members are accountable for fulfilling the organization's mandates in meeting patient care needs. Standards, quality assurance, education, and all activities supporting those processes were traditionally conceived to be a fundamental role of the management team.

In shared governance, however, those elements are no longer fundamental to the operation of the management group. In the shared governance framework, standards, practice, quality assurance, education, and delineation of all those responsibilities and accountabilities in the division of nursing transfer to the professional staff as part of their operational imperative. Because the obligation for making decisions and controlling outcomes is transferred, determining appropriate responses and making decisions for those councils and their subgroups no longer rests with the nursing management group. The group's frame of reference is considerably altered in a shared governance framework.

This narrowing of the role of management, perhaps more than any other concept under shared governance, is controversial and fraught with debate. It may cause the rejection of shared governance as a legitimate organizational framework in most hospitals. While it is easier to understand this particular framework upon reviewing its historical and operational context, it is still difficult to conceive that accountability for clinical functional elements need not rest with management. It is difficult for most people to accept that no provision is made permitting final accountability to rest with the individuals responsible for exercising the obligations traditionally defined, controlled, and managed by the administrative group. With the appropriate trusts, a well-developed organizational context, and the ability to provide a structure that controls variables at a higher level than is permitted in the traditional organization, however, there is little basis to believe that the nursing division cannot be integrated just as equitably in a shared governance framework as it has in the traditional bureaucratic framework. This is enhanced by the additional benefits the organization gains through the involvement and participation of all the professional nursing staff in the decision-making processes affecting clinical practice and patient care.

Under shared governance, the management responsibility becomes centralized and directed specifically to assure appropriate support of the nursing staff. The resources and assistance required by the staff to accomplish its task now become the sole obligation of the nursing management group. Those responsibilities associated with providing appropriate administrative, financial, material, system, and human resources are the key functions of the council on nursing management. The nurse manager must be clinically prepared and broadly exposed to professional clinical practice to comprehend and articulate the unit's nursing needs, but the core of her operation is to implement nursing practice on the unit and in the institution.

In shared governance, the management group is often responsible for carrying out the mandate of the clinical councils and incorporating their decisions into the operational activities of the nursing organization. Frequently, in addition to accountability being invested in the manager for operationalizing decisions rendered in the various councils, authority may also be given to the nurse manager to take corrective action and disciplinary processes. However, the management council also has a responsibility in educating staff and directing activity to the other councils when accountability for those activities most appropriately rests with those councils. The council on nursing management is therefore precluded from making decisions related to the work of other councils. It must forward the information, questions, or processes to the individual nursing council responsible.

Nurse managers need to be relatively free from the day-to-day direct delivery of clinical nursing care. They should have the opportunity, like any other manager, to have a full range of activities associated with providing supports and resources to the nursing unit. If the nurse manager is directly involved in providing nursing care, she is unable to attend to the full range of activities that are part of her responsibilities. Since this nurse has sometimes been involved in direct patient care, her responsibility to patients will always come before the activities of managing the nursing resource. Separating the management function from the practice of nursing is vital to the success of management on any nursing unit.

The nurse manager's responsibilities include matters of staffing, program evaluation, personnel evaluation consistent with peer review, decisions about unit coordination, allocation of human resources, material, supplies, ordering, financial and budgeting activities, and long-range planning activities. In collaboration with her peers on individual nursing units, the nurse manager is responsible for identifying and remedying problems that affect nursing care. Conversely, problems that originate from the clinical practice of nursing become the obligation and accountability of the clinical nursing resources on each unit—not the nurse manager, the nursing management council, or its committees.

This discussion of the role of the nurse manager and the nursing management council has named several elements of nursing management accountability. Nursing management is responsible for:

1. allocating fiscal resources, which include budgetary, operational, capital, and contingent financial resources essential to the practice of nursing;
2. providing all material services necessary to meet patient care needs in all clinical nursing areas;
3. providing support and clerical and functional services so nursing care can be administered in an appropriate clinical environment;
4. undertaking the mandates of the nursing organization as provided

by the nursing councils to ensure that council decisions are communicated and implemented;

5. providing and describing the human resources necessary to meet applicable standards in the delivery of nursing care in all areas of the nursing service;
6. providing the operational and leadership liaison with other hospital department heads to solve problems related to the support necessary for delivering patient care;
7. integrating the activities of each nursing unit, providing both the environment and the communication mechanisms so that maximum lateral relationships can exist between all unit nursing staff members;
8. identifying organizational problems related to supporting clinical practice and undertaking mechanisms for problem resolution;
9. establishing communications with all other governance councils to facilitate information sharing and other appropriate actions between the councils;
10. articulating mechanisms for developing staff leadership in individuals and groups to ensure the organization's movement from a dependent to an independent professional nursing model;
11. providing a developmental and educational program for nurse managers subject to the approval of the council on nursing education; and
12. providing for the appointment of a committee of the council on nursing management, with a broad cross section of nursing representation to recommend action on such issues as the quality of work life, salary and wages, benefits, and other employee programs.

The functions of the nurse manager and the nursing management council change as the organization moves toward a fully developed shared governance structure. The change, however, involves facilitation and encouragement of accountability and responsibility by professional nursing staff for obligations connected to their clinical function. In moving to a shared governance organization, management must obviously divest itself of roles that belong to the staff. Since much individual ego strength and power are invested in some of these accountabilities, the transition from the typical bureaucracy toward the staff framework is obviously fraught with difficulty. Monitoring the movement of accountability to staff nurses and dismantling some traditional nursing management responsibilities will become a basic administrative function. The role requirements of the nursing administrator are awesome in this transition, and her ability to assess elements of the organization and implement appropriate change strategies is a key to a successful transition. Strategies for making the change are discussed in detail later. Nursing management's active support for the activities within this changing framework, however, will be vital to a successful transition.

Helping the managers focus on elements in their areas of accountability will be a product of both time and attention. The change process will be encouraged when managers start to recognize the staff's successes as they begin assuming more and more of their clinical accountability for nursing affairs associated with patient care.

THE COORDINATING COUNCIL

The role and responsibility of the coordinating council is discussed in more detail later. It is important now, however, to mention its operation in relation to the other councils and their activities. Coordination of the nursing organization is essential to the successful completion of the councils' work and the appropriate delivery of clinical nursing practice. To ensure this, a mechanism must be established that allows communication between the councils in a decision-making framework. When decision making is spread over a broader base, as it is in the council format, the obligation for ensuring communication becomes even more urgent than usual. Establishing mechanisms for decision-making communication, integration of functions, resolution of conflicts and critical decision making between councils must be incorporated into nursing's framework. To do this, a coordinating council is set up to centralize all the activities of the individual council and to convene the council chairpersons for dialogue. The council chairpersons make up the centralized decision-making group within the nursing organization; through its auspices and activities, the group discusses and facilitates decisions affecting the entire division of nursing. Council chairpersons also take up issues related to council coordination. The relationship between the coordinating council and the nursing administrative body must be well established; the reasons for this will become clear as we discuss coordinating activity and integration of the nursing division.

THE CORPORATE NURSING STAFF

While the governance councils and the coordinating council assume major responsibility for the ongoing governance of the nursing organization, the nursing staff as a whole maintains the ultimate obligation for its activities and decisions. A mechanism needs to be built into the organization that provides a corporate role for the nursing staff. Thus, the nursing staff in session can collectively review, approve, revise, adopt, and undertake activities deemed appropriate and necessary to its role. Most of the organization's activities will be undertaken by the appropriate governance council. Reports of activities, questions, concerns, and related issues, however, should be provided within the corporate structure.

The corporate nursing staff should meet at least once a year to ensure staff involvement in at least the following activities:

1. review, revise, and approve the nursing staff bylaws;
2. review, discuss, and approve the governance council's activities;
3. vote on issues of concern to the nursing division;
4. review, comment on, revise, and approve the nursing organization's goals and objectives, its long- and short-range planning process;
5. debate issues of professional concern affecting the role and practice of professional nursing;
6. mandate the specific consideration of issues by the appropriate nursing governance council as a whole, with a commission to report back to the staff as required;
7. hold a special education session for the corporate nursing staff on a topic of interest to the profession;
8. provide an opportunity to meet informally to network and discuss issues of individual concern; and
9. provide a forum for interaction with the hospital administration, nursing administration and management, and other individuals chosen by the corporate nursing staff.

Other items of interest to the nursing staff may be added to the list. The truly professional organization provides as many opportunities as possible for staff involvement in governance activities. Using a forum that meets at least once yearly provides limited, but at least regular, access for the nursing staff to those people who represent their interests in the councils and clinical management areas. If the institution can offer these gatherings on a quarterly basis, making one of the quarterly meetings the annual meeting, it will provide more frequent opportunities.

Whatever form is provided, the professional nursing staff should participate collectively in the shared governance process; each member is ultimately responsible for full participation in activities for which they have some accountability. Developing a forum in which each practicing nurse can express this role facilitates the move of the nursing staff to a professional framework of operation. It also reaffirms the organization's commitment to participation and inclusion of nursing staff in all activities affecting their practice and function. A statement of expectation and accountability is also facilitated through delineation of the nursing staff's responsibility in governance activities. Each time the nursing staff meet in their professional forum, the collaborative nature and professional character of the organization are reaffirmed.

What should become apparent through the development of the councils is the organization's movement from a traditional line staff authority structure to an integrative governance framework that shares authority and involves the staff in both participatory measures and actual decision-making capacities. The structural components of this organizational framework, consistent with identified elements of operation, show a different way the organization of nursing can be structured. Again, it must be emphasized: key to the success of this process is the transition of decision making from centralized bodies of authority in the management structure to diffuse and interrelated organs within nursing. In shared governance, the councils are accountable for specific decisions and for implementing and determining the outcome of those decisions. Accountability for determining the success or failure of individual councils belongs to a coordinating council consisting of governance chairpersons. Also, building evaluation mechanisms into the council activity and attaching the appropriate objectives framework to attaining council tasks helps make sure their work is done and evaluated. Therefore, checks and balances of outcomes are in place on three levels:

1. The nursing administrative overview of the activities of all the councils must be consistent with overall organizational goals and objectives.
2. The councils' activities, mandates, and performance must be measured against predefined goals, objectives, and standards.
3. The evaluation and interaction undertaken by the coordinating council (consisting of the chairpersons of all the councils)—identifying issues, problems, concerns, and processes associated with the integration of council activity—is a central focus of this group (see Figure 5-1).

Through the entire process, the nursing division's accomplishment of its tasks and responsibilities, as well as the determination of outcomes, is handled in a radically new way. The challenges inherent in this approach are obvious. The opportunities, when compared to the risks, are also impressive. At this point we can begin to conceptualize the possibilities that emerge from using shared governance in a dynamic nursing organi-

Figure 5-1 Nursing Operational Framework Organizational Structure

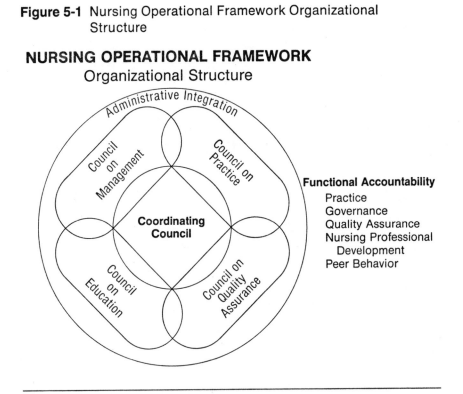

NURSING OPERATIONAL FRAMEWORK
Organizational Structure

Functional Accountability
Practice
Governance
Quality Assurance
Nursing Professional
  Development
Peer Behavior

zation. Creative energy provides the beginning point for change—altering the very structures of the organization is but the first step.

NOTES

1. *Webster's New World Dictionary* (New York: World Publishing Company, 1982), p. 286.

2. *Roget's International Thesaurus* (New York: Thomas White Crowell Company, 1980), pp. 740, 999.

3. J. Naisbitt, *Megatrends* (New York: Warner Communications, 1982), pp. 190–205.

Chapter 6

Planned Change: The Organization in Transition

Any organization that seeks to undertake a change with such broad implications as the move from the traditional organizational structure to a shared governance framework must be fully cognizant of the mechanics and intricacies of the change process. The process is a logical, systematic approach to change that examines all the factors involved in moving an organization from one point to another, more desirable situation or circumstance.

One hears much discussion about the change process. What is usually involved is a fundamental examination of where one is, where one is going, and the best way (within the context of the organization) to reach a defined destination. The change process encourages the individual to look prospectively at all the characteristics, elements, and behaviors involved in moving from one state to a new state or condition. In examining and understanding elements of the change process, the change agent must become familiar not only with the processes that must be addressed in making change but also with the responses, behaviors, characteristics, and other appropriate corollaries to initiating change. The lack of understanding that comes from not being involved in the mechanics of change is frequently used by nursing administrators as an excuse for slowing or delaying real change.

It is important to recognize that there are times when reaction, anger, and animosity are appropriate responses to a particular point in making changes. Similarly, there are times when acknowledgment, encouragement, appropriate response, and universal acceptance of actions and situations occur as goals are met in the quest for change.

An understanding of the change process alone is insufficient. The leader in the process must be committed to a full understanding of how to implement change and use it as an encouraging, as well as modulating, modifying influence in moving through the steps of a radical organizational change.

A leader without this understanding will be hindered in his or her role. Change itself has no value unless the outcomes identified as achievable are reached. If one has succeeded in changing but has not arrived at the desired point, the change process has essentially failed. The change agent must build on the understanding available through implementing the change process and must recognize its various stages so that change will occur in a logical, consistent manner. Planned transition also allows the change agent or innovator to assess the positions of the transition so that actions specific to that stage of change can be logically and consistently undertaken. This initial assessment will ensure that each part of the organization's movement to a new state can be fully implemented and integrated into the organizational process.

It is always wise to begin with a review of the theoretical framework for the change process. Examination can then be undertaken of some of the practical applications of the change process in moving the organization from the traditional hierarchic bureaucracy to a shared governance structure.

THE THEORY OF THE CHANGE PROCESS

Providing the environment to support the change event and understanding the role of the nurse leader as a change agent are the beginning points for making planned changes. When the supporting structures and mechanisms are in place, there are a number of strategies that can be used to initiate the change process in a logical, consistent, and measurable manner. This is especially so in the case of a major step, such as moving the organization from its old framework into a new model for professional behavior.

Much of current change modeling has its origin in the work of Kurt Lewin, who believed that change processes had three basic steps: unfreezing, movement, and refreezing (See Figure 6-1).[1] Lewin described unfreezing as a motivational event in which some change initiation occurs. It is during unfreezing that the social/environmental system or individual acknowledges the need for some change. In this framework, deficits in the current situation are diagnosed, and essential directions that create the need for change are established. After this diagnosis, Lewin suggests that alternatives be identified and assessed. He indicates further that the initial forces subsequent to the creation of change are frequently evidenced by:

1. a lack of confirmation or disconfirmation
2. the introduction of guilt or anxiety
3. the creation of psychological safety

Figure 6-1 A Representation of Lewin's Concept of Managing
Change

MANAGING CHANGE

PROCESS
Know the mechanics
Use the system.

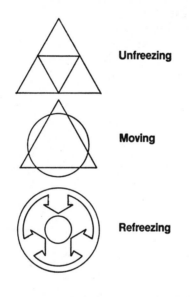

Unfreezing

Moving

Refreezing

Specifically, as individuals become aware of change requirements, their perceptions may not immediately be satisfied. This yields a lack of information about their expectations of the environment. The individual may feel uncomfortable. This initially leads to some action or perhaps to inaction. This discomfort can frequently result in guilt or anxiety in the person being influenced by the change. Further sentiments at this time affect the individual's perceptions and feelings of change. This is often displayed by the individual as a compromise, creating a sense of psychological safety.

The process of unfreezing, therefore, moves through several processes between problem identification and the recognition that the environment must ultimately be altered (see Figures 6-2 through 6-5). When this recognition is achieved, after going through the previous anxieties, concerns. and insecurities, a resultant wide variety of states of uncertainty result. This affects both the environment and the individual participants who work within it. Confusion, discord, anxiety, and reaction are frequent signs of the unfreezing stage. However, this disturbance and uncertainty

Figure 6-2 Step I of Lewin's Concept of Unfreezing

UNFREEZING

Step I ASSESS:

- examine critically present status of
  organization and situation
- definition of present system
- current organizational behaviors/
  expectations
- key formal and informal leaders.

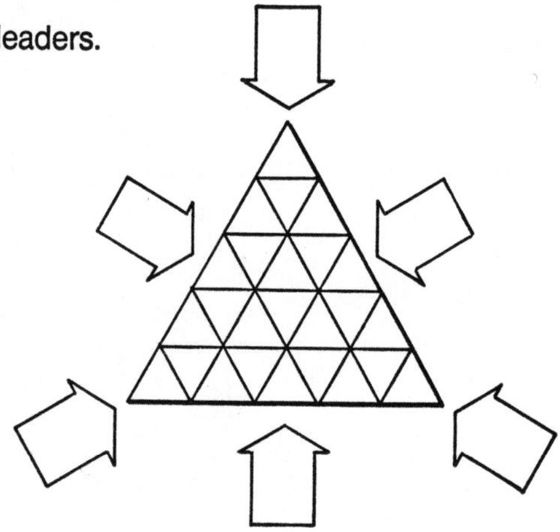

provide the initial volatility that is essential to start the change and begin the fundamental steps in moving from the old state to a new one sought by the organization.

Lewin's second stage of change, movement, contains the social change events that actually move from the old situations to the new anticipated responses (see Figures 6-6 and 6-7). This stage expands on the collectivity of information required to initiate the change process fully. This is the data generation, information-gathering, and support-building portion of the change process.

Information can be identified and clarified after the initial problem identification. It is then combined with other information and directed by the change agent in a logical and organized format, providing a framework for the new direction. Lewin indicates that cognitive redefinition through processes such as identification and scanning occurs at this time. Identification is described as an association established with a particular knowledgeable, respected, or powerful peer or superior in the organization. This

Figure 6-3 Step II of Lewin's Concept of Unfreezing

UNFREEZING

Step II IDENTIFY:

- organizational supports
- organizational constraints
  (personnel and institutional)
- outcomes/expectations both
  behavioral and system
- rationale for change event.

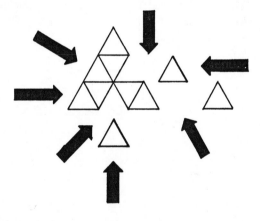

---

peer may influence the decisions of the organization, its participants, and even the change agent. The scanning process permits those directly involved in the change process to pursue a number of possible ways to resolve the problem.

While peer identification may facilitate the success of change, it can also tend to limit the number of alternatives sought. On the other hand, scanning provides the same kind of information from a number of different sources that facilitate movement from the stable situation to an unclear, yet more desirable new state.

Broad availability of data and resources, however, may increase the amount of time involved by lengthening the time for decision making and consensus seeking. To foster understanding and subsequent commitment

Figure 6-4 Step III of Lewin's Concept of Unfreezing

UNFREEZING

Step III DETERMINE CHANGE FACTORS:

- tools
  - personnel
  - plans
  - resources
- process
  - strategies
  - beginning place
  - knowledge framework

Educate key managers and other leaders.
Reframe input and revise program plan.

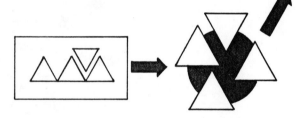

to risk taking, which releases participants from the old and encourages them to reach out to the new, the organization should consider investing time to share information and address their concerns. Chances that more appropriate decisions will be made are enhanced when all information data bases are used and all participants have a knowledge of and a share in the application of information.

This second stage of change, according to Lewin, contains a strong element of planning and examining. At this point, planning steps become clearly defined, organized, and systematically used, building upon all available resources and developmental strategies. The direction established by change begins to solidify and be understood by the organization. Specific choices are selected and applied. Processes are defined. The change agent selects and applies criteria for measuring and monitoring change. He or she undertakes the first steps to make sure that change moves in the anticipated direction.

Figure 6-5 Step IV of Lewin's Concept of Unfreezing

UNFREEZING
Step IV BUILD ORGANIZATION SUPPORT:

- inform staff of outcomes.
- involve staff in program definition.
- utilize levels process as building block.
- transfer control to key clinical leadership.
- don't worry about majority not yet "on board."
- begin to establish credibility.

Construct Informational Resource
- develop a strong data base.
- disseminate information broadly.
- discuss, deliberate, argue, disagree, and stimulate.

Formulate Action Groups
- broadly representative.
- communicate, communicate, communicate.
- provide direction and let go.
- work for specific goals, not generalized ones.

In the movement stage, the organization begins to see some of the new becoming successfully applied, and some of the old becoming unbundled from the practices and expectations of participants. Here again, however, a high level of insecurity, doubt, and need for validation occur. Encouragement, support, and energy are required to propel people toward the change goals.

The third stage of Lewin's change process is called refreezing (see Figures 6-8 and 6-9). During this stage, new changes become fully initiated, integrated, and stabilized. It is becoming evident that these new behaviors are part of the values and operational system of the work environment. Formalization and development of the policy and behavioral and disciplinary supports that direct and maintain the changes are begun here.

Figure 6-6 Step I of Lewin's Concept of Movement

MOVEMENT
Step I ASK QUESTION:

1. Is your direction clear, responsible with some hope of success?
2. Is your task framework specific rather than general?
3. Is there an immediate outcome that can gratify and stimulate further action?
4. Is your power base established — know who is with you, who is not, and who will work?

Action Strategies

1. **Personal** - if individual needs (power, prestige, growth, economics) can be enhanced collaboration will result.
2. **Clout** - change — move — friction — conflict. Involvement and negotiation are the key.
3. **Negotiation** - do things at the right time for the right people. Touch base, touch base and touch base . . .

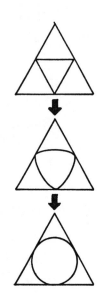

Refreezing involves strategies for stabilizing and maintaining the new environment and for reducing the number and degree of alternatives and the varieties of response and action available to participants in the new environment. Stabilizing the environment includes such items as clearly defining acceptable and unacceptable behavior, and establishing new policy and new mechanisms for authority in providing routines upon which the new expected behaviors can be continually exhibited and approved.

Throughout the entire process, Lewin recognizes that there are driving forces that either impede or facilitate the process of change. He identifies those forces as restraining forces. He indicates that it is essential to recognize them early in the change process. Frequent observation during all stages of the change process ensures that the change agent will continually be aware of the strong influence of the restraining forces. The agent will also see the need to develop strategies and resources in the environment throughout the process to offset the forces' influence. If these forces are known to the change agent, their impact and effect can be carefully con-

Figure 6-7 Step II of Lewin's Concept of Movement

MOVEMENT
Step II PLAN:

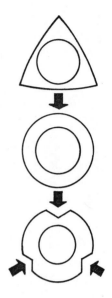

1. Make sure those involved are aware of **specific** tasks they can accomplish.
2. Activity must be **realizable** — goals should be able to be accomplished.
3. Allow for **immediate** rewards to serve as motivators for future action.
4. Monitor; Review; Step back; Review again.
5. Make time frames realistic.
6. Establish a tight-knit organization that can take pressure from outside and in.
7. Support each other; one to one communications; "pep" sessions.

---

sidered and incorporated in the planning and implementation of any change event.

Driving forces must be capitalized on and used frequently since they maintain the momentum for change. Recognizing and utilizing these forces balance the effort and influence of the restraining forces. Positive driving influences provide a continual equilibrium that permits the change agent to maintain a balance between possibilities described and hoped for and the organizational constraints that validate security and stability. The tension between these two factors must be offset by the change agent, who provides the momentum to create the environment, the forces, and the urges for obtaining change. These driving forces are an essential consideration for the change agent, whose ability to manage them successfully can ensure that the process remains a motivated, continuous, and ultimately successful one.

Many theories have been built upon Kurt Lewin's ideas. Everett Rogers saw change as having many characteristics that can have an impact on the success or failure of the process.[2] Rogers maintains there are five stages in the process of change: awareness, interest, evaluation, trial, and adoption.

At the level of awareness, denial of the need for change is eliminated. Interested individuals identify a point in the change process where there is individual or group desire to start a change. Evaluation processes examine the essential change strategies, along with the original content. Trial centers on the initiation of change events. Trial is used to select those particular processes that will be most successful in making changes. Adoption represents the group's selection of specific actions that result from identifying change strategies. Selecting trials assures a validation of actions as a major effort in creating a new environment.

Rogers' stages of awareness and interest correlate well with Lewin's stages of unfreezing. Trial and evaluation correspond with Lewin's process of movement, and adoption parallels Lewin's refreezing and stabilizing the change event.

Havelock also expanded the work of Kurt Lewin and established a model for planning change.[3] His model contains six basic elements in building change processes:

1. building a relationship
2. diagnosing the problem
3. acquiring the relevant resources
4. choosing the solution
5. gaining acceptance
6. stabilizing the environment

Havelock puts special emphasis on the major role planning plays in the change process. It is his belief that appropriate planning skills and techniques will facilitate the appropriate and successful development of change events in a logical and systematic manner. Attention to planning ensures that the change will develop in an orderly and systematic way. Building exception monitoring and dealing with contingencies in the system are also essential, especially in planning, in Havelock's view. Havelock's

---

Figure 6-8 Step I of Lewin's Concept of Refreezing

REFREEZING

Step I CHANGE COMPLETION:
1. Completion Internalization
2. Acquired behaviors entrenched
3. Behaviors do not extinguish
4. New routine reinforced

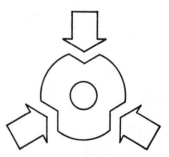

Figure 6-9 Step II of Lewin's Concept of Refreezing

REFREEZING

Step II EVIDENCE OF CHANGE:

1. Validation of changed situation
2. Environment reflects appropriate action
3. Judgements reflect new Values
4. Past practices are not evident

---

emphasis on planning indicates that, if appropriately planned, the actual implementation of phases of change will involve far less time and energy than would otherwise be the case.

Reinkemeyer identifies seven steps in the change process.[4] These outline some clear demarcations between levels of the change process that are essential to the change agent. If these are not identified, change cannot be implemented.

1. development of a felt need and a desire for change
2. development of a relationship of change between the agent and the patient or client system
3. clarification/diagnosis of the system's problems, needs, or objectives
4. examination of alternatives and the beginning goals and action intended
5. transformation of these intentions into changed behavior
6. stabilization of change
7. ending the relationship in the change process between the agent and the system

Reinkemeyer recognizes that not all aspects of change unfold in a logical manner. Change is a dynamic process that may seek alternative directions during any of its events. In this system, identifying needs parallels the unfreezing phase of Lewin's model. The relationship phase identified by Reinkemeyer, initially vital to the evolution of the change process, occurs at the beginning of the interaction with the change system. Openness and responsiveness are required at this initiating phase. Also, the extent of the change involved should be indicated at its opening phases. Correct problem identification becomes a very important step so that the change event can unfold clearly to meet defined and articulated needs. Skills in assessing cause and effect must be used at this point. Defining directions for resolving problems that may arise on initiating change events will require alternative routes. Setting priorities and selecting the most appropriate routes are essential during this phase.

In Reinkemeyer's model, planning also plays a major role in initiating change processes. It is from sound planning, which transforms intention into action and gives it substance and framework, that the dynamic process of change emerges. Strategy development for initiating change events as well as motivational and supportive techniques are all important in helping start the change process. Since new behaviors will ultimately be expected, attention to factors related to support and growth of the participants is essential. In Reinkemeyer's next-to-the-last step, stabilization, all efforts at moving the change process have been well planned, carefully initiated, and evaluated. This demonstrates creation of new behavioral characteristics for individuals in the work environment. New routines and standards based on the new behaviors are indexes of the stabilization phase. High levels of variable activity are reduced or minimized, since change becomes self-supporting and self-perpetuating at this point. During and after this stage, termination of the relationship between the change agent and the system begins. The need for continuing intervention by the change agent diminishes, and those operating within the system become self-directed and secure. They successfully carry out their obligations and responsibilities in the new system.

Lippitt also builds on Lewin's change theory by identifying seven phases in the change process:[5]

1. diagnosing a problem
2. assessing the motivation and capacity for change
3. assessing the change agent's motivation and resources
4. selecting progressive change objectives
5. choosing the appropriate role for the change agent
6. maintaining the change once implemented
7. terminating the change relationship

Lippitt identifies the need for process skills, as well as skills related to human interaction and group dynamics. His model, therefore, is also a dynamic model and remains essentially unstratified. Any element of the process may occur or recur at any given moment. Because change processes are dynamic and must allow for a free flow of activity that does not follow rigid progressions, the change agent must be skilled in assessing responses to change. Lippitt's seven stages address progressive components that are characteristic of change strategies. His stages are clearly well integrated with the context of Lewin's three major processes:

Unfreezing

1. diagnosing the problem
2. assessing the motivation and capacity for change
3. assessing the change agent's motivation and resources

Movement

4. selecting progressive change objectives
5. choosing the appropriate role for the change agent

Refreezing

6. maintaining the change once implemented
7. terminating the change relationship

In Lippitt's seven stages, diagnosis is vitally important. The problem or change condition must first be clearly identified before appropriate directions can be established. He considers definition of the problem extremely important to the successful evolution of subsequent change. Without accurate diagnosis, follow-up action and behavior may ultimately be based on inappropriate first steps. Here again, constraints and resources need to be identified. The key policymakers and change groups upon whom the process may have an impact must be included in defining the need for change and undertaking activity to that end. Sharing and collaborating in all change events is inherent to successful evolution of the change process.

Lippitt requires a thorough assessment of the environment, including its capacity for change. Motives and motivation for change should be determined at the outset. He considers this the beginning step in the planning phase. A review of policy, social imperatives, resources and constraints in the environment, individual characteristics of the participants, power relationships, organizational structure and authority, and abilities and skills of the group are all subject to assessment prior to beginning any change processes. Understanding these factors provides support for building the change process on a firm foundation and moving it carefully toward its intended outcome. Economic, social, and financial constraints must also be reviewed carefully to determine their impact on the development of change.

Lippitt clearly focuses on the change agent's need to be well prepared and able to initiate change. The agent's ability to motivate others and guide the complex interrelationships of the change process through its various stages must be evident. The change agent may be drawn from the organizational environment or from outside. Decisions about using an internal or external change agent must be negotiated and resolved according to the needs of the environment. The change agent's skills and other character- istics must be clearly understood before implementation, because the agent's attitudes and abilities frequently affect outcome. Matters of per- sonality, behavior, leadership, and motivational skill need to be resolved prior to the action phases.

At this point in Lippitt's model, decisions occur regarding the selection of change objectives. When the previous matters have been addressed, the planning phase begins to involve itself in the change. Identification of steps in the change process and of the mechanism for implementing those steps are begun at this second phase point. Specific timetables, processes, deadlines, and outcomes are defined and correlated to ensure that activities and events flow logically and meaningfully toward change. Goal setting, evaluation, and innovation are defined and implemented now. Beginning evaluation occurs early enough so that necessary assessments are com- pleted in accord with each succeeding step. This helps the change agent determine the organization's location within the process.

FROM THEORY TO IMPLEMENTING CHANGE

The Role of the Change Agent

The role of the change agent now begins to unfold as she leads the process. A change agent's roles include behaviors that are supportive, facilitating, directing, coordinating, and integrating. The change agent will recognize situations and events that can constrain or support attainment of change. It is important for those involved in the change system to have a clear understanding of the agent's roles so as to know how best to use the agent to facilitate the transition. Identifying and confronting problems along the continuum help motivate changes and direct them toward antic- ipated outcomes, and this occurs at the outset of the change process. Consistency and logical flow, resulting from ongoing monitoring and inter- action between agent and system, are required to validate movement toward change expectations.

Communication takes on an increasingly important role in a change project. Well-developed feedback mechanisms, facilitation, policy sup- port, and human group dynamics are necessary to maintain momentum. Plans that permit the change events to spread and diffuse throughout the entire operation must be made and implemented, and evaluation becomes a basis upon which to validate each change event. Innovation and flexibility should build upon the change to further establish subsequent adaptive strategies. Adaptation to the change process must be clearly defined, and expected behaviors should be described, monitored, and, finally, assured through discipline.

Termination of the Change Agent's Role

After the change has been firmly entrenched, mechanisms for maintaining it and evaluating its ongoing effectiveness should be put in place. Termination of the relationship between the change agent and the environment begins here. If the change is appropriately planned and executed, the environment soon becomes self-supporting and the agent's interaction becomes less essential. It is expected that at these final points of change, many of those involved are now self-directed in fulfilling the recommended mandates. They should maintain the basic operational characteristics of a new, firmly entrenched change. Policies and procedural processes that support the change will provide a framework for ensuring compliance and perpetuation of the events themselves.

Here the change agent must undertake strategies to make sure that her separation from the change process is not traumatic but supportive of the organization. Lippitt suggests that a clear time frame be established for the change agent's extraction from the process and that time mandates be clearly understood and accepted by both the system and the agent. If the change agent is involved in the environment, a role change—from director, implementor, and facilitator to supporter and model—the new, operational environment becomes essential. Designation by the agent of others, who will be responsible for maintaining and monitoring subsequent events as they continue to solidify, will assist in this transition.

CHANGE IN THE NURSING CARE DELIVERY SYSTEM

Initiation of change is a complex and involved process in any organizational environment. The hospital environment is a dynamic system subject to growth and change. To minimize stresses inherent in the process, it is necessary to manage complexity and to plan change consistently and logically. Because of the identified need for change in the nursing care delivery system—especially in a change to something as dramatic as shared governance—change strategies within the frameworks previously described must be used.

The change process is very important to a dynamic organizational transition. If organizational change is to have meaning and success, this change must be planned carefully and undertaken so that it is consistent with the needs and the pace of the particular organization. Radical, quick implementation of a new organizational system such as shared governance can only court danger and ensure failure. Emphasis on the change process described herein will bolster the transition of a new organizational design and operational framework.

No theoretical framework for change can provide any meaning for an organization unless it is successfully applied. Perhaps the most difficult part of the change process is applying its elements in the operational environment carefully and systematically, in such a way that it truly influences and moderates not only the direction of change but also its successful outcomes. Using the change process and understanding all its characteristics require the most highly developed skills of the nursing administrator and nursing management, as well as those of the clinical leadership team. In a highly complex organization, such as the nursing profession in a hospital, many interacting change elements occur simultaneously. Attention to each of these elements demands highly developed skills and constant effort from nursing leadership. Systematic change can be undertaken, however, and elements of the process can be successfully applied and used to guide the change carefully and meaningfully.

Discussing many of these elements and reviewing the appendix in this text can help the change leader begin to think about and strategize change processes toward shared governance in the nursing organization.

WHERE DO WE BEGIN?

The process to change an organization usually begins with one individual, the primary change agent. In a nursing organization, the nursing administrator must be the prime mover. This is indeed a risk for this person. In the traditional system, the nursing administrator is the single most powerful individual. Her position is the focus of control and the final authority when decisions must be made. From her emphasis, personality, leadership style, and conceptual characteristics, the nursing organization takes its substance and form. Because of her primary role, it is evident even to the casual observer that this person must be the major element in initiating any processes that will fundamentally alter the nursing organization.

The kind of leader who is willing to face the risks that come with such a change must obviously be someone who is comfortable with her leadership and has a high degree of trust and commitment to the professional character of nursing. Further, she must believe in the staff's ability to participate and share in the governance of the nursing profession within the hospital framework. This high degree of trust, professional commitment, and belief is perhaps a cornerstone to the belief system so essential to achieving a shared governance framework. The nursing administrator who is uncomfortable at the thought of giving up her place at the center of the decision-making process and who does not yet have the needed trust and beliefs will have difficulty facing the risks that accompany developing a truly professional organization.

Many doubts and fears attend this particular concept, and great commitments in time, patience, energy, and just plain work are involved in this major undertaking. Much development, growth, pain, and struggle are associated with the activities involved. It is a major commitment not only for the nursing administrator but also for the organization she directs. While the rewards of this change are great, so are the struggles to attain it. When she weighs the concept and this change in balance with a fully committed, truly professional, and involved nursing organization, however, the nursing administrator quickly becomes aware that the energies and risks invested will reap many meaningful and tangible outcomes.

Commitment: The First Step

The first step, then, is a conscious, concerted commitment by the nursing administrator to move the organization into a new framework. That decision, made within the bureaucratic context, is the foundation upon which subsequent decisions and activities will be built. Making the personal commitment, and articulating the beliefs associated with that commitment, begins to set in motion a whole new set of objectives, processes, and programs as well as a new mechanism for planning and undertaking the steps necessary to implement this change. The commitment will require her energies and activities and those of other leaders in the organization, including those in the clinical area. The use of new resources will be required, and individuals will be tapped for input who have not before contributed to the development and success of nursing practice.

The energy generated from this one decision of commitment by the nursing administrator can transform the organization. That energy becomes self-perpetuating and continues to impel the organization in a positive way. The nursing administrator who makes this decision must also realize that once the door has been opened and people begin to experience shared governance, that door can never be closed again. Therefore, the commitment is not for the short term. It is not periodic, or temporary, or just a trial. It is one that makes a statement that will have a lasting impact on the nursing organization. This commitment identifies nurses as true professionals, behaving as such. Therefore, the new organization shall facilitate, encourage, and expect all the activities that represent professional behavior. This commitment, which only can be made by the nursing administrator, is the key factor in initiating change from a bureaucratic framework to one of shared governance.

From Commitment to Strategy

Once the nursing administrator has taken the risk and entrusted her resources, beliefs, and personal values to the process, a series of actions must immediately be undertaken that will affect the progress and success of the program. The nursing administrator must recognize that the organization is not going to undertake the process toward shared governance readily, nor will it immediately accept her enthusiasm about the change. Enthusiasm, commitment, energy, and drive for the program grow and develop as more nurses become committed to it. It is the responsibility and purpose of the nursing administrator, however, to help involve others in it initially. Thus, through strategizing, developing, and structuring elements of the organization she can help its energy grow.

Before she begins to make such changes, some individual planning must take place. She must begin to strategize the next move. She must address issues related to her own role, those of her key managers, the management team specifically, and all management processes in general. Since management has the primary responsibility for governing and moving the organization, she must begin with management to transform the organization. Her thinking must first relate to this process, and the person she must begin with is her own superior, the chief executive or operating officer. Most hospital administrators have limited preparation related to major clinical services such as nursing. They tend to view nursing from outside the profession, within a context considerably different from that of the nursing leadership. The hospital administrator's preparation and experience have been in a broader area, providing leadership for a multitude of services within the organization. The administrator's major concern, therefore, is neither nursing nor the governance system. This administrative person will have a wide variety of insights related to the practice and operation of nursing within the hospital framework. The administrator will bring all the knowledge and experience acquired in that position to his or her concept of the nursing organization. The nursing administrator must have a clear idea of what that concept is: how it emerges and how it works to facilitate or constrain nursing practice. Most hospital chief executive officers and operating officers are committed to the delivery of optimum clinical services and, further, to offering those services at reasonable cost. That will be the administrator's frame of reference.

The wise nursing administrator will know the chief executive officer's manner of thinking, behaving, and interacting with the nursing division. Within that context she can carefully strategize those elements and descriptors of the move to the shared governance concept that will be most palatable and most productive.

It is not essential to report the complete anticipated outcome of any change, expecting the chief executive or operating officer to "buy into" all the pieces of shared governance right at the start. The nurse administrator may reveal the early stages of change. Then, as each stage achieves more success and exerts a greater impact on the organization, she may expand the executive's frame of reference for the shared governance concept. The nursing administrator should remember that nothing builds confidence like success. Change processes that are carefully planned and structured gain broader commitment, involve more staff participation, and provide more success and positive exposure for the hospital. Though not directly involved in reducing costs, they do contribute to improved patient care. Such processes facilitate employee/employer relations, create a strong basis for success, and result in intense interest in their value by appropriate administrative officers.

Like any effort, success is built over time and usually is the outcome of a series of carefully structured steps. Developing the executive's impression successfully—within the context of his value system, hopes, and wishes for the organization—is part of carefully planning and strategizing for the development of shared governance.

The nursing administrator needs to remember, too, that the chief executive officer has been brought up within the same traditional management framework as she and will probably be considering all operational issues within that context. It will take time to persuade him of the need for a change of reference. However, the chief operating officer, like the nursing administrator, has been exposed to the current literature outlining new, more productive concepts of managing human resources. Building on these resources and facilitating his own knowledge base, he can expand his conception of the professional organization and its operation (see Figure 6-10).

After strategizing her role with the operating officer and working out mechanisms that can assist in either supporting and explaining the move to shared governance, the nursing administrator must identify with her peer leadership the internal plans, programs, and strategies that will be essential to the process. Obviously, the move to shared governance is not going to be a short-term program. The change will demand a series of steps that will take a considerable period of time to implement and evaluate fully. Therefore it will demand a concerted, long-term commitment to be

Figure 6-10 Unfreezing Your Administrator

Some clues to "unfreezing" your administrator

1. Determine his philosphy and his point of view.
2. Articulate your relationship with him/her.
3. Remember to negotiate, not demand (provide alternatives).
4. Document, validate in terms he can understand.
5. Help him/her see how it affects his own best interests.
6. Show how the organization is hurting without the proposed change.
7. Obtain support from other administrative heads.

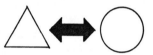

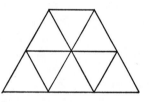

successful and address each of the major components of nursing identified in earlier chapters.

Achieving shared governance in nursing involves many subprocesses that must be articulately addressed and evaluated. The move from most traditional nursing organizations to one of real shared governance will take from three to five years to implement. Often this is enough to keep nursing administrators from undertaking the process. But looking ahead three years certainly seems a longer time than looking backward three years. It might be encouraging to the nursing administrator to look back at the last three years of tenure and see how quickly they have passed, how much has been accomplished. The nursing administrator should view the three-to five-year operational plan the same way.

Many of the elements of the plan already exist in the organization. Many pieces of the organization meeting Joint Commission on Accreditation requirements for hospitals will certainly provide the basis for making required changes for shared governance. It is important, however, to articulate the progress the nursing organization is making on each item. Through the assessment of activities and progress in meeting defined expectations, a clear picture of the starting place from which the organization can grow will be established. This data base will give the organization the change agent tools for determining where to begin.

All the issues related to the five major components of nursing should be included in the operational plan: practice, peer relations, quality assurance, professional development, and governance. Development of the objectives within each of those major headings should help the nursing leadership get a clear picture of progress in accomplishing professional goals for the organization. The three- to five-year operational plan for shared governance will require periodic updating and revision as requirements of the organization change. While outlining the direction of the nursing organization in specified time frames, it will require some accommodation and adjustment based on the variety of responses obtained as it proceeds. Revising the plan should clearly articulate changes in time, expectations, and goals as the organization matures and as shared governance is integrated within the activities of the nursing division.

The change agent should begin here, as in any major change process involving organizational dynamics, with the strengths and positive characteristics of the organization. The agent should always capitalize on the organization's success, the things that represent professional behaviors, the elements already working in the organization. By beginning with the organization's positive characteristics and adapting them to new processes, the change agent can transform the structure by providing a new kind of activity. That activity can represent not only shared governance beliefs but also the activities associated with those beliefs. At this point some important first steps can be undertaken.

The management group is the primary tool for articulating and carrying out the operational directions of the nursing organization. The nursing administrator usually has an executive committee or a management committee that includes all the managers in the organization. Sometimes this group is broken into smaller subgroups to include executive-level managers, such as division directors, and mid- or front-line managers, who are usually head nurses, patient care managers, unit managers, and so forth. Since the work of nursing and decision-making activities are usually done in these groups, facilitating their development may be the first step for the nursing administrator. Changing management's frame of reference, developing commitment to shared governance ideals and concepts, and altering management styles and behaviors will all be important early points for the nursing administrator. Just because the nursing administrator has changed her thinking about shared governance does not automatically mean her nursing management is enthusiastic about the transition.

The nursing administrator must remember that power equals status. Collectively, power and status render value to the position and the person in it. Any activity that threatens the power base of the individual will obviously not be encouraged by that person. Initially, much activity will have to be undertaken by the nursing administrator. Discussion about shared governance concepts and delineation of managers' roles and responsibilities within that context will be required of the nursing administrator. She must recognize that this process must not be abbreviated; it must be dealt with directly and in some detail if management is to understand the concept of shared governance and encourage its development.

One of the most difficult processes in making this change relates to defining the role and responsibility of the individual manager and the management team. As previously indicated, clearly delineating this role of management, defining the nurse manager as a manager of human, fiscal, material, and support resources, can create a great deal of dissonance in the nurse manager, especially the front-line nurse manager. Her last-stand adherence to the clinical role that is, in the final analysis, so valued by the nurse is obviously a symptom of the difficulty inherent in encouraging transformation of her own role from one of clinical management to one of organizational management.

Further key steps in the development of the management group as the first phase of management change will involve discussions and decisions that relate to most of the following items:

- the role of the nurse at various levels in the organization; determining what functions and responsibilities are part of that role and which are not
- the work of the nurse management council and other management groups; delineating collective management's accountability in the council as well as the individual manager's accountability in the context of various management roles in the organization
- determining the role of management individuals in facilitating and developing accountabilities and responsibilities in the professional staff for functions and responsibilities consistent with their clinical roles
- articulating the executive nurse's legislative elements and management responsibility for unfolding mandates of both the clinical and management councils
- peer evaluation, discipline, and application process to the nursing division and transition of management's role to the clinical practitioner when appropriate
- emotional, behavioral, and organizational attitudes, actions, and responses of the nursing management group to the changes in responsibility, function, and scope of the management role

- political and social implications of the commitment to a transition to shared governance, with special emphasis on maintaining the internal and collective integrity and support of the nurse management group and the nursing division
- appropriate management styles that are most successful in facilitating staff development and movement to a shared governance model
- forum, process, and activity that address problems, failures, and concerns in building the shared governance transition; mechanisms for their resolution
- appropriate provision of necessary supports to individuals in the group in making the transition toward new roles and in developing new behaviors and processes related to decision making, responsibility, and role definition

While these items include some of the basic discussions and concerns that must be addressed by the management group, they in no way articulate the full range of concerns that will arise in transition to the shared governance approach.

Each institution will have its own concerns reflecting its unique environment and issues. Whatever issues arise are appropriate for discussion and deliberation by the managers. Sensitivity to the demands this transition places on all managers is a basic requirement of the nursing executive group and, most especially, the nursing administrator. As the group begins to struggle with the process and the mechanics of the shared governance framework, careful monitoring and moderating of the influence of these activities, issues, and needs must be emphasized if the process is to succeed—even marginally. The nursing administrator's role in this process is vital.

GETTING STARTED WITH THE STAFF

Along with the nursing administrator's work with the management group, seeds of the shared governance process should be filtering through the nursing organization in a very informal way. Consideration of the move to shared governance should be discussed by the nursing division. At this point the change should have no major effect on other services in the hospital; it is still primarily an internally generated process. Through this informal exposure to the concept of shared governance, the staff can begin to conceive some of the possibilities, obligations, and responsibilities that might be part of such a move. Formally, however, the nurse administrator should begin to look at existing structures through which some of the work gets accomplished. Thus, she can think of ways those structures can be used to move shared governance into clinical areas.

Perhaps one of the best places to begin is with those formal processes that address policy and procedure or standards development through specific committee structure. Most hospitals have policy and procedure committees that encourage some representation from staff.

Practice Council

In the practice council, issues related to the formal support of nursing practice are discussed and deliberated. The council usually makes decisions, forwards recommendations to appropriate administrative bodies, and incorporates standards into the organization's formal structure. Since this approach reflects the traditional system, changes in format and process should be undertaken that reflect more professional handling of matters that affect delivery of clinical care. The practice council should begin to consider ways to articulate its accountability and responsibility more clearly and represent staff participation in major decision making more fully.

The first issue that must be addressed is composition of the practice council membership. In any organization, membership distribution is broadly representative of management and narrowly so of clinical staff nurses. Leadership on the practice council is usually assumed by someone from management, who then becomes responsible for ensuring that organizational processes and practices unfold within the standards format. Some of the first changes can occur here. Changing the membership distribution of the practice council so that the majority represents professional staff from all major clinical areas is advised. Chairperson of the council should be a clinical practicing nurse instead of a manager.

One should not be disappointed, however, to see that a change in membership does not produce major changes in outcomes or participation in the standards process. Remember that this is a long-term effort. Many things will have to occur in the organization before significant changes take place. Through altering the structure and membership of the council, however, the organization begins to make a statement about the roles and responsibilities of the group.

After such changes have been made in the council structure, the nursing administrator should begin to help the council formulate its authority over matters of clinical practice. One must begin this process carefully, reviewing each element with an eye toward its impact on the work of nursing.

Discussions and formal arrangements related to the role and responsibility of the council as it moves toward formalization as a governance council should focus on the following issues:

1. the clinical staff's role in the formulation, recommendation, implementation, and evaluation of standards for specific clinical areas
2. the format for the standards design, implementation, and approval process
3. determination of a mechanism for reducing and eventually eliminating administrative and management roles in standards development, approval, implementation, and evaluation
4. the communication process essential to integrating the decision-making functions of the practice committee/council into the nursing division
5. the role, responsibility, representation, membership, and term of office of each member of the practice committee/council
6. the appropriate learning process and orientation program of each committee/council member on the role, function, and responsibilities of membership and action on the committee/council
7. the manner in which the functions and responsibilities of this committee/council integrate with other policy functions of the organization in relation to other services and departments and to the medical staff
8. the role of the nursing administrator representative on the council, the extent of authority, and this representative's expectation for advice and service to the committee/council
9. the power and authority of the chairperson to act on behalf of the council and the final approving accountability invested in that role

A broad base of issues must be incorporated into discussions on the growth and development of this committee/council. As this body develops, it needs to assume more and more power to reflect the organization's commitment to the function of the clinical practitioner in decisions that clearly affect practice. Delineating what practice is and is not, what is or is not appropriate for consideration, are all parts of the deliberation of this group. Much of this group's formative time will be spent discussing these major role transformations. Much support and group identification will have to be included in the initial changes essential to building staff involvement and accountability in clinical decision making.

At this point, some discussion is needed on the traditional veto power of the nursing administration or the nursing administrator in relation to decisions made in other settings. In moving an organization from bureaucracy to shared governance, certain kinds of absolutes must be deliberated. The final absolute that remains invested in the nursing administrator in most bureaucracies is the right to veto or reverse decisions made elsewhere in the nursing organization. In the shared governance concept, the impact of final authority has major implications.

In shared governance, authority, accountability for decision making, and the exercise of responsibility move from the nursing administrator into the operational areas of the organization. The issue of final authority must be discussed in detail by the nursing administrator and her peers. The process of removing final authority from the administrative structure of the organization must be carefully planned. Implementing this major change may be one of the keys to building trust, commitment, and belief that a shared governance structure will eventually emerge within the organization.

Many organizations that have approached the development of shared governance have participatory structures that already reflect many of the components of shared governance. However, that final stage of transition—where accountability and authority are invested in the membership—is frequently not achieved because the nursing administrator remains at the center of the decision-making process. In such instances, the message conveyed, although not explicitly expressed, is that the nursing administrator cannot fully trust the organization to support itself. Therefore, she must maintain final summary authority for all the activities of the professional staff.

Perhaps the reason for the nursing administrator's maintaining this final veto in relation to nursing staff activities is her belief that this system ultimately will not work or that the staff is not ultimately worthy of complete trust in performing the work of the nursing organization. She may believe that decisions made by the staff will somehow be in conflict with the mandates, philosophy, and direction of the nursing organization at large. She may also fear that what the nursing organization brings forth may not necessarily be in the best interests of the hospital as a system, that it may threaten the integrity of both the nursing organization and the hospital. A fully trusting and committed nursing administrator, one who understands the process of shared governance, will ensure that three factors are considered and adhered to:

1. that the organization is carefully structured and well mandated, with accountability, including appropriate checks and balances, spread throughout the organization; that it is trustworthy;
2. that decisions not in compliance with the hospital or the nursing organization are not made; and
3. that key decision-making processes affecting operation of the nursing organization are carefully considered.

To be sure, this last point is one of the more controversial ones in moving toward a total shared governance concept; it will demand much discussion, personal thought, and careful unfolding.

As the practice council begins to define accountability and establish its role in relation to standards of clinical practice, it may be appropriate for the nursing administrator to invest in that council's chairperson the final authority for approving and promulgating nursing standards of practice throughout the organization. This means that the chairperson's signature will represent the final authority on clinical standards of practice implemented in the organization. The council therefore, becomes the formal mechanism through which all standards processes must proceed. While the nursing administrator is represented by an advisor to the council, all the processes, elements, decisions, and authority of the council become invested in the staff itself. Much is accomplished by the nursing administrator's investing that final authority in the group. The transition of clinical decision making and responsibility to the clinical staff nurse is encouraged, and trust in the quality and outcome of that process transfer to the group. As a result, the group develops a stronger sense of accountability and a commitment to responsible action, especially when its members realize that they are truly the final authority on matters related to clinical standards of practice.

The same elements of the change process that are undertaken system-wide apply to changes within the practice council. It cannot be expected that merely providing opportunities for growth will yield the desired outcomes in the professional staff members. For decades, the professional staff have been in a dependent position in the bureaucratic organization. Shifting from a position of dependency on management for making decisions and taking risks on their behalf to one requiring independence and individual and collective risk taking is not a move that the staff will undertake with ease. Participation, involvement, and commitment within the professional framework is work. That work is no longer the obligation of the management team. It now becomes the business of the whole professional nursing organization. Those traditionally protected from the risks of decision making will now be intimately involved in all the processes associated with making decisions. That transition is an intimidating and risky process for the professional staff nurse, who is new at such deliberations. The organization's nursing administration advisor, clinical specialists, and other leaders committed to developing the professional staff within this framework must work to orient such individuals and help them grow toward shared governance. Of course, there will be disappointments, slow movement, and sometimes reaction by staff as the process evolves. The staff also have many traditional bureaucratic beliefs, which the organization has heretofore accommodated. The nursing staff members, too, will have to reconceptualize roles, responsibilities, accountabilities, and functions of themselves and other members of the nursing team.

DEVELOPING STAFF'S ROLE IN QUALITY ASSURANCE

In many organizations quality assurance has been viewed as a painful, interruptive process—one that monitors and sometimes interferes with the nurses' caring process and that seems always to reveal problems with practice. Quality assurance should be a very positive, ongoing process, but it is frequently considered negative, fault finding, problem centered, and not terribly encouraging. The staff play a limited role in this process, and most of the activity in quality assurance is the responsibility of quality assurance persons.

In shared governance, quality assurance is an intimate part of practice. The narrow view of the purpose of quality assurance is eliminated. Concepts related to research, staff development, creation of new knowledge, and other factors are all incorporated into the process. Staff involvement in the quality assurance mechanism helped incorporate the outcomes of quality assurance into the ongoing activities of nursing; it lends some strength to the transition of nursing into a fully professional organization within the hospital.

The transitional process of the quality assurance council is similar to that required for the standards council. Changing the membership, incorporating new decision-making processes, creating a chairperson at the clinical level, making the quality assurance individual and the nursing administrative representatives advisory and supportive—all these activities help turn the quality assurance council into the basic structure for movement toward a council framework. Again, defining membership, terms of office, and other functional responsibilities within the quality assurance process are important to developing the group's basic membership strengths. The quality assurance council has broader accountabilities than those traditionally invested in nursing quality assurance committees. The council is responsible not only for identifying areas of concern in the nursing organization but also for recommending, even mandating, corrective action that must be undertaken by peers in the nursing organization.

The quality assurance council has unique power and authority in defining which corrective action is appropriate in disciplinary processes the staff will take on noncompliance. Again, the authority and accountability are invested with the professional staff at the peer level; this creates peer accountability for maintaining minimum standards of practice. Investing accountability for recommending disciplinary processes and for undertaking corrective action commits the organization at the staff level to action that is consistent with both the function and operation of the staff in carrying out nursing practice. It is with professional nursing peers that issues related to the action of all nursing professionals are reviewed, discussed, and acted upon.

There will be many issues that the council must discuss to fully understand and develop its role. Specific to this deliberation are the following issues:

1. the role and responsibility of the quality assurance council in problem definition and deliberation
2. the authority of the quality assurance council in making decisions on compliance and discipline
3. determination of the quality assurance plan and mechanisms for undertaking quality assurance activities throughout the nursing organization
4. integration of quality assurance activities into the practice of individual professional nurses in the clinical setting
5. discussion and development of a system for monitoring compliance, undertaking corrective action, and assuring follow-through
6. development of an effective mechanism for communicating the council's activities to the professional staff and to the other governance councils, so that appropriate decision-making activities are incorporated into the council system
7. development of a system for making recommendations to the standards council for review of quality assurance outcomes in relation to standards; the need to develop new standards and revise old ones and to specify problems with compliance
8. discussion and development of communication and interactional processes between quality assurance and managers to ensure that corrective action and discipline recommended by the council are carried out by individual units and by specified management individuals
9. establishment of ethics and a process for assuring confidentiality and collegial respect when discussing issues of individual practice, compliance, corrective action, and discipline within the council framework
10. development of a mechanism for the approval of both internal and external research activities directed toward improving nursing practice; the possibility of the development of new standards of clinical practice

11. integration of nursing quality assurance activities with those of the hospital and with the board of directors responsible for reviewing quality assurance activities

Again, while individual hospitals implementing a shared governance approach may have a whole range of unique concerns and considerations, the preceding items represent a necessary minimum. The process should be undertaken in a step-by-step, organized manner. Activities of the nursing quality assurance council will accelerate slowly because many issues related to expansion of quality assurance are sensitive and will involve processes traditionally reserved for the management team. Frustrations associated with peer review, peer decision making about compromises of individual and collective practice, undertaking disciplinary processes, and monitoring compliance can create many emotional concerns for the membership. Again, accepting the value of peer decision making and involvement in those matters traditionally reserved for management will be a struggle for many of the practitioners involved. Continual growth, support, and encouragement by clinical and management leaders in making this transition, with an organized orientation to the system and the process, will be helpful. Involvement in learning strategies to help the staff develop the skills of the roles associated with quality assurance is also needed.

MOVING EDUCATION TO THE STAFF

Traditionally, articulating and implementing educational processes have been handled by a division of nursing education or by a separate department of education with a nursing component. Educational development, programs, curricula and the like have been the responsibility of this group. As a result of the current transition of accountability, education is now viewed by most nursing staff as the responsibility of those especially prepared in educational matters. It is not integrated into the behaviors of the individual practicing staff nurse. In most institutions the process is currently considered outside the activities of the practicing nurse.

While the nursing profession has frequently characterized the educational role as a vital piece of professional nursing practice, evidence of its incorporation into institutional practice has been slow. Many fears relate to using principles of adult education and exercising clinical responsibility in delivering educational services. Other fears center on delivering information that may not be approved or accepted by other practitioners, notably physicians, or on some internal inadequacy in meeting the needs in an educational framework. As a result, many new kinds of nursing practitioners, including patient educators, program developers, staff educators, and developers, have developed. The practicing nurse also has a long-held claim that with all the other responsibilities of her daily work role, she cannot readily assume the time-consuming effort of education as well. A close examination of the activities of the practicing nurse, however, might reveal that there are many ways in which functional obligations can be adjusted to leave more time for professional development activities associated with meeting patients' educational and long-term needs. This, of course, will be an integral part of the role of the council on nursing education.

The nursing administrator will have to develop the structure, role, and responsibility of the council on nursing education carefully. Since most of this accountability has hitherto been assumed by specialized, mandated departmental function, transferring responsibility and accountability for both policy and process in education to the operational area of the nursing division—specifically, into the hands of the professional staff—can create some strong reactions from this group. Involving the education department with the clinical and management leadership team in discussions on the development of nursing staff in education can be a major first step in bringing the process to fruition. An entire educating process on the role and responsibility the staff, for their own development and for patient education, will also consume a major portion of the responsibility and time of the nursing leadership.

The ultimate goal, of course, is to make education—both for professional development and for patient education—the role of the professional staff. This should not be an interruptive process but an ongoing portion of their practice. In order to do this, the staff must be intimately involved not only in the delivery of education but also in its review, approval, implementation, and evaluation. This occurs in both the nursing division and at the unit level, within a specific clinical area. The intent to move education from a broad, division-wide basis to the smallest base of operation at the unit level and to provide for support of ongoing educational activities at this level is invested in unit nursing personnel. The council on nursing education mandate necessitates movement of education in the direction of unit-based activities and provides a mechanism to support that movement. Therefore the focus of the council is twofold: first, to provide educational services for the division and, second, to provide unit-based professional development and patient education. Subsequent to that provision, the council will be responsible for monitoring and evaluating mechanisms, as well as the usual review and approval processes, to assure that nursing education has been integrated and is operating effectively on a day-by-day basis. Staff leadership will have to spend considerable time in discussion and deliberation in this area to assure that the special needs of each institution are addressed.

In implementing this new governance activity and the processes associated with it, specific issues should be undertaken at the inception of the council on nursing education. They should include at least the following items:

- representation, assignment, role, and responsibility for membership
- a mechanism for delineating, reviewing, and approving the institutional nursing education program and individual unit education programs, in relationship to both staff development and patient education
- the relationship of the council on nursing education with the education service or department; the interaction between the leadership of the education department and the council on nursing education
- basic educational expectations for staff development and patient education programs and services
- development of appropriate communication mechanisms between the council on nursing education and the other councils on the promulgation of educational needs, education about appropriate standards and new processes, and education about corrective action in the quality assurance program
- review and approval of management education consistent with priorities established by the division of nursing
- delineation of the role and responsibility of the council in devising and evaluating the annual educational calendar for the division of nursing, and in integrating it with other educational activities in the hospital
- determination of the role and responsibility of the council on nursing education in relation to external educational activities carried out under the auspices of the institution and the division of nursing— specifically, graduate and undergraduate nursing education using hospital nursing facilities
- discussion and deliberation on the role of nursing in community education and outreach
- specification of minimal expectations for staff development by hour requirements and integration of the council in the allocation of fiscal resources for educational activities in the division of nursing.

These items are not all-inclusive but they do represent a minimum for initiating discussion and formulation of the council on nursing education. Again, many issues unique to each institution will have to be addressed to assure that the council's work is integrated into the nursing organization.

Much groundwork must be done in the formative stages of the activities of each of the councils. Timing the work of each council is necessary, both on when to initiate each council and the appropriate time frames for initiation. Each institution must base its decisions on its own situation. Some institutions are strong in one area and need more time to develop that same strength in other areas of the nursing operation. In moving the organization to a staff-generated governance system, careful assessment of initiation, progress, and the change process for each of the councils will help determine the next step. Each successful step will be the indicator or symptom of the next element of movement in the organization. As each group builds upon its smaller successes, the interests, abilities, and facilities of each of the governance councils will steadily grow. At the end of the change process, the work of the councils will emerge with confidence, clarity, and some highly visible positive outcomes for the nursing organization and the hospital.

NOTES

1. K. Lewin, "Frontiers in Group Dynamics: Concept, Method and Reality in Social Science, Social Equilibrium and Social Change," *Human Relations* vol. 16, no. 1 (June 1947): 5-41.

2. E. Rogers, *Diffusion of Innovations* (New York: Free Press of Glenclou, 1962).

3. R. Havelock, *The Change Agent's Guide to Innovation and Education* (Englewood Cliffs, N.J.: Educational Technology Publications, 1973).

4. A. Reinkemeyer, "Nursing's Need, Commitment to the Ideology of Change," *Nursing Forum*, (1970): 341–350.

5. G. Lippitt, *Visualizing Change, Model Building and the Change Process* (La Jolla, Calif.: University Associates, 1973).

Chapter 7

Coordination and Integration: A New Role for the Nursing Administrator

As indicated previously the nursing administrator's role in moving the organization from the traditional bureaucratic framework into one of fully participating shared governance is absolutely essential to its success. While the nursing administrator in the traditional framework is at the center of the decision-making process and has final authority and accountability, her importance to the success of shared governance is not changed by the transition. Her role, function, and responsibility may be significantly altered in the transitional process, and her ultimate roles in the organization may be different; but her continual facilitating, monitoring, coordinating, and integrating the process will still demand all her skills and resources.

One of the great concerns of nursing administrators as they begin to initiate this new governance framework is whether or not the nursing organizational system will remain integrated, operational, and successful without creating a new bureaucracy that, though decentralized, will further complicate the interrelationships of personnel, functions, and practice. Reviewing other sections of this book can create an overwhelming fear that the process is too broad and complex to meet the requirements of the nursing division's day-to-day operation. On the other hand, if the nursing administrator compares the complexity, functional support, and broad range of activities currently operating in the bureaucratic process against the anticipated outcome in shared governance, she will find that while the structure is altered, the complexity is not increased. A detailed examination of any organizational structure, especially that of clinical nursing, may lead the reader to believe that nursing is a highly complex and functionally valuable component of the delivery of health care services. Both the focus and intent of the shared governance framework are to broaden the base of involvement in that complexity, reduce the burden on the system, and bring to the level of practice those issues and concerns that are rightful constituents of that practice.

Thus, the overriding responsibility of the nursing administrator in this transition is to provide information and to monitor, support, facilitate, and integrate the processes and functions. It is important to develop a mechanism in which the councils' activities are integrated into those of the nursing division, so that the impact of the councils' decisions can be provided for in the ongoing operation of the nursing division. If the councils are responsible for both initiating decisions and evaluating responsive actions, there must be a mechanism that ensures that these decisions and activities are carried out, monitored and evaluated, corrected and improved where necessary, and supported as an ongoing part of the function of the nursing division. The nursing administrator's role takes on meaning and value at the center of this process.

COORDINATING COUNCIL

The nursing administrator cannot coordinate the multifocal activities of developing the shared governance system single-handedly. The mechanism must be developed to provide opportunities for the nursing administration and the leadership of the governance councils to interact. Further, they must be able to direct, integrate, communicate, and coordinate the council's activities with the responsibilities of supporting and developing patient care on a day-to-day basis.

Function of the Coordinating Council

The coordinating council is the mechanism that provides the opportunities to integrate and coordinate the nursing division and all the functions related to its governance (see Figure 7-1). The coordinating council takes its impetus from the leadership role of each of the members of the coordinating council, in conjunction with the nursing administrator, and works within shared governance to provide some direction for the nursing organization. Coordinating council tasks specifically address issues related to:

1. questions and concerns between the councils regarding territoriality and appropriateness of issues
2. communication strategies and mechanisms within the nursing division to facilitate interaction among the individual councils that make up the coordinating council
3. communication between council leadership and nursing administration to integrate the decision-making function with the operational processes constructed to carry out the decision making

Figure 7-1 The Organizational Structure of Nursing's Operational
Framework

NURSING OPERATIONAL FRAMEWORK
Organizational Structure

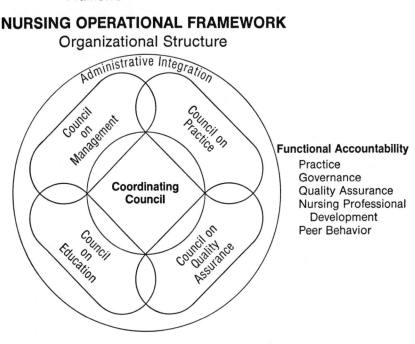

Functional Accountability
Practice
Governance
Quality Assurance
Nursing Professional
  Development
Peer Behavior

---

4. resolution of the collective problems of all the councils and the
   nursing administration having broad, division-wide implications
5. devising, monitoring, and reviewing annual divisional goals and
   objectives, quarterly governance activity, articulation of divisional
   goals and objectives, and reports of the various committees and
   task forces of the governance councils named for specified business
   of the nursing staff
6. development of strategies for taking up issues and concerns regarding interdepartmental problems and those arising from the relationship of the medical staff to the nursing staff
7. delineation and determination of appropriate nursing representatives on the board level, hospital-wide, and medical–staff committees
8. a collective review of the work and outcomes of the councils'
   subgroups with an impact on the governance councils and operational functions of the nursing division

9. development, review, refinement, dissemination, and submission to nursing staff for its approval the nursing staff bylaws that will govern all functional elements and activities of the governance councils and members of the nursing division
10. guidance to the nursing administrator in her role as representative of the nursing division and staff to other forums on issues of concern to the nursing division and the professional nursing staff
11. collective review of all the governance councils' and professional nursing staff activity and evaluation of all the operating components of the governance system in relation to facilitating the activity of the nursing profession within the division of nursing
12. devising alternative mechanisms within the governance structure of the nursing division as a whole to adjust for "noise" in the system or problems that may compromise the facility and the success of the governance system in the hospital organization

The coordinating council consists of the chairpersons of each of the governance councils and the nursing administrator. The chairpersons of these councils also represent the subgroups that are mandated specific tasks by the councils. For example, the chairperson of the practice council may represent the delivery-of-care committee and the career ladder committee, both of which are mandated by the nursing practice council. The chairperson for the council on quality assurance may also be representing the peer review committee, the unusual occurrence committee, or the incident reporting committee. The management council chairperson will also represent its staffing task force or its wage/benefits/working conditions committee. The same holds true for the council on nursing education and the nursing administrative representative on the coordinating council. Thus, the full responsibilities for unifying all the functional elements of the shared governance system will be invested in the chairpersons of each of the councils and the nursing administrator. Working together, members of the coordinating council begin to focus all nursing activities within the context of the division's philosophies, goals and objectives, and anticipated outcomes and in relation to its role, function, purposes, and anticipated outcomes.

Within this group, specific items affecting implementation of the shared governance system can be discussed and deliberated. Thus a common baseline of expectations and activities for each council can be established. Some consistency and conformity in each member council's functions and operations must be integrated and ensured through the coordinating efforts of the chairpersons. Discussions related to issues and decisions that must be rendered in a number of different areas should be undertaken. Suggested areas of concern might include:

- the role of the clinical specialist in council membership, advice, and service
- the role of the nursing administrative advisor and the management council representative on each of the governance councils and that individual's relationship to the rest of the council
- the staff nurse orientation process to the council role
- nomination and approval of membership, term of office, and number of reappointments
- the appropriate size of the council and the clinical specialties represented in the councils
- scheduling meetings (i.e., date, length of time, frequency) to provide opportunity for membership to participate fully in council activities without interrupting clinical practice
- the number, function, and role of the appropriate subgroups, committees, and task forces of each council and their accountability to the appointing council
- problems with council activity, members, and nursing administrative representatives in ongoing council activities
- monitoring and assurance of appropriate application of the Joint Commission on Accreditation of Hospitals' standards applicable to each of the governance councils

While these activities are specific, others may be added to fit the unique needs of the institution. It is important to recognize that the coordinating council is responsible for (1) integrating the individual accountabilities of each council; (2) successfully bringing together the diverse operational expectations found in each of the councils; and (3) coordinating and supporting all the functional aspects of operating the nursing division.

Through this council's activity, the nursing administrator becomes fully integrated into the centralized decision-making processes that have an impact on division operations. Since the clear intent of shared governance is to move the organization toward that professional framework, however, clinical staff assume major responsibility for governance activities. The power equation, even in the coordinating council, rests primarily with the clinical staff. Their representation on the coordinating council clearly indicates this power equation. There are two nurse manager representatives on the coordinating council and three clinical staff members representing the clinical councils of practice, quality assurance, and education. Even in the functional coordinating council, the professional nursing staff remain collectively accountable, with the attendant power and authority necessary to maintain that standard. In a truly professional nursing organization, this should create no dissonance or disharmony since the trusts attendant in developing the shared governance system already ensure that that power equation does not create discord. The inherent trusts establishing that equation will, as has been shown in those organizations that have taken this risk, return the greatest possible rewards to the nursing division and the profession responsible for its activities.

THE ROLE OF THE CHAIRPERSON

The governance council chairpersons, working closely with the nursing administrator, must be oriented as they are elected to their respective council activities. The chairperson's role is obviously a key one requiring a great deal of effectiveness, commitment, and assertive leadership in representing the staff and the nursing division. Understanding the role and assuming responsibility for its successful expression require a great deal of skill and commitment. It is advisable that those who are to assume full responsibility for leadership of the governance councils first have a year as chairperson-elect to work with previous chairpersons in developing the necessary skills, ability, and leadership and to become oriented to the council's responsibilities. That whole process should be accurately described by the coordinating council and should be incorporated into the bylaws developed by this group.

THE NURSING ADMINISTRATOR'S TRANSITIONAL ROLES

The skills required of the nursing administrator operating within this group are significantly different from those required of the individual with sole decision-making responsibility in the organization. In the traditional bureaucratic framework, those skills, abilities, and decision-making responsibilities center on the manager as executive. The shift of power that occurs in the shared governance framework requires the nursing administrator to develop a different set of skills to facilitate the work of nursing within her new role. The nursing administrator's skills in negotiation, dialogue, group dynamics, process, change management, communication, diverse loci of control, and being able and willing to risk are all necessary to her success. Rather than being director, controller, initiator, and power representative of the nursing organization, the nursing administrator must now change to become facilitator, coordinator, integrator, and representative of the nursing organization. She will frequently be required to represent the mandates, interests, and decisions of the nursing staff to other forums and areas of the hospital organization and community. She assumes a new task in her role, representing the interests of the staff at large and ensuring that representation is expressed in the forums in which she is a member—the hospital board and medical executive groups.

As a shared governance concept begins to shift toward the unified system within the hospital, many representative functions will be shared by a diverse group of nursing representatives. As previously indicated, the change to shared governance is primarily an internal one. While it does have an external impact in the long term, most of the functional processes are internally generated and directed in terms of the activities of the nursing profession.

At the time the nursing organization is in transition, however, the nursing administrator becomes the agent of the nursing staff and assumes responsibilities for strategizing, defending, encouraging, supporting, and deflecting the transition. This is a demanding and often emotionally frustrating role. On one hand, she loses centralized decision-making authority by sharing it with the entire nursing organization; on the other, she becomes increasingly accountable, through her administrative position in the hospital, for the success of the outcomes of her staff. The nursing staff assume the obligation for achieving success in shared governance, but the nursing administrator is held accountable by her administrative peers for their success. Obviously, a great deal of trust, belief, commitment, and valuing of nursing staff processes and operations in shared governance will be part of the nursing administrator's belief and behavioral system.

One of the additional demands on the nursing administrator in a shared governance framework is the consultative and collaborative relationship she establishes with the staff directly and through its governance representatives (see Figure 7-2). Working closely with the chairpersons from the governance councils, the nursing administrator establishes collaborative and communicative relationships before taking action that may require critical decision making. Since in most shared governance organizations the chairperson should be invested with critical decision-making authority, for acting on behalf of the council between regularly scheduled meetings, the nursing administrator can consult with the appropriate council chairperson for advice, recommendations, and appropriate decision support for a critical action that must be undertaken in a relatively brief period of time. This kind of critical action, however, should be minimal at best. Since long-term planning and decision-making processes are inherent in the shared governance structure, critical or emergency decision-making

Figure 7-2 The Support Role of the Nursing Administrator

SUPPORT ROLE OF THE NURSING ADMINISTRATOR

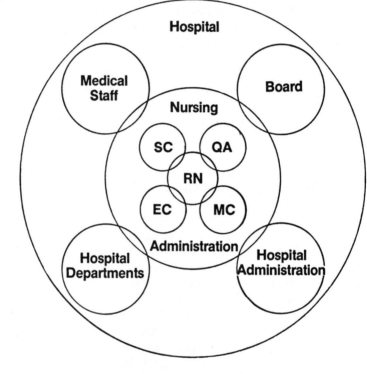

processes should be minimized. Here, however, as in any human dynamic organization, there will be some need for immediate decision making. As a result, the cooperative consultation between chairperson and nursing administrator will be essential to rendering appropriate critical decisions effectively. This same rule can apply to all management levels with regard to specific decisions that may have to be rendered and that will have an effect on specific activities of one or more of the governance councils.

Where all governance activities are involved, an emergency meeting of the coordinating council can be called by the nursing administrator to deliberate questions and issues relating to resolving a division-wide problem. Since provision for governance council activities is made available in the work load productivity standards, dollars spent in these deliberations should already have been incorporated into the cost of delivering those services.[1]

THE FINANCIAL IMPACT

As with any new program or approach to management of nursing resources, the issue of the dollars involved must be addressed. It would first appear that the design of this approach would require some major investments of time and, therefore, of money. Though this assumption is true, more dollars are not required for this program, just a better allocation of the money already being spent in nursing support activities with a minimum of committed and measurable outcomes.

For example, many nursing organizations presently have staff and management involved in the committee and task force work that is necessary to accomplish ongoing and special projects in nursing. Some institutions have even hired special projects personnel or assigned individuals to design and/or manage a new, necessary program. Staff support services, clerical support, and unit managers (the non-nurse kind) all contribute to the "bottom line" costs of traditional nursing organizations. Even in the settings that do not have additional nonpatient care personnel, much of the support time and costs used are long on work and short on application or follow-through. A problem frequently verbalized by nurses is the lack of follow-through on efforts that are essential to assure quality, provide standards, measure productivity, improve performance, and provide commitment on behalf of nursing staff.

Another major area of financial concern frequently decried by hospital management is the lack of front-line commitment to the control of institutional costs, especially within the current prospective payment system. There frequently appears to be no real investment of the staff in the necessity of developing processes and mechanisms that address the cost of delivering nursing care at the bedside. The frustration in all this is that in order for hospitals to be successful in confronting the prospective payment system, all levels of hospital staff will have to be involved.

In most hospitals, staff have often been insulated from the realities of the financial process. While frequent recipients of its impact, the staff are virtually unaware of the mechanics of financing and supporting a hospital. Investment and involvement of nursing staff have been difficult precisely because of a general lack of understanding or insight into the whys and wherefores of hospital finances. The financial considerations specifically regarding the staffing issue, always of major concern to nursing staff, reflect that narrow scope. Staff's reflection of staffing needs is generally unidirectional: the staff needed or requested to render appropriate nursing care. Management's direction is also often narrowly directed: how much staff can we have for the fewest dollars? There is lip service to the concerns of one for the other on this issue; unfortunately, it remains often only lip service.

Quite simply, to bring the staff insights and obtain an appropriate response, the staff will have to be involved in the issues. Not only should they be viewed as part of the problem; they also need to be included as the source of its solution. Designating or delegating accountabilities for this issue to a management person skirts both the problem and its solution. In the shared governance framework, responsibilities for all issues with an impact on staff belong to those who represent and make decisions on behalf of staff. It seems ludicrous to assume that we can entrust life-and-death decisions to nursing staff but fear trusting them with financial choices.

Assuming the cost of operating within a shared governance framework will, of course, have to be the decision of each institution. Initial planning and implementation time does involve costs that must be incorporated into the budget. Some of these costs, however, can be shifted from the inevitable termination of nonproductive or strictly management-oriented meetings that may be dealing with issues that nursing staff are already addressing in the shared governance organization. A careful management audit of meeting and task force time and process can often find that some meeting time can be exchanged and some activities reduced.[2]

Activities associated with devising programs that will affect productivity or enhance performance may by themselves have some obvious cost value. The tradeoff in these situations is at the outcome and, only in higher levels of performance. Therefore, time spent in programs that address the clinical ladder concept, minimum performance measures, and activities that deal with cost and care in the practice setting have some long-term and deeply felt cost or efficiency considerations.

The amount of time spent in meetings, with the possible exception of divisional management meetings, can actually be reduced overall in the shared governance system. The frequent and interruptive meeting schedule that pulls staff away from their patient care assignments will minimize productivity in such circumstances. In shared governance, where the staff is doing much of the organizational work of the nursing division, having monthly one-day staff meetings will accomplish more and demand considerably less management and staff time. Having the councils operate this way puts an end to brief, segmented, interruptive weekly or biweekly meetings, with their generally poor attendance and low level of output. At one hospital that instituted a shared governance structure, much of the cost associated with such meeting times was reduced.[3]

There should be no other additional cost considerations that accrue to the attention of the hospital's financial concerns in a shared governance system. It is not designed to raise costs, nor does it suggest that they must be increased in any way to obtain staff involvement in governance. If anything, this new organizational system provides the hospital with additional opportunities to involve nursing staff in addressing the issue of cost and prospective strategies to reduce and prevent further cost escalation. As always, having the staff participate in, or even originate, suggestions and processes that provide for better productivity, cost reduction, new service markets, or alternative revenue sources can provide an added value to the institution not previously available. In the traditional system, nursing staff are not invested; they do not "buy into" the financial and product concerns of the hospital of which they are an integral part. Since providing "ownership" for nursing activities to the staff responsible for carrying them out is the cornerstone of the shared governance concept, all concerns, including financial ones, will be essential to the success of the truly professional nursing organization.

MANAGEMENT ISSUES

Besides issues related to costs and administrative concerns generated from that interest, there are other management processes and issues that are subject to change during the transition phase. The role of the nurse manager at all levels of the organization, like that of the nursing administrator, moves from one of direction and control to one of facilitation, coordination, and integration. The front-line manager or head nurse will feel the strongest impact from role change of any individual in the nursing organization except the professional staff nurse. In the decentralized system, the unit's nurse manager has a lot of responsibility and accountability. In that role she has traditionally become accountable and responsible for all activities that occur within her purview. In the shared governance system, through the limitations of her role in relation to practice, quality assurance, and education, a good portion of her accountability is distributed to other individuals. While the unit is a microcosm of the nursing division as a whole and therefore reflects its character, it becomes more focused and directed to specific components of nursing's work. Like the nursing administrator, this person must develop some of the same skills related to negotiation, collaboration, group process, and collective deliberation, as well as highly developed communication skills, as an ongoing portion of her role. Much of her traditional responsibility in relation to discipline and control has also changed in developing the shared governance system at the unit level. Development of peer evaluation processes that include professionals who share responsibilities for delivering patient care with the individual being evaluated; involvement in quality assurance in relation to compromises in clinical practice; and undertaking and ensuring the development of council-mandated activities in the individual nursing unit and reflecting compliance with those council mandates back to the appropriate council—these are all parts of shared governance. Being represented on the clinical councils by nursing management staff articulates the management point of view in council decisions. This process further reflects the changing character of the nurse manager's role. A centralized, directive nurse manager with a high need for control cannot be successful in a shared governance framework. The ability to make the transition to professional models of management behavior, similar to the behavior expected of the professional nursing staff, will be a requirement for success by the nurse manager in a shared governance system. To ensure the success of the shared governance process, scheduling systems must be developed that permit the professional nurse to participate fully in shared governance activities both at scheduled meeting times and in special activities carried out on behalf of the governance council. She must develop a higher level of trust in the nursing staff for making patient assignments, for staff schedule discussions, and for resolving unit-based problems in practice and in unit operations. Further, she must subject her own role to peer review and peer evaluation both from other managers and from clinical staff who operate within her sphere of influence. It will be necessary for this nurse manager to act as a conduit of information, resources, support, material, and dialogue in relation to various aspects of the operational implications of shared governance. The nursing staff meetings should be held on a regular basis, and part of them should be used for unit-based problem solving, peer interaction, communication of governance activity, staff development, and fulfillment of other specified governance activities as determined by the entire organization. Obviously, the ability to provide leadership in an open and responsive environment and the willingness to learn, to share, and to grow with the professional staff are vital characteristics for the unit-level nurse manager in this professional mode of operation.

The nursing administrator assumes a great degree of responsibility for ensuring that the unit-level nurse manager is prepared and has the information, resources, material, and supports necessary for transition. Regardless of the governance system devised and implemented, this front-line management group will still be central to its success. These groups always have some accountability for making sure that, at the practice level in the fundamental unit of clinical operation, all the aspirations, work, accomplishments, and positive outcomes of the nursing organization emerge. It is clearly in that setting that change will reveal evidence of success or failure. Close collaboration and coordination of all changes toward the new governance framework must be developed in relation with the primary unit nurse management group. Individual and collective relationships between the nursing administrator and the unit nurse manager produce ongoing expectations that must be carefully and consciously maintained by the nursing administrator and the administrative staff. One particularly insidious and dangerous possibility must be avoided as the organization moves toward shared governance. This is the concerted and successful application of change strategies to the professional nursing staff, permitting them opportunities to mature and function at higher levels of behavior, but with the absence of corresponding development and growth in the unit's nursing management staff. No greater potential for frustration, discouragement, and overt sabotage of the move toward shared governance exists than when the nursing management group is not continually developed to be assimilated and to provide leadership in coordinating and integrating the transitional activities and processes.

In both unilateral and collective action with the nurse management group, one of the primary roles of the nursing administrator is to create the environment and the operational framework that sets the basis for later development of shared governance and the practice standards essential for its maintenance. A key process here is for the nursing administrator to provide a frame of operation in which behaviors representing the dominant views and beliefs in the nursing organization are expressed and permit little latitude for alternative or optional behaviors in relation to those beliefs.

In bureaucratic nursing organizations, a wide variety of practice standards, abilities, competencies, and behaviors have traditionally been accepted. As a result, while the nursing organization has been staffing itself with larger and larger components of professional practitioners, the wide variety of preparation and standards applied to individual practice have not permitted the organization to develop a consistent idea of minimum practice performance, corollary to acceptable standards of practice articulated through the professional societies and associations. Usually the standards promulgated by professional groups responsible for such delineations have been of a higher level than those accepted by the organizations employing professionals who claim to adhere to those standards. Thus, the hospital structures and delivery of nursing practice have been somewhat different from the expectations articulated through the educational and professional bodies and processes. Operationalizing the organization to reflect these standards creates a significant area of transition for the nursing organization. The nursing administrator assumes a primary role in this area of responsibility.

EXPECTATIONS OF PROFESSIONAL BEHAVIOR

Since it is clear that higher levels of professional behavior will be demanded of practitioners, a framework within which those expectations can develop successfully and can be maintained with some consistency must be developed for the nursing division. A number of mechanisms can be undertaken to ensure this process:

- revision of the job description
- initiation of a detailed peer review process
- revision of the patient care delivery system
- definitive determination of disciplinary and corrective action measures, compromises, and clinical practice
- development of a divisional clinical practice monitoring process
- implementation of multidimensional approaches to compliance with practice

Each of the preceding items is an appropriate starting place for raising the level of clinical practice and expectations and maintaining a narrowly defined framework within which those expectations can develop. It is clear that if the nursing organization is going to fulfill the inherent obligations of a professional organization within the shared governance context, the parameters of practice must be defined more narrowly than those of a traditional organization framework. Narrowly defining parameters of practice, raising the levels of expectation, and creating definitive measures for monitoring them are relatively easy steps in making the transition toward a higher level of professional behavior. The difficult part is creating an organizational framework and environment in which behaviors that differ from expectations can be diminished or eliminated and where appropriate organizational supports can be placed to facilitate appropriate professional behavior.

Parallel Levels Program

Perhaps one of the best ways to provide for this definitive range of professional behavior expectations is through a well-developed clinical career ladder or parallel levels program. One of the reasons for identifying a levels program as an appropriate process for developing a higher level of professional behavior and expectations relates to the fact that a levels program is generally developed through a process that incorporates all professional roles within the organization as well as the individuals who fulfill those roles. Thus the development of a professional levels program is a process in which each member has some investment. Through their representatives on the levels committee or task force, the staff participate fully in defining various parameters of practice at accelerating levels of expectation, so that they can accept the criteria established for delineating and measuring performance at various levels of practice. The levels program accomplishes a number of the previously listed items within one program. It also provides the organization, through its peer review processes as well as its management process, with opportunities and mechanisms for not only monitoring, but also controlling, the delineations of competence, practice behavior, and performance expectations within the context of the criteria.

The levels program should include a system of peer review that permits the peers of people who operate within the context of levels to make parallel judgments in relation to those items of practice on which they would have some insight and influence. The peer review process is sometimes perceived as intimidating and threatening. Yet it can be devised so that the confidentiality of the participants is protected while delivering information required to make appropriate clinical practice and behavior judgments. In establishing the criteria that peers use to evaluate others' performances, the assurance that the criteria are succinct, definitive, and articulate in defining expectations is important. In many evaluation systems and levels programs in a number of institutions, the criteria for performance are either nonmeasurable or too general to clearly indicate compliance with standards. The criteria that identify the role of responsibility and function within a specified level should be clear, succinct, and refined to the highest level. Criteria should be evidenced in outcome expectations so that participants in evaluation will know, clearly and without question, the specific expectations attendant on their roles at the level for which they have assumed responsibility. In measuring expectations for professional practice and performance, it should be clearly stated which professional expectations should be articulated in the elements clearly displaying behaviors reflecting professional performance.

The levels program addresses all aspects of professional behavior within the organization, including the role of the nurse in relation to governance activities, self-development, patient care, education, and peer relations. Consequently, the system helps to narrow the definition of acceptable performance levels. When staff members recognize that specific expectations and defined performance levels are related to their practice role, they are more likely to achieve those levels. It has often been said that people always perform as they are expected to when the expectations are generally accepted and well known by the participants. In other words, successful achievement can be ensured by clearly defining the criteria so that expectations, in addition to being well founded, can also be understood by participants. The participants then become a part of the framework for higher levels of clinical practice and behavior and will act more consistently with those expectations and values. By clearly defining criteria, the nursing organization creates a professional culture with narrow ranges of performance and behavior that the nursing staff will both understand and maintain.

Having High Hopes

The nursing administrator's responsibility is to ensure that mechanisms that, if absent, would prevent the growth of nursing staff, are part of the development of the professional organization. Nursing administrators should understand that it is not inappropriate to have high levels of expectation. It is only when those expectations remain unfulfilled that there is dissonance between the behavior and function of the professional and the expectations the organization has of the individual professional nurse. Incorporating the formation of the criteria in a career ladder program into the shared governance transition provides the nursing administrator another environment within which the staff can begin to participate and articulate their roles in self-development and monitoring the clinical affairs of the nursing division. Using the group process and appropriate structures inherent in the governance councils and framework of the nursing organization helps build expectations of professional behavior into the organizational transition. It is in that framework, therefore, that "buying in" to these expectations by the professional staff is built into their role in the practice component of the shared governance system. Therefore, because the appropriate group processes were used and incorporated into the change strategies of the organization, the need to convince, cajole, and discipline the nursing staff into compliance is avoided and the role of nursing administrator as monitor and controller is essentially vacated. Of personal benefit to the nursing administrator is the fact that her efforts in the transition from director to facilitator, integrator, and coordinator are successful. Since the process itself is generated by the nursing staff's involvement and since the momentum of change can be maintained in their hands, the nursing administrator is free to devote her time and energies to some of the more challenging administrative activities of developing shared governance with her peers and administration and in the role of coordinating the nursing division with the coordinating council. By permitting the staff to develop the career ladder parallel levels program in their behalf and to invest some financial and benefits rewards in the outcome, the nursing administrator continues to reinforce her trust, commitment, and belief in the nursing staff.

An examination of the change in the role of the nursing administrator will give some idea of how that role can be expanded and how the organization's perception of it can be enhanced. We are already aware of the nursing administrator's work as an advisory member of the governance councils. Here, the nursing administrator primarily counsels, communicates, and coordinates information and resources to support the work of the councils. Frequently, at the position of staff nurse, the information essential to make decisions that may have broad-based implications for the division of nursing may not be available. This may occur because the nursing administrator has a broader vision and access to much more information and resources; thus, she may be able to support the data base needed to generate appropriate and meaningful decisions. Her information, views, and resources can be balanced against those of other membership representatives and advisors to the councils. Also, the clinical specialist and other leaders in the nursing organization may add additional information or supplement information from the nursing administrator to assist the council in using a full range of resources and information in considering an issue.

A Nonvoting Position

To ensure that the role of the nursing administrator is truly changed and truly viewed as supportive to and representative of the staff in the clinical councils, it is important that the nursing administrator not hold a voting position. In not holding a voting position, she makes a statement to the clinical councils regarding their independence as clinical professional nurses making decisions that meet their specific needs. Of course, consideration of the effect of the nursing administrator's informal power is important. Initially, as the councils begin their work and council members remain dependent on the nursing administrator in her exercise of authority as articulated in the traditional behavioral framework, that influence may be more formative than will be the case at a later stage in the process. As the nursing administrator reinforces the council's independence by pulling away from being involved in their decision-making process, the councils will become more assured of her support, as well as her facilitation of their decision making; they will then grow less dependent on her as decision generator.

In the change process, the transition is necessary from deep involvement in the decision making of the council to less and less involvement—up to the point at which the councils' independence in decision making is evident. In terms of the nursing administrator's role, the point is to produce an environment where growth toward independence in decision making is developed in councils, and where providing the skills, resources, and information necessary for council members to make this transition becomes part of the provisional role of the nursing administrator at the council level.

It is clear, therefore, that her role, besides being supportive and representative of the nursing staff, is also that of challenger, teacher, and developer.
Activities that had normally been directed toward governance decision
making and centralized authority are now put into another frame of reference. She assumes the major portion of her responsibility, as the organization moves from being a bureaucratic framework to being a shared
governance system, in this role.

Working closely with the management group to assist them in their
development also becomes a central concern of the nursing administrator
and her assistants and associates. As previously mentioned, a great deal
of time and energy must be spent by this group in helping front-line
management develop and grow at a rate consistent with the growth expected
and generated by the staff. Frequent meetings using group process, as well
as individual conferences and goal setting, will be important parts of the
role of the nursing administrator as the management team develops. Since
the management team's role will also be supportive, generative, and educational, skills and tools necessary to assume those responsibilities will
be essential to keeping the front-line nurse managers' role vital and vibrant
in the transitional phase. Skills, understanding, monitoring, and moderating the change process will also be important tools of the unit nurse
manager. Helping the unit nurse manager with the resources, information,
and tools essential to fulfilling new sets of obligations, as well as valuing
her growth and transition, will assist the system and the organization's
successful implementation of shared governance measurably.

In the transition toward a shared governance system, many of the outcomes anticipated at the end of the change process will initially be mandated by the remaining decision-making authority of the nurse administrator. As in any transition, authority to the staff does not automatically
transfer in a shared governance system. The particular program discussed
in this text usually takes from three to five years to implement fully. In
the initial stages of transition, the decision-making authority of the nursing
administrator should be directed to mandating certain behaviors, expectations, and processes that will generate a response from the staff and
facilitate the move to staff-level participation and decision making. Decisions such as refusing to review, approve, and sign off on standards of
clinical practice, or mandating the quality assurance council to make
decisions regarding corrective action for unresolved problems in a given
clinical situation, will begin to demonstrate behaviors and characteristics
acceptable in a shared governance model. Implementing peer review performance evaluations within the management group, as an effort to exemplify commitment to peer review, is another example. In this way, the
nursing administrator begins to transfer accountability.

In this framework, creating within her own role the behavioral expectations she hopes to see in all the professional staff will be a major focus of facilitating the change toward shared governance. The nursing staff at all levels will look to her management role and will be able to take their example and their encouragement from, and measure their progress in comparison to, her commitment and behavior change in the shared governance framework. There will be much temptation for the nurse administrator to assist the staff by making decisions on their behalf or by shortening the time frame of their decision-making process and assuming some of the responsibilities herself. By shortcutting the system this way, however, she begins to make a statement to the nursing staff that may be difficult to reverse later. As painful as it may be for her, it may be more important and appropriate, in terms of the change process, to allow the staff to go through the painful and sometimes consuming process of making appropriate decisions so that they can more fully own those decisions and recognize that they are fully accountable for them. By assuming their responsibility, albeit temporary, short term, and sometimes interruptive, the nursing administrator delays the staff's transition by breaking the trust continuum. She reinforces the dependent belief that when the going gets rough, the nursing administrator will relieve the pressure on the staff and will assume some of their obligation for decision making. The wise nursing administrator will undertake a number of processes to facilitate the staff's successful arrival at appropriate decisions; it will not always be easy.

The nursing administrator will assume a facilitating role in an effort to encourage shared decision making and to bring skills and decision making to a high level through the group process. As the councils and professional staff become more skilled in decision making and group dynamics—as well as in managing their shared governance activities at the terminal end of the change process—decision making by the staff will become smoother, quicker, and more clearly understood by all. The initial delays, complications, and slowness of decision making, while frequently frustrating, are part of the necessary team and group building. They will provide participants with the skills, ability, trust, and confidence necessary to assume full control of governance activities.

Work Outside the Division

As demanding as the internal activities in the nursing division are for the nursing administrator, she will have additional obligations outside the immediate concerns of the nursing division. As the administrative executive for the nursing division, she represents the interests of the staff, its governance councils, and its activities to the other forums in the hospital in which she holds membership. In her role as clinical executive, she relates to the executive group of the medical staff, the administrative body, the board of trustees, and the external community the interests that are impacted by the services of the hospital. In this position she is an articulator, defender, supporter, and representative of the shared governance system to the hospital system and the community as a whole. While in conjunction with the coordinating council, membership on the medical staff and hospital committees is filled by appropriate nursing staff representatives, and the nursing administrator's role is to represent the nursing staff at the formal organizational executive level in at least the transitional phase of the movement to shared governance. As this nursing staff is growing and maturing to assume additional responsibilities for its affairs, the impact of that independence and growing responsibility will be felt by groups outside the nursing division. Groups and other departments at the administrative level and in key positions on the medical staff will be interested in the development of the nursing division and its impact on them. The impact on most of these bodies can be positive; however, the change in the decision-making framework that deflects the control of decision-making process from the nursing administrator to the organization through its constituent bodies can create some communication problems and confusion with other departments and forums in the hospital. The nursing administrator articulates changes in the system and facilitates movement of groups outside the system toward accepting the decision-making loci and refining mechanisms to assure that appropriate communication and leadership support occurs.

Touching base with these external groups periodically during the change process, bringing them up-to-date with the transitional elements and alterations in the governance structure of the nursing organization, can help establish a relationship with these groups before any problems arise. It can provide an open, informative, and sharing environment with these individuals and can help offset any of the discord or problems that might conceivably occur. Information sharing should be considered developmental, as the change process clearly indicates. It may be appropriate to share information regarding the transition at various points in the change process. It may be inappropriate, however, to share the total process of change at the outset of movement toward that new system. Carefully determining what kinds of information are essential to the leadership group and other forums in the hospital and what kind of impact the change may have on other groups is part of the careful strategy development included in the role of the nursing administrator.

Aid to Her Administrative Head

As moderator between the nursing division and other areas of the hospital, the nurse manager maintains continual sensitivity to the changing influence and impact the movement toward shared governance may have on other leaders. Negotiating for support from her peers and from leaders will also be incorporated into her primary role, as will keeping her administrative head informed and updated on the transition toward shared governance. She also provides information related to the constraints and possibilities involved in making this change, and assists in providing her administrative head with the information necessary to offset any problems and concerns that may come to his or her attention.

Besides arming her administrative head with the appropriate responses to questions or concerns, the nursing administrator should incorporate this individual into the change process itself. Through careful planning, she can keep the administrator involved throughout all of the stages of the process.

One of the best ways to keep all parties informed in relation to the activities of the nursing division, and incorporating those activities into the processes of the hospital as a whole, may be to establish a regular meeting for the chief executive officer, the chief medical officer, and the chief nursing officer (nursing administrator), at least biweekly. In these sessions, the nursing administrator can discuss the activities and processes unfolding in the nursing division that will have an impact on the administrative and medical staff areas of the hospital. Keeping these officials informed, negotiating and seeking common solutions, establishing a peer relationship on a continual basis for information sharing, collaboration, and collective problem solving can all be major tools in establishing positive relationships and encouraging a framework within which shared governance can develop. A further benefit of this conference is the development of a trusting and open relationship with the medical staff through its chief officer. Developing a more collaborative and peer-level relationship between the chief nursing officer and the chief medical officer can only result in more positive relations and a better framework for clinical problem solving.

Presenting the shared governance model and its activities to the medical staff organization and the board level also presents an opportunity for the executive not only to expose the activities of the nursing division over a broad base but also to help offset concerns that both groups have in relation to nursing's growth and development in the organization. Many of the concerns should be offset by raising the level of practice and professional behavior and by developing a governance organization that models those professional behaviors.

As long as these key groups are well informed and able to articulate what is occurring within the nursing division, support and encouragement from them should be forthcoming. The secondary benefit to the nursing administrator in exposing her role and providing opportunities for others to understand the professional practice of nursing certainly accrues benefits to the entire organization of nursing. Any dialogue or exchange generated within these forums can obviously benefit the system.

Questions should arise from these bodies that will demand answers from the nursing administrator. These key leaders can suggest how shared governance can be refined to fit better within the hospital organization. They can also provide some understanding of the accountabilities of their own groups in regard to patient care and the effectiveness of the organization in distributing patient care responsibilities. All this can help the nursing administrator in refining and guiding the organization through the move to being a truly professional one. This dialogue between members of the executive and board levels of the hospital and the nursing administrator provides a positive input and sharing of many varieties of information essential to making the system work.

Clearly, the role of the nursing administrator is truly one of an integrator, facilitator, communicator, and coordinator of the whole transition toward shared governance. While the basic functional activities of the nursing administrator's role may change as the organization moves to shared governance, the importance of her role is in no way diminished. Indeed, that role is even more vital and dynamic in the shared governance organization than it could ever have become in a traditional bureaucratic system. The nursing administrator's ability to keep her finger on the pulse of the organization, diagnosing elements of the change process and the position of the organization of transition, will help her understand the problems, issues, and concerns of the developing nursing organization in a state of change. Her sensitivity to the differing momentums of change and the various ways in which change affects the nursing organization at different times and places will help her lead the transition to a successful outcome.

Professional Parallels

One of the claims frequently heard by nursing administrators is that this system is invalid and will not work, that the organizational system is being created to model very closely a medical staff organization, and that it will be rife with the problems inherent in the medical staff system. While there clearly are parallels between the medical staff organizational model and nursing's professional model, those parallels exist in other professional structures, as well—notably, the university system and employment settings where such professionals as engineers, psychologists, social workers, and others have their practices. The parallels involve some fairly common organizational structures necessary to support the independent and collaborative bases of professional organizations. While those parallels are appropriate and meaningful, there is one circumstance that influences the nursing organization and the professional nursing staff that makes it particularly different from the medical staff organization within a hospital framework. Physicians associated with the hospital are primarily independent entrepreneurs or businessmen. Other than those directly employed by the hospital, they generally maintain their own practice and independent settings. The hospital is used by physicians to render special kinds of care necessary to meet the treatment needs of their patients. The relationship between the hospital and the physician is built on the recognition of this independent practice framework. The hospital makes no claims on the physician's practice, and the physician makes no claims in relation to the control and administration of the hospital. The nature of their relationship, then, is clearly described in a set of bylaws that protect the independence of the two entities.

Within the context of the relationship between the professional nursing staff and the hospital, there remains a commitment between the two that goes beyond that generally displayed between physician and hospital. The nursing staff is employed by the hospital to fulfill the professional nursing responsibilities articulated through the hospital structure as part of the service it offers. Because of that unique interdependence and the integration of the role of the hospital with that of the professional nurse, the nature of the relationship is more one of interdependence and support.

Because the role of the professional nursing staff is internally interdependent, the work of nursing within the context of the hospital is more integrative and less competitive than that of the physician in relation to both his peers and the hospital. Because of this unique and strong interrelationship between the hospital—which offers the nursing service—and the nursing practitioners rendering that service, the claim that nursing staff will be just like the medical staff in a shared governance framework does not correlate with reality. Shared governance will in no way diminish the highly developed and necessary interrelationship between the hospital and professional nurse, nor will it introduce the competitive model behavior displayed in the medical model.

In the long term it is anticipated that the very integrated and interdependent relationship of professional nurses in exercising their role will preclude support and facilitation of competitive behaviors among these practitioners. The nursing administrator will constantly be called on to articulate this relationship and differentiate the nature of nursing and nursing practice from that of other professional models. Offsetting some of the presumptions about the impact of this new organizational model with appropriate and valuable information on the nature of the shared governance system will frequently fall within the context of the nursing administrator's role.

The nursing administrator in a shared governance framework has a full opportunity to avail herself of all her skills and abilities developed in this role. These skills are essential to the successful development of the shared governance system. While the nursing administrator's role will change fundamentally, her new behaviors in that role will be as fulfilling as rewarding, and as challenging as any she has previously performed in the bureaucratic model. As innovator and change agent, the nursing administrator will constantly assess the transition of the organization, identify new behaviors and alterations in structure and function, and fine tune and refine the organization to reflect fully the professional model that nursing staff so ardently seek. Representing the nursing organization internally and externally will refine her skills in group process and in dialogue, negotiation, and articulation. It will be a most satisfying growth experience for the nursing administrator. Each time she represents the nursing organization, she becomes more and more comfortable and skilled at conceptualizing and articulating the shared governance nursing organization to both her peers and other interested people in the nursing organization. The excitement, challenge, and creativity in her new role will offer her many opportunities for her own growth and, ultimately, the growth of the profession.

NOTES

1. P. Schwartz, *Patient Classification Systems for Saint Joseph's Hospital, Nurse Staffing Based on Patient Classification* (Chicago Illinois: American Hospital Association, 1983), pp. 29–36.

2. T. Porter-O'Grady, *Computerized Operational Variance Report* (Atlanta, Ga.: Saint Joseph's Hospital, 1983).

3. ———, *Developing a Nurse Staffing Standard* (Atlanta, Ga.: Saint Joseph's Hospital, 1981).

Chapter 8

Bylaws: The Tools For Self-Governance

A professional organization that is structured to reflect professional relationships, interactions, and communication systems must have guidelines that clearly describe the relationship between the components and the functional processes inherent in these components. What usually occurs in an organizational structure is that some descriptor is defined that clearly outlines for the objective viewer a systematic approach to describing the mechanics of the organization.

In the organization, each participant committed to supporting the shared governance structure must have some idea of his or her role and those of the organization's components in order to assume the role expectations that are part of that person's position. To do this in the traditional bureaucratic structure, a set of organizational definitions, protocols, policies, and procedures governing activities is outlined and usually placed in a personnel information document available during orientation to all new employees. In shared governance, however, the broad procedural and policy structures apparent in the bureaucratic organization no longer exist. Since the organization is governed at the operational level and since professional practitioners have some obligation in managing its structure, a new kind of informational resource must be devised to describe both the relationships between members of the professional nursing staff and the roles and responsibilities in governance activities that each member of the nursing staff is to undertake.

PURPOSE

All professional organizations have a set of documented descriptors that describe the organization and the relationship of its members to the function of the organization. The governance and decision-making structure is usually included in this framework. This framework is usually a set of bylaws that fully outline all elements of the organization and functional components that carry out the responsibilities of the organization in rendering its service.

Bylaws usually reflect the character of the organization. Through a review of the bylaws, a leader becomes familiar with the organization, its purposes, structure, and operating processes that carry out its work. The bylaws outline each of the elements and how they function within the organization. Through the bylaws, a full understanding of the basic processes that support the organization's activities can be obtained. The bylaws indicate the system for professional governance, the degree and kind of participation that are included in the governance system, and the activities of the organization. Bylaws usually express, in some form or other, the organization as an accountability-based organization, defining those accountabilities in terms that are understood by both its members and the individuals it serves.

Bylaws should be unique to the purpose of the organization so that the organization's goals are clear, the members' roles and responsibilities necessary to accomplish the goals are specific, and the system is maintained and supported. Because the professional organization is dynamic, responding to change both in its knowledge base and its practice framework, its bylaws also are dynamic and can be adjusted to reflect the changing character of practice and responsibility. A mechanism is built into the bylaws' process that permits the organization to participate in defining the bylaws, implementing subsequent rules and regulations to carry out the bylaw's mandates, and altering and adjusting them as appropriate to reflect organizational changes. It is especially important that bylaws be structured so that they favor no single element of the organization but rather clearly and objectively describe its operation so that all components work efficiently and effectively. Since bylaws are primarily descriptors of the organization's activity process, they should not include any activities designed to benefit any one parochial interest over another. In a professional organization, the bylaws should be as free from political consideration as possible but should be directed as much as possible toward describing the organization in a clear and precise manner.

INTRODUCTION TO SHARED GOVERNANCE

Introducing the concept of bylaws into the governance framework of the hospital organization will be a challenging process. Most administrative heads in hospital organizations do not look at employed professionals in the context of bylaws, other than as they outline the role of the medical staff. Since medical staff generally are the sole group that is viewed in a totally professional framework, a great deal of political and communication activity will need to be undertaken by the organization to facilitate the process. Some organizations, looking at shared governance, will implement bylaw structure first; thus they will provide form and substance to the unfolding shared governance activities that will develop subsequently. While this may be successful for some organizations, it can be a problem in that initially the bylaws describe a framework that has not yet developed. The framework that ultimately accrues to the organization may be one that is significantly different from that planned. This is so because of the necessary adjustments, growth, and changes in the structure as the organization adapts the structure to meet the needs of the system. The bylaws should reflect what actually occurs. It would be recommended that the bylaws not be the initial step in developing shared governance, but perhaps be one of the final stages to best articulate, inform, and document the operating processes of shared governance already under way.

The nursing administrator along with the council chairpersons will spend a great deal of time deliberating over the political problems associated with the bylaw structure. While it is the responsibility of the governance council chairpersons to see that the bylaws are created and reflect the operation of the nursing organization, much of the activity associated with bylaws will have little to do with their formulation. It will be related to obtaining interest, support, and ultimate approval by the formal approving bodies of the organization, the administrative staff, and ultimately the board level of the hospital organization. The move to bylaws, therefore, should not be taken lightly, since they carefully define the relationships and functions of the organization in terms that will be understood, accepted, monitored, and disciplined by the organization. They should be carefully designed to reflect the specific needs and the operational behavior of the organization.

It is hoped that much of the work will be done with the administrative heads in describing the need for bylaws for a truly professional organization. If the appropriate information base has been developed, the communication system may have the greatest impact administratively or professionally. Obtaining initial support for the bylaws should not be difficult; however, developing a mechanism for assuring its approval at the board level of the organization will demand much strategy planning and program design to ensure that each member of the board approving the nursing staff bylaws will understand the reason for bylaws and what they outline and describe, and can in good conscious support the bylaws and what they purport to do. Here, again, if board members have been kept well informed and are aware of the progress of the professionalization of the nursing staff, if they are familiar with the successful outcomes and impact this professionalization is having on the purposes and services of the hospital, much will be done to dispel any discord prospectively.

The key to obtaining support for the bylaws after the political processes have been addressed is to have clearly defined, well-structured, carefully laid out bylaws that are understandable and that outline the shared governance activities of the division of nursing. The process of design and restructuring will require careful review and and perhaps a number of drafts before it is acceptable. Legal review of the final drafts of the bylaws in order to make sure that they do not comprise federal, state, local, and corporate regulations related to professional employees should be part of their final construction.

BASIC ARTICLES OF THE BYLAWS

Bylaws should be as uncomplicated as possible. They should be able to break down the elements of the governance structures of the organization and clearly define them in terms that are understandable, yet fully descriptive. Heavily detailed, long, complex bylaws will ultimately serve no purpose and will not provide the kind of information and governance guidance necessary to those who will function under the auspices of the bylaws. There are, however, basic elements of the bylaws that should be consistent with any bylaw structure. These elements provide the framework for the activity of the organization within them.

The framework that generally provides the chapter, the summary outline, of the bylaws are called articles. These articles are the structural framework for the bylaws. They address the functional operation of the organization, and they provide for a mechanism that integrates the activities of the organization under their various delineations. The articles contain the content of specific sections of the bylaws that address pieces of the work of the organization. For purposes of the professional nursing organization, the articles of the bylaws should address the following basic elements:

1. Preamble
2. Role
3. Services
4. Membership
5. Governance
6. Discipline and Removal
7. Organizational Coordination

8. Bylaws Revision
9. Rules and Regulations
10. Adoption

Under these general outlines or articles, much of the description of the organization, its relationship, and its functional attributes can be described. It is within this framework that all of the work done thus far within the development of the shared governance framework will be clearly evident. Through the bylaws, a clear picture of the organization, its structure, function, and operation will be described to the individual unexposed to the governance framework of the organization. Since the bylaws will be the basic tool that describes the organization, understanding the bylaws— perhaps outlining them in the orientation program, communicating them to the professional staff through the educational process—will be essential to fully incorporate the bylaws' piece of the structure into the ongoing operation of the nursing organization. It should also be noted that development of the staff in relationship to the bylaws should indicate to them that the bylaws are their governance tool, utilized by every member of the nursing staff as a framework for understanding the organization and their roles and responsibilities within the context of the nursing profession. Under the article headings, each section of the organization and its responsibilities becomes clear to members of the nursing staff. In reference to each of these articles, the elements contained in the bylaws can be articulated, reviewed, and referred to by the nursing staff as the need arises.

Preamble

The preamble of the bylaws usually outlines the purpose, philosophy, and critical objectives of the organization such that, through its review, the individual interested in the nursing organization can achieve a clear idea of what the organization is about, what it means for that individual, and how it describes its role and function in terms of its critical objectives. Under each article of the bylaws, sections identify specific components of the bylaws that address key issues in describing the organization. In the preamble, there are several sections that specifically address the general nature of the organization, its philosophy, purpose, and objectives in the manner in which the organization describes itself.

The purpose of the bylaws should direct itself to the governance of the division of nursing. It should direct itself to providing a framework for the operation of the division of nursing and should describe the organization's accountability and the professional staff within the shared governance framework. Under the purpose, or perhaps under a section of its own, a definition of nursing as it applies to that individual institution may be appropriate to give the reader some idea of how nursing describes itself in the context of its service. A good framework for the description of nursing would be the American Nurses Association description of nursing in its social policy statement.

Philosophy of the Division of Nursing

A subsequent section of the bylaws should address the philosophy of the division of nursing. That philosophy should be clearly outlined and should be as nonesoteric as possible. An ethereal, nondirective definition of philosophy provides no value or meaning for anyone in the organization. The philosophy should be a clear description of the beliefs of the division of nursing that can be translated into action and articulated into objectives, such that they provide the belief and philosophical framework in concrete activities that will emerge in the division of nursing. Because nursing is a clinical profession, some reference should be made to the client or patient that is served, health care economics, excellence in nursing practice, quality assurance, statements of confidentiality, and fulfillment of the mandates of the board of trustees. Other constituents of the philosophy of the division of nursing should acknowledge the needs of nursing in the system, providing some belief system that supports the education, practice, evaluation, and increasing need for a broadened knowledge base within the nursing organization. The function and role of nursing practice within the organization, however, should not be limited to an internal focus. The philosophy should also address the nursing services' responsibility to the community outside the organization so as to provide a broader range of focus of services offered by the nursing division in the hospital, consistent with the hospital's own community identity and philosophy.

Some definition of nursing's research base and the development of a knowledge base within the organizational structure should be made in the philosophical statement. Commitment to broadening research and to applying it in the practice environment is consistent with the goals of the profession at large. When defining the philosophy, the professional goals outlined on a national and regional basis should be incorporated into the philosophy of the division of nursing. After all, it is important to recognize that nursing is a broad-based profession, reflecting a number of different service bases. Tying into the national character of nurses is an important step in unifying nursing activity from its practice setting with its corporate, political, and social responsibilities.

Some reference should be made in the philosophy to the environment in which professional practice is performed in the institution. The philosophy in relation to the governance framework, the belief of the practitioner's role in decision making and in self-governance, and some statement in relationship to the accountability of the professional practitioner for cares and services rendered should be made in the philosophy statement. Through this process the philosophy statement does not become a set of theoretical beliefs that somehow cannot be translated into action. Through concretely identifying statements of belief in terms of the profession's responsibility for practice, a framework is provided for the subsequent sections of the bylaws that will articulate how this philosophy is to be carried out in the organization.

Of course, the philosophy of the division of nursing should reflect the summary values of the institution it serves. The philosophy of the corporate body of the institution should integrate well with that articulated by the nursing division. Through careful examination of how they interrelate, a merging of the purposes and intents of the philosophy of the hospital and of the division of nursing should clearly exemplify the commitment of nursing to fulfill the obligations of its own professional service and the obligations of the hospital through which it offers those services.

Purposes of the Nursing Division

While the purpose of the bylaws has been articulated in the first section of the preamble, a section should be devoted to outlining specific purposes of the division of nursing. The purposes outlined in relation to the division of nursing specifically identify in a very brief format, nursing's reason for being within the context of that institution. Those reasons for being should be clearly and succinctly articulated within the first sections of the bylaws, under the preamble article. The purposes should address the specific service rendered to the organization and under what authority it is rendered; nursing's commitment to research, education, and the application of new knowledge to patient care; and, finally, some reference to creating in the organization the work environment essential to the successful professional practice of nursing within the institution. While these purposes may not be the sum of all of the purposes appropriate to a nursing organization, any purposes outlined should contain these basic elements. It is from the purposes that the nursing-critical objectives will take their substance and form.

Critical Objectives of the Nursing Division

From the purpose statements in the bylaws, the nursing organization should be able to begin to define its critical objectives in relation to the operational character of the division of nursing. The critical objectives should address the functional operational elements of the organization that articulate the context within which the work of nursing will be done. Those objectives should also relate specifically to the performance criteria through which those who hold leaders in nursing accountable can measure the outcomes, not only of individuals in the division of nursing but of the entire division of nursing collectively. Those performance objectives should relate to nursing, planning, leading, organizing, and controlling. While the critical objectives should not specifically mandate individual accountabilities for these critical objectives, they should be such that the whole division of nursing can be held accountable for their successful performance.

Within the context of nursing performance, issues related to the nature of the relationship between the nurse and the client, the assessment and care process, the nursing delivery system, and the quality assurance function should be clearly outlined in the delivery of service. Since critical objectives are outcome oriented, those behaviors that are essential to the delivery of services must be emphasized in terms of their actual accountability for successful delivery. Looking at relationships, the delivery system has individual accountability within the nursing performance criteria for the critical objectives addresses the basic character of nursing's clinical responsibility.

In relationship to its performance in planning, the nursing organization has a role in participating with the institution in meeting its long-term and short-term needs—specifically in relationship to its clinical goals. Therefore, a definition of nursing's planning system and its approach to participating in the ongoing planning process should be incorporated into the critical objectives of the division of nursing. A planning system should be outlined: the mechanics of the planning system—the skills, requirements, and systems undertaken—should be articulated within the context of the planning objectives. Some reference should also be made to the financial and systems application of the planning process within the division of nursing, such that those responsible for leadership of the division of nursing will recognize the importance of the economic and long-term planning components of the institution in rendering its service.

The role of the leadership-critical performance objectives is directed specifically to providing that the professional organization of nursing meets the needs of the hospital and the client the hospital serves. Therefore, in the planning and performance of critical objectives, a statement that relates to maintaining that environment and the system that supports the environment should be made. The decision-making process and the accountability of the nurse manager, as well as the professional practicing nurse on an individual and departmental level, should be outlined and defined. Mention should be made of the growth and development process of the staff; the credentialing process, as well as the performance evaluation process, should be incorporated into the leadership strategies essential to meeting the basic needs of the nursing organization. Through these objectives, the values of the organization in relation to how it monitors and articulates expectations for leadership should be fair and clear.

There is responsibility in the division of nursing for organizing the division in such a way that it facilitates the effectiveness of the organization and the work it is directed to accomplish. In the organizational framework, it should be clear through the standards that measure the objective related to appropriate organization of the division of nursing that the patterns of the organization are clearly understood and articulated, that the organizational charts reflect the relationships within the division of nursing. Some statement relating to the decision-making process and the commitment of the organization to the shared governance framework should be clearly defined. Finally, in order to maintain its integrity and its unity, the organization must have a controlling system built in, one that will measure all results against objectives and against the organizational plan derived from maintaining the integrity of the system. Some mechanism for undertaking corrective action for deficiencies and for maintaining this integrity should be identified through the standards, which articulate the controlling performance in the nursing organization. Some indication of results measurement in the planning process should be identified.

The controlling mechanism should also look at the exception report mechanisms and the corrective action undertaken in relation to exceptions that exist in the division of nursing and that are unacceptable and fall outside the standards for operation of the division of nursing. Exception reporting should also be included under the controlling function in relation to the effectiveness of the shared governance system, so that review of the bylaws can determine that there is a mechanism to monitor the practices and behaviors of the professional within the organization.

Roles

In this section appears the description of the professional character of the organization and the professional nature of the membership of the organization. The authority under which the profession describes its accountability, as articulated in state law in the Nurse Practice Act and other regulatory delineations, should be identified in this section. The role of the professional nurse in delivering nursing care should be outlined here, too. It should be clear to the reader in reviewing the role statement in the bylaws what is and is not included in the role of the professional nurse in the organization. This statement should be fairly summative of the role and obligation of the professional in the organization and should discuss in detail those role expectations that unfold within the specific individual institution.

It is appropriate to include here the functional elements of carrying out the role of nursing practice in the organization. Such delineation as collaboration, nursing care planning, fulfilling appropriate prescriptions of other professionals, responsibilities on hospital committees and governance councils, and other functional responsibilities can all be appropriately outlined within the role statement. However the role statement is articulated, it should be clear to anyone reviewing the bylaws what the expectations of the role are, and what the individual will be held accountable for in performing nursing practice. Finally, some statement of the mandates for that role from the board of trustees should be included under the role delineation of the professional nursing staff.

Major Clinical Nursing Services

This article of the bylaws contains several sections related to the specific services within which nursing emerges. Those major clinical services that are offered in relation to nursing practice should be articulated and described in detail here. In the description of each clinical service, the role and responsibility of professional nursing unfolding those clinical functions and the clinical obligations of the service should be articulated. It is important to undertake this delineation so that the services to which nursing is committed in the institution can clearly be understood by all members of the staff.

Since nursing practices in a number of different settings renders a number of different services, each of those services has specific requirements and criteria for their practitioners that are different and involve special and unique preparation. It is here that we begin to see that the specialization that has occurred in nursing is articulated and the demands of that specialization can be defined. It is unreasonable to expect that the definition of the medical nursing service should incorporate the same criteria for exercising nursing practice responsibility as those delineations that might describe neonatal intensive care nursing. The responsibilities, obligation, training, education, and practice components of each of those areas are significantly different and, should therefore be described in a different context.

In describing the services and unique characteristics, the following items should be considered:

- the definition and nature of the service itself
- the special qualifications and requirements of those delivering nursing care services within the specified nursing division
- the special and unique practice considerations essential for assuming responsibilities and the service
- the specific standards that apply to the service being outlined
- the relationship of the specific service with other nursing services offered within the hospital
- the unique admission, discharge planning, and transfer requirements of the clinical service being described
- the relationship of the nursing staff to medical protocols that apply to the service
- any special activities or actions that may describe the unique characteristic of the section or service being identified

A clear description of the service should not be limited to those items already identified. Any characteristic that clearly outlines and describes the services in which nursing participates should be incorporated into the description of that service in the bylaws. The clearer the description of the service, the more thorough the understanding of the role of nursing in that service will be to those who refer to the bylaws.

Nursing Staff Membership

Sections incorporated into the article related to nursing staff membership are vitally important to every member of the nursing staff, as well as those individuals who will seek to obtain privileges of membership on the nursing staff. This section of the bylaws should begin with a clear, succinct definition of membership. Some indication of membership privileges that accrue to the individual by seeking a position on the nursing staff and some indication of the requirements for those privileges once membership is achieved should be provided.

Specific delineations of the qualifications for membership should be outlined within the article on membership. Basic requirements related to licensure, background and experience, education, demonstrated competence, evaluation, references, and all indicators necessary to determine the appropriateness of an individual who seeks privileges on the nursing staff of the institution should all be included. Some indication of what is not acceptable for those seeking privileges on the nursing staff of the institution should also be identified in the initial sections covering qualifications.

There should be some discussion in the bylaws of special criteria for applications for privileges in defined areas of the nursing organization. Those special requirements related to critical care, perioperative nursing, specific demands in relationship to specified clinical areas should be clearly outlined within the bylaws. The individual seeking privileges on the nursing staff, in reviewing the bylaws, should get a clear picture of the basic minimum expectations for practice demanded by the institution. If there is a career or parallel ladders program in the institution and if that is part of the ongoing shared governance system, some indication of the demands of that system should also be incorporated into the initial statements of criteria for appointment to the nursing staff.

In outlining employment of nursing staff, it is important to recognize that some inclusion related to the conditions and duration of appointment to the staff be indicated. The various conditions and time frames attached to appointment to the nursing staff allow the individual and the organization to assess the professional nurse's progress in meeting her requirements as a nurse and the needs of the institution. In the traditional bureaucratic system, this has commonly been called the orientation period. Under the bylaws of a shared governance system, however, membership on the nursing staff is determined to be a privilege. Because of that, it is the obligation of the nurse to see that both her contributions and her needs are adequate to expectations placed on her in the position she assumes. This section addresses condition and duration of appointment, issues related to the initial appointment period, the requirements for permanent appointment after the initial period has been successfully completed, what particular privileges are conferred upon completion of this initial period, and the credentialing process requirement essential to assuming the role as a professional nurse on the nursing staff.

Also included in this section is appointment to the nursing staff in positions other than the professional slots in the nursing organization. These persons supply specific services under the direction of a professional nurse. The individual should be identified, their role should be described, and the limitations on that role should be outlined. There are many who may have problems with the delineation of allied or assistive nursing personnel within the content of the bylaws—especially since the bylaws are to govern the activities of professionals. Also, there may be some problem with the issue of classifying individuals other than professional nurses in a subsequent or secondary category. One of the things that we must recognize as professional nurses is that in order to be a professional nurse, one must meet specified criteria. If one does not meet the specific criteria that essentially describe a professional nurse, then one is not a professional nurse. Benefits that accrue to those who have met those requirements and fulfill those criteria are benefits that attend the position of the professional nurse. Under the bylaws, these benefits are articulated. While any member of the nursing staff is assured of equal rights and basic privileges in protecting their employment and their role in the institution, it must be recognized that their role can in no way reflect the role of the professional nurse in the same content, with the same expectations and benefits that accrue to that role. In order for that to occur, those individuals must pursue activities that prepare them to achieve the privileges of the profession.

Nurses have a traditional reputation of assuming the cares of all groups and trying to adjust their own status, commitment, preparation, interests, and control to accommodate the needs of other individuals associated with nursing. Such accommodation has colored our history and severely complicated our professional growth and progress. Professional nurses must take time to consider that, in order to facilitate the role of professional nursing and to successfully integrate it into the health care delivery system as an equal partner in meeting needs of health care, that individual and that role must be clearly described, understood, and defended by members of the profession. It should become the responsibility of other groups to articulate, define, and defend their own roles in delivering health care services. The political reality for the nursing professional should be to support the nursing profession. This is a primary consideration of the role they assume in delivering health care services. Support of other groups and other professions must correlate with the needs and values of the nursing profession. When benefit accrues to both groups as an outcome of that support, then and only then is it appropriate to render that support.

Therefore it is important in the bylaws to delineate clearly the differences in role and in expectations between various groups in the nursing division who offer patient care services. Delineating the roles and responsibilities makes it clear to members of the nursing staff, and the allied and associated nursing staff especially, which role expectations fall within the text of their work and which expectations do not. Clarifying and negotiating those roles and responsibility expectations is a part of developing the shared governance system within the division of nursing.

Other delineations of the professional nursing staff that may have some impact on the patient care process in the nursing division should also be incorporated into the bylaws. The consulting nursing staff identifies those professional staff who may be granted privileges on a temporary basis, who provide per diem consulting and temporary practice services to the nursing staff in the division of nursing. They may also provide specified services upon demand of those asking them in the division of nursing. Consultation to the nursing staff should have a specific mechanism through which the consulting professional nurse can obtain privileges prior to meeting consultation needs within the organization. This process should be incorporated into the credentials review system. Part of the process of reviewing and approving credentials for appointment to the consulting nursing staff is one that looks at background education, experience, appropriate liability insurance, affiliation with physicians (if that is a part of the individual's practice), and some credentials review of the individual's consulting service to assure that they are appropriate and consistent with the goals, philosophy, and needs of the nursing organization.

A major section that should be incorporated into the article on nursing staff membership is the entire credentialing process. This section should detail the credentialing process so that those seeking the proper credentials may know the process that must be undertaken to obtain privileges on the nursing staff. The credentialing process, of course, should reflect the professional delineation of the nursing organization. The credentialing process should include the review of credentials by peers designated under the auspices of one of the councils—preferably, the council on nursing quality assurance. In it should be some mechanism that identifies the application essentials, the career ladder or parallel levels program requirements, special certificates or diplomas, degrees, or any other evidence of special preparation for the role the candidate is seeking to assume. The applicant for membership on the nursing staff should also have a personal interview with the representative of the credentials review process. In some organizations that have moved to shared governance, the personnel office has a credentials review officer who represents the credentials review committee of the nursing staff. This person reviews the candidate's preparation and material for achieving membership on the nursing staff and then approves the candidate's application to the nursing staff to facilitate the process of making use of the individual in the appropriate clinical role. However, in those organizations that have such an officer, the credentials and the review process must be validated by the credentials review committee within a specified time frame, permitting the staff an opportunity to make decisions regarding the approval of peers for appointment to the nursing staff. Since the initial period or the provisional period of employment is one that allows both the institution and the candidate to determine whether the role and situation are appropriate to each, decisions affecting the continued appointment of the candidate to the provisional nursing staff can be rendered by the credentials committee.

The credentials committee membership, role, responsibility, and activities must be articulated in the bylaws with an opportunity for those who are seeking membership to have the right of appeal should membership be denied. The process must be as clearly defined as possible, so the candidate is aware of the opportunities and obligations she has in assuming her role as a provisional member of the nursing staff. From this provisional status, within 90 days or whatever the probationary period on the nursing staff is for the individual institution, after having met all criteria for provisional appointment, the person may automatically attain permanent privileges on the nursing staff. There may be some fear mentioned on behalf of the nursing staff that the credentialing process could be a complex and difficult one. However, when one considers carefully the components and the mechanics of the credentialing process, it is very similar to that taken by the institution in viewing candidates for employment in a traditional system. The only alteration is the shift in role and responsibility for review of the credentials of candidates. The only different aspect of review, other than the title and involvement of the credentials review officer, is the summary review of candidates' credentials by the credentials review committee. While that may appear complex to some, there are many ways in which the credentials review process can be invested in the professional nursing staff without involving a delay of the candidate's successful integration into the organization. Appointment of specified professional staff individuals to review and approve credentials on behalf of the committee; a regular short-term credentials review committee meeting— scheduled on a frequent basis or whenever employment occurs—to review a number of candidates' applications for privileges all can be undertaken to facilitate the process of credentials review. When one carefully examines the process in a shared governance system, the benefits both in nursing staff response and accountability of staff for its own membership and the trade-offs in time and energy are more than worth the adjustment.

The Governance Structure of the Nursing Staff

The description of the shared governance system and the various pieces of the system and its operation should be incorporated into the articles. Specific definitions of the governance council, their roles, activities, responsibilities, and membership should be defined within the specific article of the bylaws. The structure should be one that is directed toward indicating its influence and power within the organization, and the operational characteristics of the structure should be described.

The governance councils should be summarily mentioned, and their integrative and coordinating function with each other should be described in the early sections of this article on governance structure. The councils should be identified by name, and each council should be clearly delineated as to their role, membership, and responsibility.

It is not essential to detail the functional aspects or the activities of each of the councils. It should be clearly understood, through a review of the bylaws, what the process, function, and activity of the councils are. Each of the councils should maintain, in a separate format, their own rules and regulations and the council activities and processes unique to that particular council's role. A later section of the bylaws deals with rules and regulations in the nursing organization.

In discussing the role of the council, the bylaws should contain summary statements of the councils' commitment within the nursing organization and the components of that commitment used to measure performance of the council. The role of the council should integrate well with the roles of the other councils and should clearly describe the functional elements so that the reader can differentiate the roles of the councils.

The responsibility statement that describes the activities of the council should also be relatively clear. The responsibility statement should be specific and identify those process elements in the council over which the council will have accountability. In the bylaws, where there may be close delineations in terms of describing roles and responsibilities in each of the councils, some manner of discriminating between those roles and responsibilities that may have similar descriptors between the councils should be identified, so that the reader, and the staff utilizing the bylaws as their tool for articulating responsibility of councils, can distinguish clearly between the roles and functions of the various governance activities.

A section related to officers and the role of the officers should be included. The appropriate delineation of officers, their election, their term of office, and the number of officers appropriate to each of the councils should be described fully under each of the councils' sections in this article of the bylaws. The officers' roles and responsibilities in relation to the nursing division as a whole should be discussed in detail. Included under the officers' section of this article should be some description of the power and authority of the chairperson and the responsibility of the chairperson to act on behalf of the council between its regularly scheduled meetings. Meeting times and duration are also appropriate considerations for inclusion in each section of the bylaws on governance council activities.

Membership should be clearly delineated as to the number, responsibility, and kind of membership on each of the councils that is considered appropriate. Council membership representation should match that article in the nursing bylaws that describes the specialty services offered by the hospital. Membership on the governance council should be representative of the interests of nursing and the interest of the councils and their various activites within the division of nursing. It may not necessarily be appropriate that council membership be the same for each of the councils. A more general membership may be expected on the practice council, and a more specific unit-based membership may be appropriate for the council on nursing education. The management membership is mandated primarily by position and therefore is different in structure from those undertaken by the other councils. It is important, in describing membership, that each member shall have a specified role and responsibility both in representing the professional staff and in fulfilling the obligations of the council. The roles and responsibilities of each member should be as clear as possible— if not in the bylaws themselves, at least in the rules and regulations of each of the councils.

A section that relates to the selection mechanism and the period of service for governance council membership should also be incorporated into this article of the bylaws. The selection process should be indicative of the character of the professional staff and should be as open, responsive, and perhaps democratic a process as possible. Representation should also be devised in such a manner that no one clinical area or service of the hospital may have all membership positions in any one council. Distribution of the council membership throughout the division of nursing should be incorporated into the bylaws. The mechanism for rendering the selection, term of service, and subsequent terms of service should be pretty clearly described within the section on service, as described within the bylaws. Some effort should be undertaken to limit the individual services of membership so that membership can be spread over a broader base within the organization. Individuals renewing membership indefinitely may limit the ability of the nursing organization to be adequately represented and to allow other members of the staff to serve on the councils according to the needs of the organization. Spreading membership throughout the nursing organization and limiting the tenure of service on the councils can help facilitate the work of the councils and involve a broader range of the nursing staff in the councils' various committees.

Incorporated under each section that addresses a specific governance council, should also be an outline of the various approved standing committees of each of the governance councils. The standing committees that address specific, ongoing needs of the nursing staff and supporting professional activity should be clearly articulated, including their role and responsibility in fulfilling the mandate from the council that sponsors the group. For example, under the practice council would be those committees and groups assigned to address specific issues related to standards development, the career ladder program, the committee that reviews and monitors the delivery system, a committee or task force that looks at intra- and interdepartmental problems related to practice. In the council on nursing quality assurance, committees that relate to the review of compromises in individual nursing practice, incident reporting review, and peer evaluation process can all be incorporated into the standing committees of the organization. Whatever standing committees are appropriate to each of the governance councils, determined by the needs of each institution, those committees should be identified in the bylaws with their roles described and articulated for the membership.

Discipline, Removal, and Appeals Process for Nursing Staff Membership

A major article within the bylaws should be the disciplinary process articulated in the organization of the professional staff who may have problems in maintaining their practice within the institution. A disciplinary process should be outlined and reviewed consistent with those processes acceptable in meeting state requirements and meeting the individual requirements of the institution. Involvement of the personnel officer in development of this article would be helpful in assuring that most of the standards necessary to assure and maintain individual rights and privileges are maintained in this section of the bylaws. The disciplinary process should address all staff members and should operate consistent with other policies and procedures approved, either through the human resources department of the institution or the standards delineation provided by the council on nursing practice.

When removal from the nursing staff is determined to be appropriate, the process for accomplishing that should also be outlined in the bylaws. Regardless of whether the nursing staff member is from the permanent, provisional, consulting, or outside nursing staff, a removal mechanism that provides the institution and the individual nurse with a framework for the removal activity should be incorporated into the ongoing function of the nursing division, and should appear in the bylaws. The opportunity to appeal such removal and to undertake the institution's peer review process, as well as the appeals process through the nursing division, the department of human resources, the administrative staff and—if the hospital is unionized—through grievance procedure, should be also articulated within this section of the bylaws. Careful distinction, however, must be made in those hospitals that are union organized and have union representation between the removal and appeals process articulated in the bylaws and the grievance process determined by contract. As much as possible, there should be a limited connection between the bylaws and the provisions of the union contract, unless bylaws delineation has been specifically addressed in the contract. Whatever mechanism is undertaken, the nursing staff should be attuned to providing as much opportunity and protection to the individual nursing staff member, regardless of reason for removal, in order to assure that all the professional mechanisms available for the protection of the individual's rights are contained within the bylaws and are protected through the institution's appeal process.

Coordination of the Nursing Division

An important part of the bylaws is a description of how the organization is integrated and coordinates its function. The role of each of the coordinating elements of the organization should be described in subsequent sections of the article on coordination of the nursing division. In discussing the coordinating role, the role of administration, coordinating council, and the professional staff at large and some indication of the role on the meeting times for each of these groups should be discussed.

In looking at the role of the administration, description related to the nursing administrator's role and the delegation of responsibilities associated with that role should be included. The accountability of the nursing administrator for the ongoing activities of the division of nursing, and the role of the nursing administrator in assuring that the mandates of the bylaws are promulgated to the nursing staff members and are supported by the institution, should be incorporated into the section on administration. The facilitating, coordinating, and integrative role of the administration should be emphasized in relation to supporting the bylaws, rules, regulations, policies, and practices promulgated by the nursing staff. Again, it should be clearly described to the extent that the nursing staff understands the role of the administrative group in the shared governance system and can act to support that resource as is appropriate.

In discussing the coordination of the nursing division, the specific role of the coordinating council—its function and responsibility, officers, membership, and coordinating process—should be articulated within its section of the article on coordination. The power and authority of the chairpersons, acting on behalf of the councils and on behalf of the division of nursing in conjunction with the nursing administrator, should be described with some clarity. Included in this description should be the meeting times, extent and duration, and the role of the coordinating council in the decision-making process for those processes having an impact on the division as a whole.

There should be some indication in the bylaws of the role of the professional staff as a whole in decisions affecting the professional staff. A professional nursing staff annual meeting should be provided by the organization in order to provide the staff the opportunity to do business attendant to the role of the staff collectively. While the coordinating councils and the governance councils act on behalf of the staff for specific operational functions within the division of nursing, there are processes and activities for which the professional staff as a whole assume some corporate responsibility. Often changes in the organization, in its construct, bylaws, and governance activities, will require review and approval by the staff as a whole. Utilization of the appropriate rules of order, time frame, agenda, schedule, and content of the quarterly professional staff should also be indicated. Quarterly meetings or more frequent meetings than those scheduled annually should also be incorporated into the bylaws and articulated in terms of the role and responsibilities of the professional staff in relation to them. Also at these meetings of the corporate professional nursing staff, the councils should have a reporting mechanism so that the professional staff are aware of the activities of the governance council and can make judgments regarding the impact of these activities and their appropriateness on behalf of the nursing staff. The scheduling, posting, and publicity of the professional nurse staff meeting should also be incorporated into the section that addresses the professional nursing staff meeting.

Bylaw Revision and Adoption

An article that briefly discusses the review, revision, and approval process of the bylaws should be incorporated under a special article of the bylaws. The review and revision process should be carefully structured to assure that when the bylaws are altered or revised, the corporate professional nursing staff play a major role. Since the bylaws are so important to the governance structure and articulate the governance form and process, review and revision of them should be taken under serious consideration and should not be entered into arbitrarily or without careful consideration. Any revision in the bylaws should ultimately come to the corporate nursing staff and be adjusted in their annual professional nursing staff meeting, most advisedly by a two-thirds majority vote of the nursing staff. This protects the bylaws from any sectional or special bias introduced by any single elements of the nursing organization in order to provide benefit to that group. Since the coordinating council has control of and is responsible for fulfilling the mandates of the bylaws, there should be some involvement of the coordinating council in the review and revision process.

The approval of the bylaws comes after all the drafts of the bylaws have been completed and the final draft of the bylaws is ready for the professional nursing staff. Of course, each member of the nursing staff should have a copy of the final draft of the bylaws in time to review it before a vote of the professional staff approves and places into operation the constituents of the bylaws formally and finally. Of course the approval mechanism of the institution as a whole, through its chief executive officer and the chairperson of the board of trustees, should also be indicated by their signature on the final draft. When the bylaws have obtained all these approvals from the professional staff, the chief executive officer, and the chairperson of the board of trustees, they then become the mandates of the nursing organization.

Rules and Regulations

Some mention should be made in the bylaws of the rules and regulations of the governance council in groups of the nursing division as a whole. Rules and regulations are appropriate to describe the parameters of the activities of each of the governing groups within the division of nursing. Those rules and regulations should apply specifically to those areas and should give some form to the activities undertaken by each of the councils and their committees. The ability of the councils and the nursing organization to undertake rules and regulations should be incorporated into the bylaws. The rules and regulations themselves should be attached to the bylaws but should not themselves be a constituent of the bylaws. All the bylaws should be directed to do is provide permission to each of the councils, and a formal structure under which each of the councils can develop their own rules and regulations governing their activities. A simple, brief, and concise statement to that end should appear under this important article of the bylaws.

The preceding outline of the bylaws is necessarily general. Each institution will want to develop bylaws consistent with its needs. Those moving toward bylaw development should be warned that replicating sample bylaw frameworks or incorporating bylaws from other nursing organizations into an individual institution's organizational structure can create many problems. The bylaws should be a clear articulation of the organization's adaptation to self-governance in the nursing service of the individual institution. Those bylaws should reflect that unique character. They should describe as clearly and as precisely as possible, how the application of shared governance within that institution operates. This provides the formal informational and operational resource that the professional nursing staff in that institution requires to operate successfully and to integrate all the activities of the councils in the shared governance system in order to facilitate the work of nursing. Utilizing objective third-party bylaws or bylaws borrowed from another institution or setting will not adequately address this issue and does not serve the primary purpose of the bylaws—to describe and to provide an integrative tool for the individual professional nursing organization.

The task of bylaws writing is arduous and long. Careful consideration to the language, the content, the constituent articles, sections, and subsections of the bylaws appropriate to the organization is necessary in order to make the bylaws a working tool for the organization. At the same time, keeping the bylaws clear, succinct, and precise is necessary to provide that they serve as a reasonable tool for all members of the nursing staff and can be read clearly and with understanding. However, when bylaws have been successfully completed and have fulfilled the purposes and needs of the institution, they provide a positive resource for the professional nursing staff in giving evidence, to the institution and to all who review it, of a professional operating character of the nursing organization. They are the documented visible witness of the professional organization's operation and the unique professional character it has in offering nursing service to the institution. A well-defined and delineated bylaws document can be the crowning statement, when finally approved by the board of trustees, of the arrival of the professional nursing staff as professional peers—equal in status, process, definition, and outcome to any other professional discipline.[1]

NOTE

1. T. Porter-O'Grady, "Bylaws—An Expression of Self-Governance," *Perspectives in Nursing 1983-1985* (New York: The National League for Nursing, 1983), pp. 122–127.

Chapter 9

The Final Stage: An Integrated Environment for Patient Care

The development and implementation of the shared governance system should not represent an end to the organization's attempt to deliver quality patient care. As the professional practice of nursing matures in the new organizational structure, it should provide a basis for reviewing the overall system of delivering patient care by the many disciplines, and for stimulating intraprofessional growth as well. In integrating professional nursing practice, the professional practice of other disciplines—specifically medical practice—is the next step to consider.

The internal systems in the shared governance framework have been designed to articulate more clearly both the professional character of nursing practice and the interactions in the organizational framework necessary to facilitate that practice. As the organization begins to reflect a more professional image, as well as more professional operation and clinical behaviors, it can then consider implications of the shared governance system on the overall delivery of patient care services. The interaction of the shared governance system's councils and other group processes with those activities and functions that also address issues of patient care will be an important goal for the fully developed shared governance organization. Many of the strategies aimed in this direction can be defined and addressed during the change from bureaucratic to shared governance, but most of these activities will only be successful when messages of the professional character, structure, and behavior of the nursing organization are communicated throughout the hospital and medical staff.

The wise, well-prepared nursing administrator will make sure that persons in key leadership positions on the medical staff are kept informed about the transition toward shared governance and the postive impact this transition can have on physicians in the organization. Through communication mechanisms and the organized medical staff, the nursing administrator will have indicated, at various periods during the change process, nursing's readiness to assume some shared responsibility for decisions affecting policy and process. The goal, of course, is some interactive parallel collaborative mechanism between medical staff and nursing staff that fosters communication; a closer working relationship; more shared responsibility in determining outcomes of patient care, appropriate processes, and evaluation systems; and programs that facilitate the delivery of patient care.

In the prospective payment system and the move to open organizations, communication between physicians and nurses, both of whom are primary providers of health care in institutions, will be essential. According to the summary report and recommendations of the National Commission on Nursing, interaction between physicians and nurses will be vital to the success of the institution.[1] The commission indicates that mutual trust and respect for each other's roles have been described by nurses and physicians as the outcome of organizational approaches that facilitate their collaboration and interaction.

A FORMAL BASIS FOR COLLABORATION

To initiate this relationship, structures must be built into the institution that allow a formal basis for communication and collaboration between the two professions. Somewhere in the shared governance and the medical staff organizations, there should be a mechanism through which parallel functions and responsibilities in nursing can interact systematically with those in medical care delivery. Areas of mutual interest and accountability should be coordinated and interrelated between both the medical staff and nursing staff processes.

The next step in the shared governance system involves taking those formal structures that have been constructed in the nursing professional organization and integrating them with parallel professional structures addressing issues of patient care into the medical staff professional governance framework. In doing this, the key providers of health care come together to address collaboratively issues of mutual concern in the delivery of patient care—reducing duplication of resources, recommendations, and outcomes and improving both groups' operations.

Mutual Respect

Of key concern in professional development is the issue of mutual respect of one profession for the other. Nursing, having been inwardly directed while developing as a profession over the years, and the shared governance framework, may not always be fully aware of the constraints and problems associated with medical practice in the institution. Physicians, because of their focus on their own practice, likewise may not be fully aware of the implications on their practice, behavior, and care needs on the delivery of nursing care services in the institution. As a result, there has been limited and sometimes antagonistic communication between the professions, although each is committed to delivering appropriate services to the patient and the institution. Integrating and coordinating these parallel functions between the nursing staff and medical staff may be the first steps to the true collaborative processes essential to a successful partnership in the delivery of patient care.

Each organization will have to determine for itself the integrative process between nursing staff and medical staff. During the time the nursing staff has been successfully developing its professional framework, its relationships with the medical staff may have suffered because of a history of benign neglect. There are, however, some areas of initial integration that would appear obvious to both medical staff and nursing staff members in addressing some approach to collaborative efforts in improving patient care.

Collaborating on Quality

Perhaps one of these areas of first consideration would be the issue of quality of both medical and nursing care, or the quality assurance process. Both medicine and nursing have a deep interest in and a strong commitment to, the issue of quality of care. The quality assurance mechanisms within hospitals have a strong component that includes both medical and nursing interests. The hospital quality assurance plan should contain mechanisms that help address areas of mutual clinical concern among the various clinical disciplines. Since the clinical association between physicians and nurses is close, there are many quality of care issues and interests that are common to both and can be addressed collectively.

In the nursing shared governance framework, the council on nursing quality assurance has a strong mandate to undertake activities related to improving clinical practice and monitoring compliance with appropriate standards of nursing practice, with appropriate corrective action strategies when necessary. The quality assurance function in the nursing division is highly structured, totally integrated into the governance system, and strongly valued—as indicated by its equal delineation of authority for decision-making processes within the nursing organizational system. Because there is such broad commitment to quality assurance activities that are articulated in all the clinical areas of the nursing division, the nursing impact on quality assurance activities throughout the organization should be significant. Thus, representation between the medical staff and the nursing staff on their respective decision-making bodies, which address issues of quality of care and quality assurance in the hospital, would seem an appropriate first step in establishing an ongoing, integrated relationship between medicine and nursing.

Because nursing has been addressing its issues in the development of its professional character in the organization through this process of moving from bureaucracy to shared governance, the division's internal focus may be one that sometimes precludes careful consideration of the broad-based needs of the delivery of patient care within the hospital as a whole. Because nursing must recognize that it is one of the major professional deliverers of care and works very much in conjunction with the medical staff, externalizing their focus and expanding the relationship in this area are key elements of planning and implementing the full scope of professional activities articulated in a shared governance system. Beginning to review externally the responsibilities of nursing for the whole health care delivery system, especially that which parallels the medical staff, should be an important planning strategy for the nursing division.

Historically, as nurses, we have had limited access to parallel and peer relationships with the medical staff. Often we have implemented programs, structures, and systems that have demanded a close interaction with medical staff but that have frequently met problems—because either nursing's behavioral system, professional organizational structure, practice, and competencies or medical staff attitudes, behaviors, and processes have not supported their relationship. Often the relationship, which is unique between two professional groups, has been one-sided because one group, most notably nursing, has behaved more as a technical and vocational practice in the organization than as a fully professional, fiercely committed health care group. As has been the theme of this entire text, if the nurse wishes to be viewed as a professional, she must exhibit behaviors, structures, and systems that reflect a fully professional character. Integrating programs and strategies, processes, communication, and collaboration too soon in the organization short-circuits the development of a mature relationship between nursing and medicine. Frequently, nurses have come to the professional relationships "table" and found themselves coming up short in negotiating with the medical staff because of its perception of nurses and nursing practice. This perception has been reinforced by nurses' practice of fractionalization, vocational behavior, and the absence of supporting structure for professional practice in the nursing organization. Unless this conflict in perception can be addressed and remedied in the nursing organization, a continued perception of subservient and second-class citizenship by the medical professional of the nursing profession can be expected.

The process of quality assurance as the instrument for initiating the collaborating relationship between physicians and nurses capitalizes on an area of mutual interest and obligation. Since nursing representation is usually requested on medical staff and hospital committees, perhaps one of the first steps in facilitating the relationship on issues of quality assurance is to appoint to the appropriate medical staff quality assurance committee the chairperson or a representative of the nursing quality assurance council. Using her role as chairperson of the nursing council on quality assurance, this person brings a level of knowledge, skill, involvement, and investment in quality assurance activities to the medical staff quality assurance forum. She can measurably facilitate medical staff considerations of quality assurance and initially develop a strong bond between the medical staff quality assurance process and that undertaken by nursing. Articulating the detail and effectiveness of the quality assurance function in the nursing division within the shared governance framework helps raise the perception of nursing quality assurance activity by the medical staff and informs medical staff members of the professional and operational commitment by nursing to deliver quality care and high levels of nursing practice. Identifying also for the medical staff quality assurance committee those places in the quality assurance where medicine and nursing may share accountabilities and undertake quality assurance activities together can begin to solidify this relationship between the medical staff and nursing and provide a basis upon which interaction between the two professions can be broadened.

While in many hospitals this relationship already exists, refining the relationship so that accountability for quality of care issues is a joint venture by both nursing and medicine takes the process to its next level of interdisciplinary interaction (see Figure 9-1). At this level, the relationship refinement creates a peer level perception and establishes equal accountability for quality assurance activities. It also eliminates the psychology evidenced in the "You say, I do" responses between medicine and nursing, producing a relationship different from that traditionally believed in or experienced by either medical staff or nursing staff in the institution.

To make this interaction and relationship valuing peer-related interdisciplinary function a balanced equation, it would be appropriate to include the chairperson or representative from the medical staff quality assurance committee in the nursing quality assurance council framework. After the functions, activities, and processes of the nursing quality assurance council have been fully articulated, integrated, and structured operationally to

Figure 9-1 Nursing and Medical Staff Members Can Share a
Commitment to Quality Patient Care

NURSING AND MEDICAL STAFF INTEGRATION

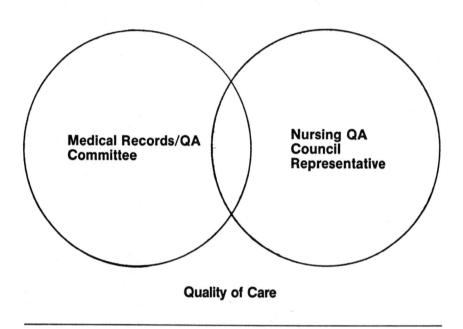

Quality of Care

produce the desired outcomes, involvement of the medical staff representative with the nursing council on quality assurance truly creates the peer-
integrated relationship that indicates a parallel commitment to issues of
quality of patient care. Having the medical staff representative working
with the official nursing quality assurance function and, conversely, the
nursing quality assurance representative working with the medical staff
quality assurance function creates both a practical operating peer relationship and a psychology of parity that provides a framework for true collaboration. It can be expected that the outcome of the work performed by
the interdisciplinary approach and the collaborative foundation established
to support that would assist the organization to address issues of quality
assurance with greater effectiveness.

As the process, relationship, and outcomes of this peer collaborative
effort to address issues of quality of patient care progress, unification of
activities, comparisons of outcomes, mutual recommendations for corrective action and higher levels of practice, and integrating reporting systems

through the hospital's quality assurance process to board review could be incorporated as outcomes of the mutual quality assurance activities. Ultimately, the trust that will develop and bind both professions, unified function, successful peer operation of quality assurance activities, and some well-defined outcomes can perpetuate the professional parity that will evolve from the relationship between medicine and nursing. Success in this area where there are significant elements of mutual concern can provide the baseline for the next steps of growth between the medical and nursing professions in sharing responsibility for patient care.

Operational Interrelationships

A subsequent major step in integrating the primary clinical practitioners in the hospital in both role and responsibility for patient care would be to move the operational aspects of the organization so that interrelationships between the two develop in an ongoing manner. The operational framework should support a mechanism wherein the medical and nursing staff can interact with governance authority at the policy-making and decision-making levels exercised in their mutual responsibilities. A carefully described, yet systematic approach to develop the quality work relationship should unfold at the unit level so that a different sense of communication, interaction, and interdisciplinary care can emerge. Structure should provide an opportunity for individual physicians and nurses working collaboratively to establish relationships and to develop practice parameters, care plans, and intervention strategies as part of the role and relationship each has in delivering patient care.

Using the governance structure framework described in this text, the unit-level practice committees, which are subsets of the council on nursing practice under the leadership of the council, would work with key physicians in specific clinical departments having admitting privileges and maintaining patients on a particular unit to define the nature of the relationship. Further, they would define both the role each would have in developing policy and practice protocols and the routines and behavioral expectations each would have of the other. They would begin to discuss the nature of the practice relationship itself. Through the integration of the nursing practice council's membership and the nursing management council representation (through the unit nurse manager) with the appropriate key medical staff individuals, the key triad would discuss, deliberate, and articulate some basic essentials in the professional relationship between medical staff members and nursing staff members (see Figure 9-2). Collectively, they could begin to set the bottom line for future collaborative

Figure 9-2 A Nursing–Medical Key Triad Can Influence the Practice Relationship

NURSING AND MEDICAL STAFF INTEGRATION

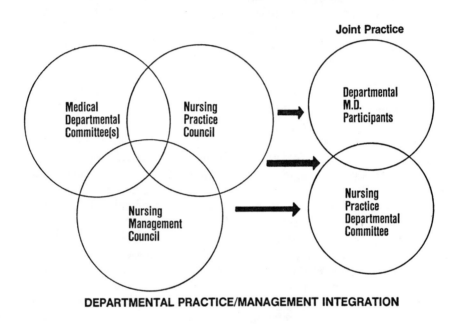

relations and ultimately some joint practice arrangements that would reflect the best professional motives and interests of each group.

In this collaborative relationship, individual problems affecting either or both professions and specified medical or nursing concerns could be addressed and resolved within the framework of the unit-level operation. This process uses the best principles of good management and facilitates an ongoing mechanism at the unit level for resolving problems within that setting and with the individuals involved. In a truly decentralized shared governance nursing organization, the staff's ability to respond to those kinds of situations with an impact at the unit level is measurably facilitated. Keeping problems at the unit level and within the specific clinical framework allows issues, concerns, and processes to be directed to unit-level needs. When problems or issues between the professions cannot be resolved in that framework or have broader implications (beyond unit control), supports from the clinical and management resources operating at the division level can be applied to assist in problem resolution. Again the goals of the interactional process are to maintain decisions within the clinical environment in which they occur and to provide the necessary supports to unfold the goals, objectives, standards, and processes determined by the staff through its council activities. It should be anticipated that this process would work directly to facilitate the relationship between physicians and nurses on an individual basis to help the two groups identify issues and concerns and practice parameters in relationships essential to clarify roles and responsibilities. One of the characteristics of professional relationships is the ability of professionals in a peer framework to identify and seek strategies for resolving issues of mutual concern. It is appropriate, of course, to indicate that one would begin this process with those physicians who would most clearly be in favor of developing this new relationship. Through working out the intricacies and implications of beginning this process and establishing a relationship routine that is effective between cooperating medical and nursing staff members, a baseline for relationships with other medical staff individuals can be established. If the process, behavior, practice, problem-solving skills, and commitment to positive outcomes can be reinforced and validated in the practice environment, it will provide the basis for more serious consideration by other members of the medical staff initially not so interested in the process. There is nothing that generates others' interests in being successful like success itself.

Joint Practice Activities

The next logical step of growth is between the professional nurses and the medical profession relates specifically to collaborative or joint practice activities undertaken at the unit level. *Joint* or *collaborative practice* is a term derived from a practice relationship proposed, implemented, and evaluated by the National Joint Practice Commision, established in 1971 to make recommendations directed at addressing the roles of physicians and nurses leading to a coordinated effort to render services related to health care in the United States.[2] Out of their work and the work of four pilot hospitals involved in developing collaborative practice strategies, some basic processes consistent with successful development of joint practice were defined. In a shared governance framework, the step of developing collaborative practice strategies is one of the more sophisticated final steps in clearly discovering the full implications of shared governance within the nursing organization. When the profession achieves that status in behavior, structure, and practice that is viewed as consistent with practice of other professions, notably the medical profession, a new basis is established for considering joint practice at a higher level than is experienced in most traditionally organized hospitals.

The collaborative practice model lends itself well to shared governance in that it demands a climate of trust and respect between the two professions, based on their complementary and mutual roles in delivering patient care. Nurses and physicians can participate when this mutuality has been agreed upon and trust has been established in defining new roles, new relationships, and new practice interaction. The guidelines for implementation of collaborative practice, as purported by the National Joint Practice Commission, parallel strategies already initiated in a nursing division that has committed itself to shared governance framework.[3]

There are generally five steps for physicians and nurses to take, with appropriate institutional support as validated in the shared governance system, that can result in a well-defined collaborative practice strategy. They are:

1. establishing joint practice committees
2. introducing primary nursing
3. encouraging nurses' individual clinical decision making
4. integrating the patient record
5. conducting joint patient care record review

When looking at each of these elements and comparing them with what has already been recommended in a shared governance nursing division, one can clearly see that a basic framework for collaborative practice already exists. Not only is the structure in place in the shared governance system that has unfolded in transition sensitive to change and the time necessary to complete it; but the collaborative structures for nurse/physician relationships also already begin to exist through the council activity and the nursing representation on the medical staff committee activity shared by representatives of both medicine and nursing in areas related to the clinical delivery of care and quality assurance process evaluating care delivery. Further, while joint practice can be an ultimate strategy of the nursing organization, identifying the medical staff and nursing groups that integrate the clinical delivery of care in a shared governance system as a joint practice committee may not be necessary if the structure of the committees in relationship to the nursing practice council, the appropriate departmental medical staff, and the nursing management council representative is in place. Since the shared governance system and strategy are to facilitate the action and opportunities for decision making of the clinical practitioners, the unit committee that addresses issues of collaborative practice would have the accountability and responsibility for defining relationships, practice, care planning, and other interprofessional activities essential to meet the work needs of both groups.

Readiness for this process has to be an individual institutional decision. The change process associated with shared governance will take varying periods of time depending upon a multitude of variables in each institution attempting to implement the shared governance process. Medical staff maturity and commitment to this process may also vary in these institutions and may require differing approaches to addressing areas of clinical mutuality between physicians and nurses. Strategies related to time, politics, relationships, finances, maturity, and competency will all play a part in the appropriate decision of any individual nursing organization to move toward shared governance. Issues related to the nursing practice delivery system, the commitment to primary nursing, and integrated records will all have an impact on the nature and intensity of the relationship between the medical and nursing staff in unfolding a collaborative relationship. Whatever patient care delivery system nursing has in the hospital, there are certain kinds of characteristics in the delivery of service that should be consistent:

- A relationship should be developed in which the patient will have the same nurse over the period of hospitalization.
- This same nurse will be responsible for planning and administering the patient's care with little or almost no delegation to others.
- The primary nurse can be clearly identified as the patient's own nurse by all those having an impact on the patient's care.
- The patient's physician will always know who the primary nurse is in relation to sharing clinical decision making regarding the care and progress of the patient.

The fact that these primary nurses must always be registered nurses in this kind of setting should be understood. The unit's departmental practice committee should freely address the practice relationship of the physician and the nurse, yet this relationship should be reinforced daily individually by each physician and nurse who participates in this collaborative process in resolving patient problems. The relationship between the two primary patient care resources is essential to the successful development of collaborative professional relationships. If shared governance is to meet staff needs in its ultimate professional characterization, the relationship between the two primary groups of nursing and medicine must be the cornerstone upon which the professional role of delivering patient care is continually reinforced and validated.

It becomes clear that developing the professional role of the nurse in the clinical application of care is central to the success of her relationship with the medical discipline in making decisions related to patient care.

The nurse's individual accountability must be supported in the system before initiating an integrated relationship between nurses and physicians for responsible decisions related to patient care. Each nurse should have a clear idea of the scope of practice, the standards of practice developed through the nursing practice council, the expectation of her role and responsibilities as developed by the council on nursing quality assurance, and the nature of her peer relations and individual responsibility on the unit through the interaction of the unit practice committee and the other peer processes that support and validate her professional role.

On the other hand, the physician encourages individual decision making when he is able to identify an individual with whom he has solid communication, trusting relationships, a belief in competency and commitment to patient care, and a systematic organizational support to the activities of practice and the relationships that help him improve his work and facilitate his interaction with the nurse. Once these trusts can be established and reinforced in the clinical environment and there is confidence in the relationship between physicians and nurses, integration of their roles will become evident. As that integration unfolds, evidence of that relationship in problem-oriented medical records and the integrated patient record become acceptable and viable tools that can be used to document and validate the mutual care process undertaken by physician and nurse. If the relational issues are addressed and attended to consistently, the format issues, such as those associated with an integrated patient record or documentation process, should be minimal. Integrating the documentation process further validates for nurses and physicians their truly collaborative role and relationship in delivering patient care.

Checking Outcomes

This process of integrating patient care can be facilitated when evaluation of the patient record and of the care delivered can demonstrate the outcomes of this new relationship. Since outcomes in patient care are vitally important and patient wellness or appropriate accommodation must be facilitated by both groups, achievement of those outcomes may be one of the mechanisms used to determine the success of the collaborative practice effort. Reviewing care outcomes through the quality assurance mechanism previously discussed is a further enhancement to moving toward true shared practice and decision making in the organization. The quality of care review by both groups collectively can only serve to improve not only the practice of both groups but also their relationship in commitment to a high level of patient care.

It is at the clinical level within this framework that the whole approach to professionalizing the nursing staff through the shared governance structure achieves its greatest value. The original intent of developing shared governance was to professionalize the nursing staff and to create satisfactions within the organization. However, in the final analysis, satisfaction is not only improved internally; it has tremendous impact outside the organization. Within this nursing structure is articulated an organizational system that finally facilitates a truly systematic care delivery approach. Through this collaborative relationship, nursing achieves its leadership status and position within the health care delivery system. The shared governance organization revalidates the clinical basis of nursing practice, and the value the organization must attach to maintaining clinical nursing practice at the center of the organizational structure of nursing services.

Clinical Executive Integration

To ensure that this application works throughout the governance system, some relational process should be undertaken at the executive levels within the governance framework of the organization that further binds the clinical relationship between the medical staff and the nursing staff in operational decisions. The difference in the nursing organization in the shared governance framework from that of the traditional bureaucracy is that the highest executive roles are invested in the governance councils in collaboration with the management and administration of the nursing division. Collectively, they are the executive body of nursing. Uniting the activities of this executive body of the nursing staff with the executive function of the medical staff will create some additional broad organizational support for the interdevelopment of the two professions. As in the clinical and quality assurance of both professions and the integration strategies used in those processes, a similar approach may be taken at the executive levels (see Figure 9-3). In a shared governance organization, it is appropriate that the official representative of the medical executive committee be a member of the nursing coordinating council and ultimately have a voting position on that council. Conversely, the medical staff executive committee would have, as a member of its body, the chairperson of the nursing coordinating council or the nursing staff holding a full voting position. While in most hospital organizations this may be considered a remote dream, it is a logical outcome of developing shared governance. Subsequently, fostering the collaborative relationship would be collaboration in the key decision-making organizations of both professions. It is certainly possible that if the professional transition of the nursing staff achieves levels of sophistication parallel with that of the medical staff,

Figure 9-3 Uniting Executive Bodies of Nursing and Medical Staff

NURSING AND MEDICAL STAFF INTEGRATION

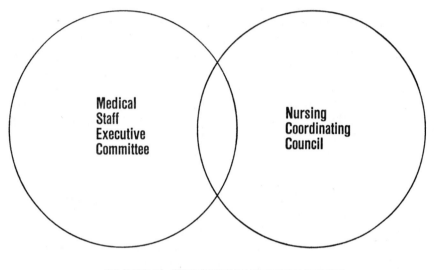

Medical Staff Executive Committee

Nursing Coordinating Council

CLINICAL EXECUTIVE INTEGRATION

sharing the decision-making processes affecting patient care within the executive function of both staffs would be both desirable and appropriate.

In establishing a basis for this transition, a beginning point could be found in the previously discussed relationship between the nursing administrator, the hospital administrator, and the chief of the medical staff. After having developed an ongoing interaction at this level, the next step for fully integrating shared governance is a transition to a relationship between the chairperson of the medical staff and the chairperson of the nursing staff. This does not necessarily mean that other individuals cannnot be involved in this process: however, a relationship between those key individuals should be fostered to facilitate patient care.

Carried one step further, it is reasonable to assume that in a fully developed professional organization in the hospital structure, the relationship between the chairpersons of the hospital board, medical staff, and nursing staff could eventually be realized. The benefits of this relationship are obvious. Involving these three key individuals in issues of mutual concern—most directly related to the appropriateness and quality of care and services within the hospital—certainly could mean value added to the operation of the institution. Again, this relationship would not necessarily indicate exclusion of other key individuals in the organization. However, involvement of these individuals with each other in the attempt to facilitate operations would certainly be appropriate and valuable. This outcome would give evidence, both externally and internally, of the commitment of the institution—not only to quality patient care but also to sound principles of good management, incorporation of all the resources having an impact on the delivery of the hospital services, and the development and utilization of appropriate resources to facilitate the successful operation of the hospital. The benefits in this approach to the hospital, physicians, and nurses would provide a strong professional base in assisting the hospital ensure both the most appropriate use of its resources and its commitment in using these resources to collectively confront the modern issues of health care delivery in a market where there is greater demand, more cost, and declining resources.

IS IT POSSIBLE?

One may, after reading this overview of the shared governance system within a community hospital setting, be tempted to say that such expectations and outcomes are not possible in a real situation. The fact that there are too many variables, too many considerations, and too much opposition to the forces that would move an organization to shared governance certainly would influence that thinking. While it is clear that this process is challenging and perhaps difficult—placing considerable demands on administrators, managers, and clinicians—it does represent the best interests of both nursing and individual professional nurses. There are many constraints that each organization will confront that will oppose a move in this direction. There are many mechanics in the organization that, by very nature of their existence, will oppose the movement of nursing to a professional delineation.

As pointed out at the beginning of this text, there are many perceptions held by those who provide leadership in the organization that indicate opposition to growing, liberating, and professionalizing the nursing staff in the organization. Many will fear that by undertaking this process, they are essentially building a cooperative labor union base in their organizations. All this thinking reflects the tradition from which we have come as administrators, managers, and clinicians. Our range of reference and experience in alternative settings, such as that articulated by shared governance, is limited at best.

The ideas that provide the basis for initiating this process are unique and new. The goals, however, are not new. Nursing has always sought to create a professional base for its practice and to create in its practitioners not only a belief but also a system of practice that would permit them to reflect those professional behaviors in their everyday activities. That process has been difficult and fraught with all kinds of dangers and limitations, to this end, nursing has not yet achieved notable large-scale success. The nursing administrator must carefully ponder these issues and questions, weighing the energies, the risks, and the demands such a change would make on all who would undertake it. Like any process of change, however, the greater the risk, the greater the possibilities. Each institution will have to determine which process, which degree of implementation, and which starting point is most appropriate for it. Each institution will have to determine what strategies work in their favor, there its strengths and weaknesses are, and what kinds of activities need to be undertaken before initiating shared governance. Needless to say, no institution will be completely free of problems and pitfalls in the process of implementating a professional governance system, no matter which route is taken, which framework outlined, or which professional strategies developed as the institution struggles to implement its professional base in nursing. Yet the outcome that creates the environment, the expectations, and the support for professional shared governance will certainly be worth the effort.

Those who undertake the risk must frequently address confrontation with others and challenge of nursing's success in the organization. As nursing becomes successful in defining its professional framework, begins to undertake responsible activities and the authority attendant to them, and begins to broaden its base of operation because of its place in the organization, there will be other disciplines and services in the hospital that will react to this change. The complaint that nursing has more influence, authority, resources, and power than it should will be heard; it will be the backdrop of many comments addressed by others in relationship to nursing. What must become well accepted in hospitals and other institutions whose primary service is returning patients to wellness or assisting them in accommodation to illness is that nursing will always be at the center of the care delivery. It is appropriate for nursing to offer and coordinate the health care services in the institution, to be a part of the central decision-making process, and to have the position and authority attendant with that role. Nurses need be neither ashamed nor reticent to accept that as part of their obligation and role in the health care institution. Others in the institution may have difficulty in accepting that reality, including those who are administrative heads, physicians, and even board members. However, it must be remembered that it is the primary activity of nursing that gives purpose, direction, and meaning to patient care within health care institutions and that, most frequently, it is the nursing practice component of the delivery of health care that most centrally facilitates and affects the success or failure of the institution. Reasonable, judicious, and appropriate use of nursing resources and incorporation of these resources in the fundamental operational decisions of the hospital are not only appropriate, they are necessary. Therefore, nurses should not be apologetic, reticent in claiming their appropriate professional place within both the governance and operational structure of the health care organization. Perhaps the best response to those who decry the role of nursing in the institution and who are uncomfortable with its centrality is to make no comment at all but to give evidence of nursing's vitality, contribution, and impact in the organization through commitment, competence, and all the professional characterizations that identify it as unique and valuable.

One of the basic tenets of this text on movement to a shared governance organization is that the change of structure is fundamental. There are many changes that can occur within the context of the structure in which one finds oneself. It is the change in structure that gives both form and force to implementing any major change in a complex organization. While it may be argued that structure is the appropriate beginning place for change, it cannot be argued that when structure begins to change, form, function, and behavior soon follow. Taking the structural route for implementing a major change begins to provide in the framework of operation those things that facilitate expected behaviors and those processes that limit undesirable or unwanted behaviors. One of the chief problems in working for transition in the practice environment is the organization's ability to alter fundamentally the behaviors of its participants, replacing past behaviors with new behaviors and practices that reflect those delineations and characteristics preferred by the professional organization. While this may tend to have a behaviorist ring, the process of making changes is not so limited. While structure is the fundamental element of the change process in moving toward shared governance, the other processes that operate concomitant to it involve not only the agents of change but also the subjects of change. Each plays a key role, to the extent of her abilities and desires, in unfolding those structures, processes, and practices that will ultimately reflect the character of the organization desired by the professionals working to achieve new organizational commitment.

Equilibrium, or Growth?

It can be said with equal certainty that attempting to change structure is perhaps the choice of change strategies that is filled with greatest risk. Structure provides a sense of solidity, security, formality, and sameness. The human condition demands balance, stability, and form to provide protection and support for its work and other activities. Each person seems to possess a spiritual need to achieve equilibrium in life. Structure provides the form that permits balance to exist in an organization. Even if the balance is not appropriate, beneficial, or positive for the participants of the organization, its continuity and stability provide some basic securities needed to maintian the sought-after equilibrium in each person's life.

It is this basic security—equilibrium—stability that is upset in the transition from the bureaucratic framework to one of shared governance. Not only is the change in the system as initiated disturbing; the new outcomes that depend more on individual accountability, participation, and involvment in the process of governance and the actions of the organization seem less stabilizing, less secure, and more variable. Regardless of its faults, the bureaucratic organization was at least *protective, dependable, stable,* and *concrete*—all terms that provide protection and security. On the other hand, for reasons previously discussed, the bureaucratic traditional management system contained many unacceptable conditions and circumstances that were limiting, rather than beneficial. The point, however, is that the going will sometimes be rough and always be challenging. While the pathway may be clear, its direction may be uncertain. Strategies may frequently have to be reviewed and altered; progress may at times need to be slowed and detours taken. Political awareness and understanding of both change and social relationships will be the keys to the work and success of all of the change agents in the organization.

Those in the United States who have undertaken the process toward shared governance and creating a professional organization for nursing have all claimed its benefits both to the profession and to the institution within which professional nurses practice. Almost universally, the problems and issues that derive from the shared governance system are preferable to those once confronted under the bureaucratic framework. The commitment, involvement, and participation of professional nurses in nursing activities in the institution are unparalled under any other governance approach. Shared governance demands broad-based activity from all the participants of nursing. Each participant, however, may contribute to the degree of her ability, time, and the balance of other commitments in life. The value to the hospital and to the medical staff is clear. The social relationships in the hospital are enhanced; problem solving, satisfaction, morale, and commitment are improved. While the direct impact of the shared governance system on the quality of patient care has not been fully evaluated, the authors have noted strong evidence in their own experience that shows that higher levels of professional behavior in the organization result in improved expectations for practice and, ultimately, in improved outcomes in patient care. Evaluation of this belief will need to continue.

A society's quality of life, both collectively and individually, may be measured by its commitment to quality for society as a whole and for each participant. To the extent that nursing professionals are a major component of the social milieu of health care delivery, improvement in the quality of work life, the quality of satisfaction, and participation by nursing staff through the process of moving toward shared goverance should be ample reason to commit to developing systems that facilitate this kind of framework for nursing. Certainly there are plenty of opportunities: for growth, development, and improvement in both individuals and in the profession. In the final analysis, the only difference between people—including those in the profession of nursing—is a willingness and ability to seize opportunity, both individually and collectively. Shared governance in nursing is just such an opportunity.

NOTES

1. National Commission on Nursing, *Summary Report and Recommendations* (Chicago: American Hospital Asssociation, 1983), pp. 5–11.

2. *Guidelines for Establishing Joint or Collaborative Practice in Hospitals* (Chicago: The National Joint Practice Commission, 1981).

3. Ibid, pp. 1-10.

Sample Bylaws for the Nursing Staff

ARTICLE 1: PREAMBLE

Section 1—Purpose of the Bylaws

These bylaws describe the governance structure of the Division of Nursing and provide a framework for its operation. They describe the organization and the accountability of the professional staff within a shared governance model.

Section 2—Definition of Nursing

Nursing is the assessment and treatment of human responses to actual or potential health problems.

Section 3—Philosophy of the Division of Nursing

It is the belief of the Division of Nursing that every individual has the right to quality health care. Because the client will come from a variety of economic backgrounds, yet will require comparable excellence in nursing care regardless of his/her economic or social status, the Division of Nursing believes it has a responsibility to render a high level of nursing care equally to all clients without exception. Such delivery of nursing care will be consistent with the mandates of the Board of Trustees under the sponsorship of the Sisters of Mercy.

Because of this economic reality, it is the belief of the Division of Nursing that the nurse be considerate of the cost to the patient of the care she/he renders and the materials she/he utilizes. Within this framework, it is essential that the nurse utilize his/her skill, knowledge, and judgment to identify and meet the client's needs in cooperation with peers and other health professionals responsible for the total health needs of the client.

It is the belief of the Division of Nursing that quality nursing practice has its basis in theory validated through ongoing nursing research. To this end, nursing must be willing to initiate and participate in research in an ongoing effort to define and improve the standards of nursing care and to seek new knowledge. Such a dynamic process will ensure the commitment of nursing as a unique profession in making a contribution to the overall state of wellness of the health care consumer. Also, new knowledge is constantly emerging within the health and social sciences that has a significant impact on nursing practice and health care in general. Since nursing is committed to excellence in practice, it is paramount that new knowledge be made available to those who will use it. Therefore, an ongoing process of continuing education in nursing is essential if quality nursing care is to be assured.

Quality nursing care would become a futile expectation if the environment in which it is practiced is rigid and tightly controlled. Professionals require an atmosphere in which participation and collaboration are encouraged. This is especially true for the nursing professional. Major decision making for care of the client must exist within the client care setting. The Division of Nursing must be structured so as to permit the nursing practitioner the freedom to use her/his knowledge and to exercise nursing judgment in order to deliver effective nursing care for and with the client. It is in this environment that the nursing practitioner can deliver responsible patient-centered nursing care for which she/he will be held accountable by the client and by his/her peers.

Section 4—Purpose of the Division of Nursing

1. To provide to the client, at a reasonable cost, quality nursing care that can be measured and evaluated consistent with the mandates of the Board of Trustees.

2. To provide an environment that facilitates nursing research and education and its application to patient-centered nursing practice.

3. To create a working milieu that encourages professional growth and personal satisfaction for nursing practitioners.

Section 5—Critical Objectives of the Division of Nursing

Critical Objective I: Nursing Performance

To provide quality nursing care to the patient.

Standards:
a. An individual nurse–client relationship is entered into upon admission, with a specific understanding between nurse and client of the client's plan of care.
b. A nursing assessment and care plan are completed with each client, organized in the problem-oriented format with measurable care objectives identified within the first 8 hours of admission.
c. The professional nurse is accountable to the client for the 24-hour plan of care. Specifics of care are identified and implemented in collaboration with appropriate other health professionals.
d. Periodic nursing quality assurance activities indicate that nursing care provided has met the objectives identified in the nursing plan of care. At the termination of the contract, the outcome of the nursing care is measured against the objectives identified in the plan of care.

Critical Objective II: Planning Performance

An ongoing planning system is utilized to ensure effective use of resources in meeting short- and long-term objectives.

Standards:
a. All planning includes clearly identified objectives and standards utilizing all available information.
b. Long-term plans reflect the long-term objectives of the Division of Nursing identified through forecasting mechanisms, outlining advances in nursing practice and technology, changing social conditions, and institutional objectives.
c. Planning is based on accurate projections of personnel, materials, and financial resources four quarters in advance. Plans are reviewed quarterly and revised as necessary, with consideration toward achieving objectives within the cost framework identified for them.
d. Unit budgets are planned for four quarters in advance by the unit's Nurse Manager within the constraints of nursing and unit objectives. Departmental budgets are reviewed quarterly and submitted to the Vice-President of Nursing. The annual nursing budget is submitted to the Hospital Administrator by the Nursing Administrator for his/her approval, prior to its submission to the hospital board.

Critical Objective III: Leading Performance

Maintain a working environment that encourages professional growth through nursing research, education, and practice, resulting in quality nursing care and personal satisfaction for nursing practitioners.

Standards:

a. Decisions are made at each level of accountability in the organization utilizing a decision-making model.

b. The Nurse Manager of the individual unit is primarily responsible for the nursing activities and personnel in her/his department and is accountable to the appropriate Vice-President of Nursing consistent with mandates of the Council on Nursing Management.

c. Individual registered nurses are directly accountable to the client for the nursing care they render in accordance with the objectives of the Division of Nursing, Council on Nursing Standards, and the individual department.

d. Each nursing department maintains an ongoing in-service education program designed to meet the educational needs of its nursing practitioners and approved by the Council on Nursing Education. Advice and service for educational programs are obtained from the Department of Education.

e. All nursing research conducted in the Division of Nursing is coordinated by the Council on Nursing Quality Assurance, Division of Nursing. All nursing departments cooperate and collaborate with nurse researchers to the extent that such research does not adversely affect individual nursing care.

f. All positions in the Nursing Division are filled by the most suitable candidates available who meet the criteria and objectives for the position, regardless of any other factor.

g. Performance appraisal is an ongoing process, with individuals appraised against identified individual objectives and departmental objectives. The professional nurse is peer appraised for her/his clinical practice, utilizing developed standards of nursing care.

Critical Objective IV: Organizing Performance

All work is organized and related so that effectiveness and personal satisfaction are maintained.

Standards:

a. The organizational chart reflects professional relationships as well as communicating mechanisms.

b. Decisions are made at the lowest possible level.

c. Position descriptions and objectives are maintained for all nursing positions in order to facilitate role description and performance evaluation.

d. Patterns of organization are reviewed and updated periodically in order to reflect actual organization and communication mechanisms accurately.

e. The organization of the Division of Nursing represents a commitment to shared governance at all levels of the division.

Critical Objective V: Controlling Performance

Results will be measured against objectives with consideration given to acceptable exceptions. Corrective action is immediately implemented where variances are not within acceptable limits.

Standards:

a. "Results measured against plans" are undertaken at all levels of the nursing service organization.

b. A time frame is established at least quarterly for corrective action of all unacceptable variances.

c. All exceptions outside acceptable limits of variance not corrected within an acceptable time frame are reported to the Nursing Administrator with recommendation for corrective action.

ARTICLE 2: THE ROLE OF THE PROFESSIONAL NURSE

Consistent with the rules and regulations of the State Board of Nursing and national standards of nursing practice, the professional registered nurse (hereinafter referred to as nurse) will assume accountability for the delivery of nursing care within the institution. The professional nurse (R.N.) delivers, coordinates, and integrates all nursing care services related to the identified needs of the patients admitted to the hospital. The professional nurse collaborates with other health professionals in fulfilling the health care needs of the hospitalized patient. Professional nurses participate in the organized delivery of patient care services through contributions to patient-care-related hospital committees, nursing governance councils, nursing care committees and task forces. Each practicing professional registered nurse is accountable for the care he or she renders to the patient. The Board of Trustees, through the institution's organizational structure, expects the accountable execution of the nursing professional's role in the delivery of nursing care at the hospital.

ARTICLE 3: MAJOR CLINICAL NURSING SERVICES

There are three (3) major clinical services within which nursing care will be rendered at the hospital.

Section 1—Critical Care Services

Critical care services will be rendered by nurses highly specialized in crisis intervention during the acute care phase of the patient's hospitalization. The critical care nurse is responsible for nursing assessment, planning, intervention, and evaluation of patients in the critical care setting.

Section 2—Medical/Surgical Nursing Services

The nurse is accountable for all nursing assessment, planning, intervention, and evaluation of patient care needs and nursing needs during the extent of the patient's hospitalization. The nurse accepts responsibility for interpreting prescriptive measures of other health professionals and incorporating the activities of the health care team into the ongoing care needs of the individual patient. Long-term care giving and discharge planning are incorporated into the appropriate role of the professional registered nurse in the medical/surgical clinical service.

Section 3—Surgical Nursing Services

The nurse in the operative environment is accountable for the appropriate care and safety of the patient who is undergoing operative intervention. This nurse is responsible for the assessment, planning, intervention, and evaluation of all preoperative, intraoperative, and postoperative nursing care needs of the patient during the surgical process. This nurse communicates and integrates the care prescriptions of other health professionals into the patient's operative plan of care and coordinates nursing care activities directed to meeting the operative care needs of the patient.

ARTICLE 4: NURSING STAFF MEMBERSHIP

Section 1–Definition of Membership

Nursing staff membership is a privilege that is extended to those who meet qualifications, standards, and requirements as set forth in these bylaws and in accordance with nursing divisional standards and the policies, procedures, and practices defined by the Department of Human Resources of the hospital.

Section 2—Professional Nursing Staff

A. Those with the nursing license to practice in the State and who can give evidence of their background experience and training; demonstrate competence; adhere to the ethics of the nursing profession; and demonstrate ability to interact with peers, patients, and other disciplines with sufficient adequacy to assure the nursing staff and the Board of Trustees that nursing care will be maintained at the highest level shall be qualified for membership on the professional nursing staff. No professional registered nurse shall be entitled to membership on the nursing staff or to the exercise of particular clinical nursing privileges in the hospital solely by virtue of his or her license to practice in the State without evidence of the preceding requirements.

B. The professional nurse applicant for appointment to the nursing staff shall be a graduate of a school of nursing approved by the National League for Nursing and shall be legally licensed to practice nursing in the State. This individual must meet all the criteria and requirements indicated in these bylaws and in the department to which the individual is applying for privileges.

C. Nursing staff privileges shall be granted within the context of these bylaws and shall not be denied for any other reason.

D. Acceptance of membership on the professional nursing staff shall constitute that the applying member will agree to abide by nursing standards promulgated by the Division of Nursing and the mandates of the Board of Trustees of the hospital.

Section 3—Conditions and Duration of Appointment to the Professional Nursing Staff

Initial appointment and reappointment to the professional nursing staff shall be made through the nursing personnel appointment process.

A. Initial appointment to the professional nursing staff shall be for a period of three months (90 days at provisional status). Permanent appointment shall be determined by the credentials review process of the nursing division and compliance with the parallel levels program.

B. Appointment to the professional nursing staff shall confer on the appointee those clinical privileges and levels of nursing practice appropriate to the competence and other pertinent evidence of the applying professional registered nurse.

C. Every application submitted for consideration by the credentialing process of the nursing division, when signed by the applicant, constitutes the applicant's specific acknowledgment of her/his obligation to provide continuous nursing care of patients consistent with the standards and rules of the hospital and to abide by the nursing staff bylaws and all other rules and regulations promulgated by the nursing staff.

Section 4—Membership on Nursing Staff

The allied nursing staff shall be composed of members of the nursing division of the hospital that performs supportive nursing, clerical, or technical tasks within specific stated job classifications. Allied nursing staff shall consist of licensed practical nurses, nursing assistants, unit secretaries, and any other supportive clerical or technical individuals as may be deemed essential to support services in the nursing division from time to time. Appointment to the allied nursing staff shall be through the usual employment mechanisms of the nursing and human resources departments of the hospital.

Section 5—Membership on Consulting Nursing Staff

Consulting nursing staff privileges will be granted to registered professional nurses duly licensed in the State, who will provide per diem consulting or temporary practice services to the nursing staff in the Division of Nursing. Each consulting nursing staff member must apply for privileges to practice within the Division of Nursing. Application and approval of consulting privileges are obtained through the following procedure:

A. A current copy of the applicant's registered nurse license is submitted for record to the Credentials Review Officer. License renewals or changes are communicated within three (3) working days to nursing administration whenever a license change occurs and the consulting privileges remain in force.

B. Consulting privileges applied for shall remain in force for no longer than twelve (12) continuous months from date of privilege acceptance, and must be renewed following this application process.

Section 6—The Provisional Nursing Staff

A. All initial appointments to the nursing staff shall be provisional for at least three (3) months (90 days). The failure to advance from provisional to permanent staff status shall be deemed as termination from the nursing staff. The provisional appointee to the nursing staff whose membership is terminated is accorded all appeal rights and privileges specified by the hospital's human resources policy and procedures.

B. Provisional nursing staff members shall be assigned to a department where their performance shall be observed by a member of the permanent nursing staff of the department to determine the eligibility of such provisional members for permanent staff membership and for exercising the clinical privileges provisionally granted to them.

C. Acceptance of clinical and active nursing staff responsibilities during the tenure of provisional status provides the basis for advancement to the permanent nursing staff category. The new staff member shall be accorded all the rights and privileges of the permanent nursing staff.

Section 7—Credentials Review

A credentials review process shall be initiated and maintained in the Division of Nursing, which reviews specific credentials of applicants to the nursing staff for potential membership thereupon. Credentials review shall be based upon, but not limited to, the following items:

A. Evidence that the applying individual has the appropriate licenses, certificates, diplomas, degrees, or other evidence indicating adequate preparation for the role candidate is applying for.

B. Applicant has successfully interviewed for a nursing staff position with the nurse manager of the clinical service in which the applicant is applying for privileges.

C. Candidate has met the levels criteria of the levels category within which the applicant is seeking privileges.

D. Applicant has been recommended for approval by the departmental nurse manager in the department in which the applicant is seeking privileges.

The credentials review process will be invested in a Credentials Review Committee, appointed by the Council on Nursing Quality Assurance. The Credentials Review Committee will take up the business of credentials review and shall consist of no more than five (5) representatives—of which one shall be a nurse manager, one shall be a clinical specialist, and the remaining three shall be appointed from the professional nursing staff. The Credentials Review Committee may be called into session by its elected chairperson at any time it is necessary to fulfill the business of the committee. However, the committee will meet at a minimum of once a month. After establishing a framework for credentials approval within the nursing organization, and consistent with these bylaws, the Credentials Review Committee shall invest responsibility in a nursing credentials review officer employed by the institution for the review of candidates for positions in the nursing division. The delegated authority of this officer shall be:

- to review and to accept credentials supplied by applicants to the nursing staff;
- to obtain appropriate approval of the nurse manager of the service candidate is applying for; and
- to accept the candidate as a provisional member of the nursing staff, subject to the usual 90-day probationary period.

Subsequent validation of the decisions of the credentials review officer by the credentials committee shall occur at a time not to exceed thirty (30) days after the credentials review officer's acceptance of the credentials of the applying candidate. The credentials review officer shall meet with the Credentials Review Commmittee at all its scheduled meetings. Final approval of all applicants to the institution's nursing staff rests solely with the appointed credentials committee.

ARTICLE 5: GOVERNANCE STRUCTURE OF THE NURSING STAFF

A governance structure shall be clearly identified through and within which the nursing staff will organize, integrate, and manage the delivery of nursing care services. The governance structure will recognize participation from all professional nursing staff members and will give evidence of shared decision making within the formal structure of the nursing staff.

Section 1—Governance Councils

There shall be four (4) governance councils that will assume responsibility for the management, operation, and integration of the nursing division. They shall be identified as follows:

- Council on Nursing Management
- Council on Standards of Nursing Practice
- Council on Nursing Quality Assurance
- Council on Nursing Education

Each council will be clearly identified in the bylaws and will operate consistent with the mandates of its roles and responsibilities as articulated in the bylaws.

Section 2—Council on Nursing Management

A. *Membership.* The Council on Nursing Management shall consist of all those individuals holding management positions in the Division of Nursing. Membership shall consist of at least the following:

- Nursing Administrator/Vice President
- service administrators/coordinators
- department heads
- one representative from the education department
- one representative from the professional nursing staff

Membership to the Council on Nursing Management is limited to those who hold line responsibilities and come within the scope of these bylaws. Each member of the Council on Nursing Management has one position on the council and may hold one vote.

B. *Role of the Council.* The council on Nursing Management is responsible for all human, material, and support resources within and affecting the continued operation of the Division of Nursing. All matters relating to the allocation, distribution, and assignment of resources to the individual clinical units and the division as a whole shall be determined, defined, and undertaken by the Council on Nursing Management.

C. *Responsibility.* The Council on Nursing Management shall devise, maintain, and control financial budgets, staffing schedules, materials acquisition and allocation mechanisms, interdepartmental communication for effective utilization, and support of nursing services. Further, the management council shall determine the adequacy of support for clinical activities and shall maintain policies, procedures, rules and regulations of the hospital, and bylaws of the nursing staff consistent with the management role.

D. *Officers.* Each year a Chairperson-Elect is elected from among the members to serve one year as Chairperson-Elect and the following year as Chairperson. The Chairperson shall be a full-time employed professional nurse manager and shall hold office for no more than one (1) year from date of election. The Chairperson shall appoint officers and committees and shall convene and manage the business of the Council on Nursing Management.

For immediate operational decisions and/or emergency situations and/ or between regularly scheduled governance council meetings, the Chairperson may act for the council. Such action must be reported to the council membership at its next regularly scheduled meeting for their review and approval.

Section 3—Council on Standards of Nursing Practice

A. *Membership.* Membership on the Council on Standards of Nursing Practice shall be drawn from the professional nursing staff with representation from each of three major clinical divisions. Members may be nominated or elected or may volunteer from the professional nursing staff. Members must be reelected annually and may serve for a period not to exceed three terms. The Chairperson of the council shall be selected from the staff nurse membership. Staff nurse membership shall not exceed ten (10) members. Additional members must include one (1) voting representative from the Council on Nursing Management, one (1) voting representative from the Department of Eduction, one (1) voting clinical specialist, and a nonvoting nursing administrative advisor.

B. *Role.* The Council on Standards of Nursing Practice will define, implement, and maintain the highest standards of clinical nursing practice consistent with national standards of practices promulgated by the appropriate national nursing specialty organizations, regional and community standards, and those promulgated by the institution. Standards of nursing practice shall be clearly defined and shall provide a framework for all nursing clinical activity to which frequent and ongoing reference can be made.

C. *Responsibility.* The Council on Standards of Nursing Practice shall be responsible for the review and approval of all materials and activities related to clinical nursing practice. Such review shall include but not be limited to:

- review and approval of all policies and procedures that relate to or specifically affect clinical nursing practice
- review and approval of all standards of nursing practice from every clinical specialty within which nursing practice occurs
- assessment and review of, and response to, all problems, concerns, issues, and other related activities with an impact on the clinical operation of the nursing division within the institution
- determination and dissemination of needed changes in practice to other appropriate councils and committees and to the nursing staff for review, education, and implementation

D. *Officers.* Each year a Chairperson and Chairperson-Elect are elected from among the members to serve one year. The Chairperson-Elect serves the following year as Chairperson. The Chairperson shall be a full-time employed professional staff nurse and shall hold office for no more than one (1) year from date of election. The Chairperson shall appoint officers and committees and shall convene and manage the business of the Council on Standards of Nursing Practice.

For immediate operational decisions and/or in emergency situations and/ or between regularly scheduled governance council meetings, the Chairperson may act for the council. Such action must be reported to the council membership at its next regularly scheduled meeting for its review and approval.

Section 4—The Council on Nursing Quality Assurance

A. *Membership*. The Council on Nursing Quality Assurance membership shall be representative of the major clinical services of the Division of Nursing. Represented on the Council on Nursing Quality Assurance shall be at least one member from the following:

- Medical Nursing
- Surgical Nursing
- Critical Care Nursing
- Perioperative Nursing
- Emergency Nursing
- Specialty Nursing
- Any other clinical specialty deemed appropriate by a majority vote of the members of the Council on Nursing Quality Assurance

Membership shall be drawn from the professional nursing staff. Total professional nursing staff membership shall not exceed ten (10) members. Also represented on the Council of Nursing Quality Assurance is one (1) voting member from the Council on Nursing Management, a clinical specialist with voting privileges, and a representative from the education department with voting privileges. A nursing administrative advisor shall also be a nonvoting member of the council.

B. *Role*. The Council on Nursing Quality Assurance shall review all current clinical practices to determine compliance with standards and the need to initiate new standards of practice based on behaviors determined through the research process or the quality assurance mechanism. The Council on Nursing Quality Assurance shall review and participate in, to the extent possible, all nursing research activities directed to providing new forums for practice, expanding current forms of practice, and ultimately improving the quality of nursing care within the institution. The Council on Nursing Quality Assurance shall report to the appropriate council, committee, department, or administrative head such outcome data as are available that affect compliance with standards of practice, the quality of nursing care, and the potential for implementing new processes, standards, and practices related to nursing care activities.

C. *Responsibilities.* The Council on Nursing Quality Assurance shall devise measurement tools for monitoring ongoing nursing care activities; shall review and compile data reflecting compliance with activities; shall make and forward recommendations to the appropriate council, committee, department head, or administrative head for action regarding care as revealed by current state-of-the-art literature and nursing research. The council will be responsible for disseminating appropriate information in order to assure continued compliance with appropriate and defined levels of nursing practice within the institution. This council shall also mandate a committee for the regular review of nursing staff credentials.

D. *Officers.* Each year a Chairperson and Chairperson-Elect are elected from among the members to serve one year. The Chairperson-Elect serves the following year as Chairperson. The Chairperson shall be a full-time employed professional staff nurse and shall hold office for no more than one (1) year from date of election. The Chairperson shall appoint officers and committees and shall convene and manage the business of the Council on Nursing Quality Assurance.

For immediate operational decisions and/or in emergency situations and/ or between regularly scheduled governance council meetings, the Chairperson may act for the council. Such action must be reported to the council membership at its next regularly scheduled meeting for its review and approval.

Section 5—Council on Nursing Education

A. *Membership.* Representation from all nursing departments shall be indicated in the membership of the Council on Nursing Education. Each nursing department shall have one (1) professional staff representative on the Council on Nursing Education, who shall be a voting member of the council. Professional nursing staff membership shall be limited to the number of nursing units represented in the institution, not to exceed eighteen (18) members. In addition, there shall be voting representation by two (2) members of the Department of Education, two (2) clinical specialist voting members, and one (1) voting member from the Council on Nursing Management. A nursing administrative advisor shall also be a nonvoting member on the Council on Nursing Education.

B. *Role.* The Council on Nursing Education shall review all annual education programs prior to instituting the education contracting process. The council shall further define educational needs on a division and departmental basis, and shall review and approve those educational offerings submitted for review by each nursing department representative. All nursing educational programs are integrated and approved for implementation by the council. The council is accountable for maintaining the highest levels of nursing care. Education is related to the ongoing portion of the responsibility of the professional practice of nursing in the institution.

C. *Responsibility.* The Council on Nursing Education is responsible for review of all annual, monthly, and special education programs undertaken within the Division of Nursing and/or under the auspices of the Department of Education on nursing's behalf. Specific educational needs, as identified by the Council on Nursing Standards of Practice, the Council on Nursing Quality Assurance, and the Council on Nursing Management, are also reviewed, approved, and undertaken by the Council on Nursing Education. Maintenance of the institution's ongoing education recording and documentation process is assured through the activities of the Council on Nursing Education.

D. *Officers.* Each year a Chairperson and Chairperson-Elect are elected from among the members to serve one year. The Chairperson-Elect serves the following year as Chairperson. The Chairperson shall be a full-time employed professional staff nurse and shall hold office for no more than one (1) year from date of election. The Chairperson shall appoint officers and committees and shall convene and manage the business of the Council on Nursing Education.

For immediate operational decisions and/or in emergency situations and/or regularly scheduled governance council meetings, the Chairperson may act for the council. Such action must be reported to the council membership at its next regularly scheduled meeting for its review and approval.

Section 6—Meeting Times

All nursing councils shall meet at least monthly and shall be responsible for the work of each council consistent with these bylaws. Minutes must be taken and duly recorded in the appropriate institutional manner. Meetings may be no longer than an hour in length unless specifically approved by the majority of the council members present. One half (½) of the total representation of a council or a constituent committee shall constitute a quorum of the council or committee and shall be deemed appropriate for conducting business of the council or committee.

Section 7—Selection of Governance Council Membership

Members to any one of the governance councils shall be selected from the designated departments, clinical services, or management roles. Membership is limited to registered nurses (R.N.) only. Potential members may volunteer or may be nominated by peers, recommended by current council members or managers, or suggested by staff for council membership. All suggested and recommended potential members must be approved by majority vote of the council in which candidate is seeking membership.

Section 8—Service of Council Member

Membership shall be rotated in April and October so that no more than one-half of the membership leaves the council at one time. Members may be reappointed for no more than two consecutive one-year terms. Members are required to attend three-fourths of all scheduled council meetings. Members not complying with attendance requirements may be removed and replaced through a majority vote of members attending the meeting at which such decision is rendered. Members may not serve another consecutive term on any governance council. After twelve (12) months not serving on a governance council, the registered nurse is again eligible for council membership.

ARTICLE 6: DISCIPLINE, APPEALS, PARALLEL LEVELS PROCESS, REVIEW, AND REMOVAL FROM THE NURSING STAFF

Section 1—Discipline and Appeals

All nursing staff members regardless of category are subject to the institution's standards of employment practices and disciplinary and appeals process, as mandated through the policies and procedures of the human resources department of the institution. All nursing staff members have the same rights and privileges and access to protection, policies, and procedural support regarding the discipline and appeals processes as any employees of the institution.

Section 2—Parallel Levels Process

Professional nursing staff shall have a levels of practice review process that shall permit the individual professional nurse to move from one level of performance to another. Such performance mechanism is practice based and shall provide the opportunity to determine objectively whether the individual professional nursing staff member has met the requirements for obtaining advanced clinical responsibilities in the Division of Nursing. (See Parallel Levels Program.)

Section 3—Removal from the Nursing Staff

When a member from the permanent, provisional, consulting, and allied nursing staff does not meet the standards provided for the individual's role in the institution consistent with the institution's policies and procedures regulating the disciplinary process, removal from the nursing staff may be undertaken. When performance indicators, peer review or evaluation processes, or developmental counseling reveals that a member of the nursing staff is not acting within the bylaws or consistent with the standards of practice acceptable at the institution, the appropriate nurse will undertake appropriate disciplinary/corrective action process. If, after due process, termination is the result, the member of the nursing staff must be informed in writing that privileges have been withdrawn and that the nurse has been terminated from membership on the nursing staff. As herein indicated, all rights of appeal may be accessed by the disciplined or terminated nurse consistent with the policies and practices of the human resources department of the institution.

ARTICLE 7: COORDINATION OF THE NURSING DIVISION

Section 1—Administration

The Administrator for the nursing division and her delegates or associates are responsible and accountable to the Chief Executive Officer and the Board of Trustees of the institution for the coordination, integration, and the administration of nursing. In her/his role, the Nursing Administrator shall be accountable for assuring that these bylaws are promulgated to all the nursing staff members of the institution, and that all responsible parties of the institution adhere to the articles and mandates of the nursing staff bylaws consistent with all existing rules, regulations, policies, and practices of the hospital.

Section 2—Coordination of Governance Activities

A Nursing Coordinating Council shall be composed of the elected Chairpersons of the four governance councils: Standards of Nursing Practice,

Nursing Quality Assurance, Nursing Education, and Nursing Management. These Chairpersons shall be identified as the officers of the nursing staff and shall serve no longer than one (1) year from the date of their appointment. A nursing administrative representative shall also sit as a voting member on the Nursing Coordinating Council. The professional nursing staff shall elect the Chairperson of the nursing staff from among the governance council Chairpersons. That person shall then serve as Chairperson of the nursing staff and shall conduct the business of the Nursing Coordinating Council and the business of the quarterly professional nursing staff meetings.

Section 3—Role and Meeting Time

The business of the Nursing Coordinating Council shall be directed to coordinating, communicating, and facilitating integration of the work of the nursing staff. The Nursing Coordinating Council shall meet at least monthly and may be called to meet at other times at the discretion of the Chairperson.

Section 4—Annual and Quarterly Professional Staff Meetings

The annual meeting shall be held in May of each year and shall include the review of the nursing division's annual objectives, activities of governance councils, and election by ballot of the Chairperson of the nursing staff and any other business as deemed appropriate. The total professional nursing staff shall meet at least quarterly every year. They shall undertake the business of the nursing staff and shall review and approve such matters as brought before it by the coordinating council. On matters submitted for staff vote, a majority of those members present shall be sufficient for passing on voting issues. The business meeting shall be chaired by the Chairperson of the nursing staff who shall conduct the meeting according to Robert's *Rules of Order*. Reports from the governance councils and their designated committees and/or task forces shall be made. Issues and motions from the staff can be addressed in this meeting following the accepted protocol.

ARTICLE 8: BYLAW REVISION

Section 1—Annual Review

These bylaws shall be changed and altered through a process to be predefined and incorporated into the bylaws' structure. This process shall be systematic and provide for annual review such that the nursing staff in their representative bod(y,-ies) may make whatever changes or alterations are appropriate to the interests of the governance of the nursing staff of the hospital.

Section 2—Amendments

The bylaws of the nursing staff may be amended at any regular annual meeting of the professional nursing staff. Any professional staff member may recommend changes in the bylaws by submitting such recommendations to any nursing council Chairperson. The council Chairperson will present the proposed bylaws change to the Nursing Coordinating Council for review and inclusion on the agenda of the next regularly scheduled annual professional nursing staff meeting. A two-thirds majority vote of the professional nursing staff attending the next regularly scheduled annual professional nursing staff meeting shall be required for adoption. Revised bylaws shall be presented to the Board of Trustees of the hospital for review and approval.

ARTICLE 9: RULES AND REGULATIONS

The nursing staff through its constituent councils shall adopt such rules and regulations as may be necessary to implement and maintain these bylaws. All new or changed rules and regulations shall be approved by the Nursing Coordinating Council prior to their implementation. Such changes shall become effective upon approval of the Nursing Coordinating Council.

ARTICLE 10: ADOPTION

These bylaws shall be adopted at the annual professional nursing staff meeting by a two-thirds majority of the members present. They shall replace any previous bylaws and shall be subject to the mandates and approval of the hospital Board of Trustees.

_____   _____
Chief Executive Officer   Chairperson, Nursing Staff

_____   _____
Chairman, Board of Trustees   Nursing Administrator/Vice President

Index

About the Authors

Tim Porter-O'Grady, Ed.D., RN, currently serves as nursing administrator in a large urban hospital and is president of Affiliated Dynamics, Inc. In addition to his years of experience as a nursing administrator, he has served as program developer and consultant to a large hospital corporation. He is the author of a number of articles for professional nursing journals and has presented programs nationally to nurse administrator groups.

Sharon Finnigan, RN, currently serves as vice-president for nursing at a large metropolitan hospital and is vice-president of Affiliated Dynamics, Inc., a consulting firm specializing in nursing development and health care management. Her background in nursing adminstration includes many years of experience as an educator, nursing adminstrator, speaker, and consultant to a large hospital corporation.